FAMILY VIOLENCE

0803928874

Volume 84 Sage L

RECENT VOLUMES IN . . .
SAGE LIBRARY OF SOCIAL RESEARCH

Second Edition

FAMILY VIOLENCE

Richard J. Gelles

Volume 84
SAGE LIBRARY OF
SOCIAL RESEARCH

 SAGE PUBLICATIONS
The International Professional Publishers
Newbury Park   London   New Delhi

SAGE Publications, Inc.
2455 Teller Road
Newbury Park, California 91320

SAGE Publications Ltd.
6 Bonhill Street
London EC2A 4PU
United Kingdom

SAGE Publications India Pvt. Ltd.
M-32 Market
Greater Kailash I
New Delhi 110 048 India

Library of Congress Cataloging-in-Publication Data

Gelles, Richard J.
    Family violence.

    (Sage library of social research; v. 84)
    Bibliography: p.
    1. Family violence—United States.   I. Title.
II. Series.
HQ809.3.U5G44   1987   362.8'2   87-26548
ISBN 0-8039-2886-6
ISBN 0-8039-2887-4 (pbk.)

93   94   10   9   8   7   6

CONTENTS

LIST OF TABLES AND FIGURES

Figures

To My Second Family: Ann and Max Isacoff

ACKNOWLEDGMENTS

I have been fortunate for the past fifteen years to have been able to draw on the help, guidance, and advice of many colleagues, friends, and students. I would not have been a student of family violence had it not been for Murray A. Straus. Murray has been a teacher, mentor, advisor, and morale booster during our partnership in the study of family violence. Each essay in this volume, each idea, each insight has much of Murray Straus's wisdom in it.

My study of family violence began at the University of New Hampshire. My colleagues and friends Howard Shapiro and Arnold Linsky provided significant guidance and support in the early years of my research.

My colleagues, students, and assistants at the University of Rhode Island have helped me, tolerated me, and counseled me since 1973. Michael Bassis, Terry Gebhart, Lucille Browning Cameron, Richard Pollnac, Martha Mulligan, Lana B. Israel, Joan Seites, Eileen Hargreaves, Claire Pedrick Cornell, and Carolyn Cole are all due heartfelt thanks.

I have been fortunate to meet and have the help of many other colleagues in writing the articles included in this book. Eli Newberger, Cecilia Sudia, David Gil, Robert Lewis, Kathy DeHaven, Howard Erlanger, Marjorie Fields, David Reiss, Jennifer Guckel, Andrea Carr, and John Scanzoni all read and provided critical comments on at least one essay in this book.

Betty Jones, Beth Underwood, Lisa Belmont, Sheryl Horwitz, and Joanne Lawrence ably typed one or more of the manuscripts and essays included in this book. I appreciate their help and tolerance. We are grateful for the invention of the "spell check" feature of the word processor we used for the second edition.

Funding for the research reported in this book came from NIMH grants MH 15521, MH 13050, MH 24002, and MH 27557, 15517, and 40027. Funding also was provided by the National Center on Child

Abuse and Neglect (Administration on Children, Youth and Families) #90-C-425.

I am grateful to Rhoda Blecker, Sara Miller McCune, and the staff of Sage Publications (past and present) for giving me an opportunity to bring these materials together into a book. I will always be in their debt for publishing my first book, *The Violent Home*.

I owe my final and most important acknowledgment to my wife Judy and my sons Jason and David. They have always been supportive and understanding. Most of all, they make my research and writing tolerable and possible.

INTRODUCTION

Twenty years ago, when people were concerned about violence they feared violence in the streets at the hands of a stranger. Today we are aware of the extent, impact, and consequences of private violence. Students of homicide were always well aware that nearly one in four murder victims is killed by a family member (Bohannan, 1960; Curtis, 1974). Research in the United States indicates that each year as many as 6 million men, women, and children are victims of severe physical attacks at the hands of their spouses, parents, siblings, or children (Straus et al., 1980).

The toll of family violence extends beyond merely the numbers of people involved, injured, and even killed in acts of violence in the home. A study published by the Centers for Disease Control (Rosenberg et al., 1984) estimated that domestic assaults account for no less than 21,000 hospitalizations, 99,800 hospital days, 28,700 emergency room visits, and 39,900 physician visits each year. In 1980 an estimated 175,500 days were lost from paid work as a result of domestic assaults. The total health-care costs of family violence were estimated at more than $44 million each year. Clearly, family violence constitutes a significant public health problem.

Although family violence has only recently been placed on the public agenda, the problem itself is not new. The history of child rearing and marital relationships are full of anecdotes, descriptions, and discussions of child abuse, infanticide, and violence toward women (Bakan, 1971; DeMause, 1974, 1975; Dobash and Dobash, 1979; Newberger et al., 1977; Radbill, 1974; Shorter, 1975). Family violence can not only be found throughout the historical record, but there is also evidence of violence between intimates across cultures (Gelles and Cornell, 1983; Korbin, 1981).

The earliest professional and popular writers conceptualized child abuse and wife abuse as aberrations, confined to relatively few homes and caused by individual pathologies. Today we know that violence is extensive and that rather than being a product of mental illness, it is a pattern of behavior woven into the fabric of family structures.

The study of violence in the home has typically focused on four major questions. First, there has been considerable concern over exactly how widespread the problem actually is. The concern with measuring the incidence of family violence is perhaps best explained as a reaction to the conventional wisdom that family violence is rare, recent, and confined to a few mentally disturbed people (Steinmetz and Straus, 1974). The second issue concerns patterns of family violence. Here the issues revolve around two contradictory points of view. On the one hand, some researchers argue that violence cannot be explained by social factors (see, for example, Steele and Pollock, 1968; 1974). On the other hand, there is the "class myth" (Steinmetz and Straus, 1974; Pelton, 1978) which says that violence is confined to one social group (e.g., the poor, blacks, and the like). The third major question concerns what causes people to be violent. Early investigations of child abuse and wife beating employed a psychodynamic model of abuse and violence. These investigations were aimed at identifying personality traits and character disorders which were associated with and caused people to physically attack family members. Other investigators developed sociological, social psychological, ecological, and various multidimensional theories of violence and abuse (for reviews of theories of violence, see Gelles and Straus, 1979; Justice and Justice, 1976). The fourth question concerns the consequences of victimization. Researchers focusing on this issue raise questions about whether battered children are likely to grow up to be abusive adults, why women who are battered remain with their assaultive spouses, and what constitutes the emotional and psychological consequences of being either the victim or an observer of prolonged intimate violence.

The study of family violence has developed from the early search for psychological disorders, which dominated the earliest investigations to social psychological models, which were popular in the early to mid-1970s, to broader family system and macro-social of the 1980s. The opening essay in this volume reviews the development of the study of family violence over the last two and one-half decades and presents a summary of the major theoretical models that have been applied to the study of violence in the home.

Violence and the Social Organization of the Family

In earlier work (Gelles and Straus, 1979) we tried to identify the unique characteristics of the family as a social group which contributed to making the family a violent-prone interaction setting. Later, Straus and Hotaling (1980), in reviewing these characteristics, noted the irony of the fact that these properties serve dual roles. On the one hand, they have the potential for making the family a warm, supportive, and intimate environment; on the other hand, they contribute to an organization which enhances the likelihood that violence will break out and escalate unchecked. Briefly, there were 11 factors:

(1) *Time at Risk.* The ratio of time spent interacting with family members far exceeds the ratio of time spent interacting with others, although the ratio will vary depending on stages in the family life cycle.

(2) *Range of Activities and Interests.* Not only do family members spend a great deal of time with one another, the interaction ranges over a much wider spectrum of activities than nonfamilial interaction.

(3) *Intensity of Involvement.* The quality of family interaction is also unique. The degree of commitment to family interaction is greater. A cutting remark made by a family member is likely to have a much larger impact than the same remark in another setting.

(4) *Impinging Activities.* Many interactions in the family are inherently conflict-structured and have a "zero sum" aspect. Whether it involves deciding what television show to watch or what car to buy, there will be both winners and losers in family relations.

(5) *Right to Influence.* Belonging to a family carries with it the implicit right to influence the values, attitudes, and behaviors of other family members.

(6) *Age and Sex Differences.* The family is unique in that it is made up of different ages and sexes. Thus, there is the potential for a battle between generations *and* sexes.

(7) *Ascribed Roles.* In addition to the problem of age and sex differences is the fact that the family is perhaps the only social institution which assigns roles and responsibilities based on age and sex rather than interest or competence.

(8) *Privacy.* The modern family is a private institution, insulated from the eyes, ears, and often rules of the wider society. Where privacy is high, the degree of social control will be low (Laslett, 1973).

(9) *Involuntary Membership.* Families are exclusive organizations. Birth relationships are involuntary and cannot be terminated. While there

can be ex-wives and ex-husbands, there are no ex-children or ex-parents (Rossi, 1968). Being in a family involves personal, social, material, and legal commitment and entrapment. When conflict arises it is not easy to break off the conflict by fleeing the scene or resigning from the group.

(10) *Stress.* Families are prone to stress. This is due in part to the theoretical notion that dyadic relationships are unstable (Simmel, 1950). Moreover, families are constantly undergoing changes and transitions. The birth of children, maturation of children, aging, retirement, and death are all changes which are recognized by family scholars (LeMasters, 1957). Moreover, stress felt by one family member (such as unemployment, illness, bad grades at school) is transmitted to other family members.

(11) *Extensive Knowledge of Social Biographies.* The intimacy and emotional involvement of family relations reveals a full range of identities to members of a family. Strengths and vulnerabilities, likes and dislikes, loves and fears are all known to family members. While this knowledge can help support a relationship, the information can also be used to attack intimates and lead to conflict (Goode, 1971).

Cultural Norms and Family Violence

It is one thing to say that the social organization of the family makes the family a conflict-prone institution and social group. However, the 11 characteristics which we listed do not supply necessary or sufficient conditions for violence. The fact that the social organization of the family which we have just described exists within a cultural context where violence is tolerated, accepted, and even mandated provides the key link between family organization and violent behavior. Opinion and attitude surveys find a high level of support for violence outside and within the home (Stark and McEvoy, 1970). In a nationally representative sample of adults 70% feel it is good for boys to get in a few fistfights while growing up (Stark and McEvoy, 1970). One in four Americans feel it is acceptable for a husband to hit his wife under certain conditions (Stark and McEvoy, 1970).

The widespread acceptability and use of physical punishment to raise children creates a situation where a conflict-prone institution serves as a training ground to teach children that it is acceptable: (1) to hit people you love, (2) for powerful people to hit less powerful people, (3) to use hitting to achieve some end or goal, and (4) to hit as an end in itself.

An Exchange Model of Family Violence

To put it simply, people hit family members because they can. Although people may learn that hitting and violence can be an appropriate or accepted response when experiencing frustration or stress, there are a number of factors which constrain people from being violent when they encounter stress and frustration. First, there is the potential of being hit back. Second, a violent assault could lead to arrest and/or imprisonment. Finally, using violence could lead to a loss of status. Thus, typically, there are costs involved in being violent (Goode, 1971).

The social organization of the family serves to reduce the potential costs of a person being violent toward a spouse or children.

Inequality. The normative power structure in the society and the family and the resulting sexual and generational inequality in the family serves to reduce the chances that victims of family violence can threaten or inflict harm on offenders. Husbands are typically bigger than wives, have higher-status positions, and earn more money. Because of this, they can use violence without worrying about being struck hard enough to be injured or having their wives take economic or social sanctions against them. Parents can use violence on children without fear that their children can strike back and injure them. By and large, women and children who are victims of family violence have no place to run, are not strong enough, or do not possess enough resources to inflict costs on their attackers.

Privacy. Victims of family violence could turn to outside agencies to redress their grievances, but the private nature of the family reduces the accessibility of outside agencies of social control. Neighbors who report that they overhear incidents of family violence also say that they fear intervening in another person's home. Police, prosecutors, and courts are reluctant to pursue cases involving domestic violence. When these cases are followed up the courts are faced with the no-win position of either doing nothing or separating the combatants. Thus, to protect a child, judges may view as their only alternative removing the child from the home. To protect the woman, the solution may be a separation or divorce. Either situation puts the legal system in the position of breaking up a family to protect individual members. Because courts typically view this as a drastic step, such court-ordered separations or removals are comparatively rare, unless there is stark evidence of repeated grievous injury.

Violence and the "real man." One last cost of being violent is the loss of social status that goes along with being labeled a "child beater" or a "wife beater." However, there are subcultural groups where aggressive sexual and violent behavior is considered proof that someone is a real man. Thus, rather than risk status loss, the violent family member may actually realize a status gain.

In situations where status can be lost by being violent, individuals employ accepted vocabularies of motive (Mills, 1940) or "accounts" (Lyman and Scott, 1970) to explain their untoward behavior. Thus a violent father or mother might explain his or her actions by saying he or she was drunk or lost control. Parents who shared the same desire to batter their children might nod in agreement without realizing that a real loss of control would have produced a much more grievous injury or even death.

Primary and Secondary Prevention of Family Violence

We said earlier that the study of family violence has focused on four major questions—incidence, social and psychological factors associated with violence, and the causes and the consequences of family violence. Implicit in each of these empirical issues is the search for knowledge which can be used to prevent and treat violence in the home.

Researchers and practitioners have been careful to point out that there are two types of "solutions" to the problem of family violence—intervention and treatment after an incident of violence occurs and prevention of violence before it takes place (see, for example, Justice and Justice, 1976).

There have been numerous suggestions and implementations of programs aimed at treating known cases of family violence and preventing further abusive behavior. Psychological and family counseling programs, behavior modification, self-help groups—such as Parents Anonymous—shelters, crisis nurseries and day-care centers, comprehensive emergency social services, and many other programs have been developed to assist families which have been publicly identified as abusive. Such programs are useful and necessary, but they serve only as ambulances at the bottom of the cliff. Given that the incidence of family violence runs to the millions of families, there are not nearly enough resources or programs to meet the needs of all violent families. A related point is that because there are insufficient resources and because child and wife beating are stigmatized behavior, only a fraction of violent families will either come to public attention or admit that they need help. The more cynical observers of current theory and practice in the field of violence in the home bemoan the fact that present treatment programs are nothing more than band-aids for bleeding arteries. While there is a grain of truth in this argument, it drastically oversimplifies the issue. If, as we argue, the widespread incidence and severity of family violence is a product of cultural norms which tolerate and approve of violence and the particular social organization of the family, then the ultimate solution and the most effective programs of primary prevention will have to recognize that no meaningful change can occur until something is done to change prevailing cultural norms and alter the social organization of the family.

To prevent violence, we need to take steps to eliminate the norms and values which legitimize and glorify violence in the society and the family. A society which creates and supports norms and values that legitimize and glorify violence will be a society that has a high level of family violence (Straus, 1977). Nearly half of all American homes have guns in them (Stark and McEvoy, 1970). Television, movies, and even children's literature (Huggins and Straus, 1980) glorify heroes who solve problems and express themselves through acts of physical aggression. Our government legitimizes violence by supporting capital punishment for severe crimes and even supporting corporal punishment in schools. We require (and are beginning to see) public awareness campaigns which outline and detail the extent and seriousness of violence in the family. America requires domestic disarmament (Straus et al., 1980). Gun control is necessary, not to keep guns out of the hands of criminals, but to protect family members—the most frequent victims of murders involving firearms! To reduce violence in the home we must reduce violence in society. The death penalty should be eliminated, and corporal punishment in schools banned. Violence on television should also be reduced. In short, the hitting license in America must be cancelled. If family violence is to be reduced, we need values and norms which say: People are not for hitting.

A second step toward reducing violence is to reduce the stress which limits the ability of individuals and families to cope with conflict in their homes. Violence in the home can possibly be reduced if we have full employment, an elimination of poverty, guaranteed health care for all individuals, and abortion on demand. The average person reading this passage will say, "but that is expensive" or "that is impossible." Granted it is expensive, granted it may seem impossible. The issue is that we have grown to accept a society which has poverty, which has unemployment, and which blocks access to health care and social positions. But society does not have to be organized in this manner, and it will have to change if we are to realize any decline in the level of family violence.

Next, the sexist character of society must change. An underlying cause of family violence is the fact that the family is perhaps the only social group where jobs, tasks, and responsibilities are assigned on the basis of gender and age, rather than interest or ability (Gelles, 1974). An elimination of the concept of "women's work"; elimination of the taken-for-granted view that the husband is and must be the head of the family; and an elimination of sex-typed family roles are all prerequisites to the reduction of family violence (Straus et al., 1980).

Fourth, we must break the cycle of violence breeding violence in the family. We must reduce and gradually eliminate the use of physical punishment of children and develop alternative parenting techniques which do not depend on hitting or force. Children should not learn that it is acceptable to hit those whom they love.

Finally, we must accelerate changes in legal codes and court systems and move the courts away from the traditional view that family conflict is an area where the courts should not intervene. Women and children require, and are entitled to, equal legal protection under the law. Wives should be able to prosecute their husbands for assault or rape. The court procedures for dealing with domestic violence need to be streamlined. And last, police should be trained to cope with and manage domestic disputes.

These solutions are all based on information gathered through research on violence in the family. The solutions proposed all involve long-term and radical changes in the fabric of a society which now tends to tolerate, encourage, and accept the use of violence in families.

Many of these proposals challenge taken-for-granted ideas of individual and group rights. Some of the proposals imply a reduction of privacy in the home and an element of intervention by government into the daily affairs of families. Clearly, some of the proposals are controversial, some are costly, and some, given the way we are taught to think about life in America, seem unworkable. However, the alternative is the continuation of a deadly tradition of domestic violence. No meaningful change will take place without some social and familial change, and this will mean a change in the fundamental way we organize our lives, our families, and our society.

Scope of the Book

In the last two decades numerous books have been published on battered children or battered wives. There have been few books which chose to conceptualize the problem as a family issue rather than a problem of children or women. Throughout our 15-year program of research we have viewed child battering and wife battering as pieces of a larger puzzle—violence in the family. Our empirical evidence confirms our early hypothesis that the various forms of family violence are related. This reaffirms our conviction that family violence is an issue of family relations rather than just a problem of child rearing or conflict between spouses. We find that children who grow up in violent homes go on to use violence on their own spouses and children. Our current research (Straus et al., 1980) finds that children who see their parents hit one another and children who are hit by their parents are more likely to use violence on their siblings and on their parents than children raised in nonviolent settings.

This book brings together 12 previously published essays (revised and updated) and one unpublished essay on family violence. These essays are the product of our program of research on family violence. The first project was an in-depth series of interviews with 80 families which focused on the incidence, types, nature, and patterns of violence between husbands and wives (Gelles, 1974). Our first book on family violence, *The Violent Home*, presented data on the extent of violence, the types of violence which are used, and the social factors which are related to marital violence. After the study and the book were completed, a number of important questions prompted us to continue to analyze our interview data. We were concerned with three questions: why did some of the women we interviewed who reported that they were beaten by their husbands choose to stay with their assaultive spouses? Over and over again we were asked why battered wives stayed at risk and did not call the police, run away, or try to get a divorce. A second issue, which we touched on briefly in the first book, was that pregnant women were extremely vulnerable to being victims of domestic violence. Why was this the case, and what could be done about it? The third question arose while the first book was being copy-edited. One of the editors wrote us a short note which asked why we failed to consider sexual violence between husbands and wives. The idea of "marital rape" had never occurred to us at any time in the design, implementation, analysis, and reporting of the research. But the more we thought about the question, the more we realized that it was a significant issue in the study of marital violence. The three essays which address these questions are contained in Part III of this volume, "Marital Violence."

The first essay we ever wrote on family violence is the second essay in this book. "Child Abuse as Psychopathology: A Sociological Critique and Reformulation" applied social psychological theory to the problem of child abuse. We found the research and theoretical conceptions of child abuse sorely lacking in sophistication and evidence. Our first article on this subject led us to a second study of family violence. Nearly all the conferences we attended in the first five years of our research devoted major blocks of time to attempts at defining child abuse. After five years, it quickly became evident that there could never be an accepted or acceptable definition of child abuse. And yet, child abuse was being defined each day by social service workers and physicians who applied labels such as "child abuse" and "child maltreator" to suspicious injuries in children they encountered. We became curious about the process which led some children to be labeled as "abused" and some children to be classified as "accidentally injured"—even though their injuries were the same. Thus, we began a three-year investigation of the social construction of child abuse. Our theoretical essay, "Community Agencies and Child Abuse: Labeling and Gatekeeping" is included in Part II of this volume, "Violence Toward Children."

Ever since we began our first exploratory study of family violence we were regularly asked, "How extensive is family violence?" and "What causes people to be violent toward family members?" Yet, despite years of research, there were no studies which satisfied basic rules of evidence and could be used to estimate the national rates of family violence. Available research suffered from a number of flaws, some of which are discussed in "Etiology of Violence: Overcoming Fallacious Reasoning in Understanding Family Violence and Child Abuse," in Part V of this volume. With Murray Straus and Suzanne Steinmetz, we spent three years planning a national survey of violence in the American family. The long planning period was needed to assess and try to overcome some of the methodological problems we anticipated encountering in such a large-scale research project. One of the first products of the study was an essay reviewing methods which could be used to study sensitive family topics ("Methods for Studying Sensitive Family Topics," in Part V of this volume). Our national survey of 2,143 families allowed us to estimate the extent of violence toward children and violence between husbands and wives. We found rates of family violence which were considerably greater than we had anticipated.

The results of the First National Family Violence Survey are presented in three essays in this volume. The data are reviewed in the opening essay, which gives an overview of the current knowledge base on family violence. Data from the survey are used to explore the possible relationship between maternal employment and violence toward children (Chapter 5). Finally, our examination of the hidden forms of family violence is aided by being able to draw on the survey questions that probed child-to-parent violence (Chapter 9).

We repeated our national survey of family violence in 1985. One aim of the Second National Family Violence Survey was to establish whether the rates of severe violence toward children and between spouses have risen, declined, or remained stable. Chapter 4 discusses the change in rates of severe violence toward children while the introduction to Part III, Marital Violence, includes our latest data on spouse abuse.

The volume concludes with our most unusual effort—an attempt to apply what we know about family violence to actual clinical practice. The constraints we encountered in attempting to apply research and theory to practice as well as our successes are reviewed in the essay, "Applying Research on Family Violence to Clinical Practice."

PART I

AN OVERVIEW OF FAMILY VIOLENCE RESEARCH

CHAPTER 1

VIOLENCE IN THE FAMILY: A REVIEW OF RESEARCH

The introductory chapter to this volume reviews research on family violence. Once viewed as rare and confined to a few mentally ill offenders, family violence has rapidly captured public and scientific attention. The first section of the chapter reviews the resarch carried out over the last two and one-half decades. Although there were abused wives and children throughout recorded time, battered women and children were among the missing persons of both popular and scientific literature until the early 1960s. Since the problem of family violence was discovered there has been an explosion of interest, attention, and literature.

Among the major problems that confront students of family violence are defining child abuse, wife abuse, and violence. Definitional issues are reviewed in the second section of the chapter. Access to cases, sampling, and measurement of violence are additional issues that are discussed.

The state of the knowledge base on family violence is reviewed with a specific focus on the extent of various forms of family violence and the factors associated with violence in the home. Seven theoretical models that have been developed to analyze the specific issue of family violence are briefly reviewed. The chapter concludes with a discussion of the new issues in the field of family violence.

Author's Note: Reproduced, with permission, from the *Annual Review of Sociology*, Vol. 11 © 1985 by Annual Reviews Inc., and from Richard J. Gelles, "Violence in the Family: A Review of Research in the Seventies," *Journal of Marriage and the Family*, 1980 42 (November): 873-885. Reprinted by permission.

Research in the Sixties

Most experts see the publication of C. Henry Kempe and his colleagues' seminal article, "The Battered Child Syndrome," as the benchmark of current concern with the issues of child abuse and family violence. Kempe's article appeared in the *Journal of the American Medical Association* in 1962. The majority of published work in the sixties was on child abuse and was authored by medical or mental health professionals.

Scholarly and even popular literature on wife abuse was virtually nonexistent in the sixties. Snell et al. (1964) wrote a profile of battered wives, while Schultz (1960) examined wife assaulters. Violence toward husbands, parents, and the elderly was neither recognized nor reported in scholarly or lay literature prior to the seventies.

The knowledge base on family violence (in reality this applies mostly, if not only, to child abuse) in the sixties was characterized by singular and narrow theoretical and methodological approaches to the problem. No reliable statistics on the incidence of family violence existed in the sixties. Estimates of child abuse varied widely, from thousands to tens of thousands (Kempe, 1971; Steele and Pollock, 1968). In 1965, David Gil and the National Opinion Research Council collaborated on a household survey of attitudes, knowledge, and opinions about child abuse. Of a nationally representative sample of 1,520 individuals, 45, or 3% of the sample, reported knowledge of 48 different incidents of child abuse. Extrapolating this to the national population, Gil estimated that between 2.53 and 4.07 million adults knew of families involved in child abuse (Gil, 1970). A 1968 survey yielded a figure of 6,000 *officially reported and confirmed* cases of child abuse (Gil, 1970). The problem with the latter estimate was that all 50 states did not, at the time of the survey, have mandatory child abuse reporting statutes, and only a fraction of known cases of abuse were being reported to official agencies. The institution of uniform reporting laws by 1968 made it seem as though there were an exponential leap in child abuse in the seventies as more and more cases of abuse were actually reported.

Gil's estimate of millions of cases of child abuse was the exception and, by and large, the prevailing attitude in the sixties was that child abuse and other forms of family violence were rare occurrences in family life.

Early research and writing on family violence were dominated by the psychopathological model (Gelles, 1973; Spinetta and Rigler, 1972).

Child abuse researchers discounted social factors as playing any causal role in violence toward children (see, for example, Steele and Pollock, 1968, 1974). Rather, the explanation was thought to lie in personality or character disorders of individual battering parents (Steele and Pollock, 1968; Galdston, 1965; Zalba, 1971). The exception to this point of view was Gil's (1970) multidimensional model of child abuse which placed heavy emphasis on factors such as inequality and poverty. The rare reports on wife abuse portrayed both the battering husband and his victim as suffering from personality disorders (Schultz, 1960; Snell et al., 1964).

The similarity of theoretical focus in the field of family violence was probably a product of the similar methods of procedure employed by investigators. Nearly all published work on child abuse and family violence was based on clinical samples (e.g., hospitalized children, patients of psychiatrists or social workers) or officially reported cases of child abuse. Early studies of family violence typically failed to employ control or comparison groups, based conclusions on post-hoc explanations, and were based on small, nonrepresentative samples (Spinetta and Rigler, 1972).

Research Issues in the Seventies

It would be fair to say that the issue of family violence, especially forms of violence other than child abuse, suffered from "selective inattention" (Dexter, 1958) prior to 1970. It would be equally fair to conclude that the decade of the seventies witnessed a wholesale increase in attention to and published reports on various aspects of violence in the home.

Straus attempted to explain the shift from "selective inattention" to "high priority social issue" by positing that the emergence of family violence as an important research topic was the result of three cultural and social forces (1974a). First, social scientists and the public alike became increasingly sensitive to violence due to a war in Southeast Asia, assassinations, civil disturbances, and increasing homicide rates in the sixties. Second, the emergence of the women's movement played a part—especially by uncovering and highlighting the problems of battered women. One of the first major books on the topic of wife battering was written by Del Martin (1976), who organized and chaired the National Organization for Women task force on wife battering. The third factor postulated by Straus was the decline of the consensus model of society employed by social scientists and the ensuing challenge by those advancing a conflict or social action model.

Perhaps a fourth factor should be added. Someone had to demonstrate that research on family violence could be conducted. Researchers commencing projects in the early seventies were constantly told that reliable and valid research on domestic violence could not be carried out. Investigators were reminded that they would literally have to ask, "Have you stopped beating your wife?" Early studies, such as those by O'Brien (1971), Levinger (1966), Straus (1971), and Steinmetz (1971) demonstrated that research could be done (using nonclinical samples) and outlined appropriate methods and sampling strategies for conducting research on domestic violence.

The main focus of research efforts in the seventies was threefold. First, researchers attempted to establish reliable empirical estimates of the incidence of various forms of family violence. Second, research was aimed at identifying the factors associated with violence in the home. Finally, scholars attempted to develop theoretical models of the causes of family violence. While most people concerned with violence in the home wanted to know more about effective prevention and treatment approaches, empirical research on prevention and treatment was rare.

Research Issues in the Eighties

The eighties saw a decline in concern for research on the incidence of domestic violence. With exception of our own Second National Family Violence Survey (Straus and Gelles, 1986; see also Chapter 4 in this volume), there were no new major studies aimed at estimating incidence. By and large, most experts felt that they had established the importance of the social problem of family violence and new and improved incidence data would be of little additional value. There was concern, however, for data on changing rates of family violence and this was the purpose of the Second National Family Violence Survey.

Additional research was carried out on factors associated with family violence. Investigators not only continued to develop causal models, they also subjected many of these models to empirical tests.

The two emerging and central issues in the 1980s are questions about the consequences of abuse for victims (both women and children) and evaluations of various prevention and treatment programs that were designed in the 1960s and 1970s.

Definitional Issues

One of the major problems confronting researchers who attempt to study violence in the family has been the quagmire of definitional dilemmas encountered. The concepts "violence" and "abuse" have frequently been used interchangeably by those who study domestic violence. These concepts, however, are not conceptually equivalent. Moreover, there are considerable variations in how each concept is nominally defined.

DEFINING ABUSE

The first form of family violence that was uncovered and recognized as a problem was child abuse, or the battered child syndrome. The first widely disseminated article defined the battered child syndrome as a clinical condition (with diagnosable physical and medical symptoms) having to do with those who have been deliberately injured by physical assault by a parent or caretaker (Kempe et al., 1962). The term "battered child syndrome" quickly gave way to the terms "child abuse," "child abuse and neglect," and "child maltreatment." Abuse was not only physical assault, but also malnutrition, failure to thrive, sexual abuse, educational neglect, medical neglect, and mental abuse. The official federal definition of child abuse, stated in the Federal Child Abuse Prevention and Treatment Act of 1974 (PL 93-237) was:

> the physical or mental injury, sexual abuse, negligent treatment, or maltreatment of a child under the age of eighteen by a person who is responsible for the child's welfare under circumstances which would indicate that the child's health or welfare is harmed or threatened thereby.

This definition is consequential because it became the model for state definitions, which are in turn the basis for state laws that require reporting of suspected cases of child abuse and neglect. Also, the federally funded national incidence survey of officially reported child abuse and neglect (Burgdorf, 1980) employed this nominal definition of child abuse. Thus, most official report data on child abuse are influenced, to one degree or another, by the federal definition.

It would be a mistake, however, to assume that since there is a federal definition of abuse, there is uniformity in how child abuse is nominally defined by researchers. In point of fact, most studies of child abuse and violence toward children cannot be compared to one another because of the wide variation of nominal definitions employed by scholars. While some investigators study only violence toward children (see, for example Gelles, 1978), others examine the full range of acts of commission and omission (see, for example, Newberger et al., 1977). Thus, reports of incidence, correlations, cause, and effect vary from study to study for many reasons, one being that researchers infrequently define child abuse the same way.

The new interest in cross-cultural research on child abuse further illustrates the definitional problem (Gelles and Cornell, 1983; Korbin, 1981). Korbin (1981) points out that since there is no universal standard for optimal child rearing, there is no universal standard for what is child abuse and neglect. Thus, those who seek to develop cross-cultural definitions of abuse face the dilemma of choosing between a culturally relative standard in which any behavior can be abusive or nonabusive depending on the cultural context, or an idiosyncratic standard whereby abusive acts are those behaviors at variance with the normal cultural standards for raising children. Korbin and others have tended toward using the latter standard as they develop and carry out cross-cultural research (Korbin, 1984).

To a lesser extent, the same definitional problems that have plagued the study of violence toward children have been part of the development of research on violence toward women. Initial definitions of wife abuse focused on acts of damaging physical violence directed toward women by their spouses or partners (Gelles, 1974; Martin, 1976). As wife abuse became recognized as a social problem, the definition was sometimes broadened to include sexual abuse, marital rape, and even pornography (London, 1978).

The major definitional controversy surrounding wife abuse emerged as a result of published research on violence toward husbands (Steinmetz, 1977a) and the use of the terms "domestic violence," "family violence," and "spouse abuse" when referring to violence between adult partners or married couples. Sociologists and psychologists, including Dobash and Dobash (1979), Pagelow (1979), and Wardell et al. (1983), have argued that to discuss violence and abuse of adults is to miss the point that the preferential victims of violence in the family are women. These authors argue that the true problem is *wife* assault, *wife* abuse, or violence toward *wives*, and that evenhanded attempts to discuss spousal violence misdirect scientific and public attention and are an example of misogyny. This controversy will be reviewed in more detail in the discussion of incidence and prevalence of violence.

DEFINING VIOLENCE

Violence has also proven to be a concept that is not easy to define. First, violence has frequently been used interchangeably with the term "aggression." While violence typically refers to a physical act, aggression frequently refers to any malevolent act that is intended to hurt another person. The hurt may not be only physical but may be emotional injury or material deprivation. Second, because of the negative connotation of the term "violence," some investigators have tried to differentiate between hurtful violence and more legitimate acts. Thus, Goode (1971) tried to distinguish between legitimate acts of force and illegitimate acts of violence. Spanking a child who runs into a street might be considered force, while beating the same child would be violence. Research on family violence has demonstrated the difficulty in distinguishing between legitimate and illegitimate acts, since offenders, victims, bystanders, and agents of social control often accept and tolerate many acts that would be considered illegitimate if committed by strangers (Gelles, 1974; Steinmetz, 1977b; Straus et al., 1980).

Additional theoretical and ideological concerns influence the ways in which the concept of violence is defined. Violence is frequently a political concept used to attract attention to undesirable behaviors or situations. Thus, some members of the political Left will define various federal programs, such as Aid to Families with Dependent Children, as violent. Members of the political Right will likewise claim that abortion is a violent act. The entire capitalist system has been derided as violent.

One frequently used nominal definition of violence, proposed by Gelles and Straus (1979), defines violence as "an act carried out with the intention, or perceived intention of physically hurting another person." This definition includes spankings and shovings as well as other forms of behavior; injury and/or death are also included under this broad definition.

By and large, the remainder of this review and the majority of research on family violence focus on the most severe and abusive forms of violence. Injurious violence or violence that has the high potential for causing an injury has captured the attention of scholars who measure the incidence of family violence, identify factors associated with violent behavior, and develop theories to explain family violence.

Methodological Approaches: Sources of Data, Operational Definitions, and the Social Construction of Family Violence

SOURCES OF DATA

Data on child abuse, wife abuse, and family violence have come from three sources. Each source has certain advantages and specific weaknesses that influence both the nature and generalizability of the findings derived from the research.

Clinical samples. The most frequent source of data on family violence are clinical studies carried out by psychiatrists, psychologists, and counselors. The clinical setting (including battered wife shelters) provides access to extensive, in-depth information about particular cases of violence. The pioneer studies of child abuse and wife abuse were based almost exclusively on such clinical samples (Steele and Pollock, 1974; Snell et al., 1964; Schultz, 1960; Kempe et al., 1962; Galdston, 1965; Walker, 1979). Such studies, while important for breaking new ground and rich in qualitative data, cannot be used to generalize information on the frequency of factors associated with violence or the representativeness of the findings or conclusions.

Studies of wife abuse and violence toward women have relied heavily on samples of women who seek help at battered wife shelters (Dobash and Dobash, 1979; Walker, 1979; Giles-Sims, 1983; Pagelow, 1981). Such samples are extremely important because they are the best and sometimes the only way of obtaining detailed data on the most severely battered women. Such data are also necessary to study the impact of intervention programs. However, these data are not generalizable to all women who experience violence; and the study designs (see, for example, Walker, 1979) frequently fail to employ comparison groups.

Official statistics. The establishment of mandatory reporting laws for suspected cases of child abuse and neglect made case-level and aggregate-level data on abuse available to researchers. The American Humane Association collects data from each state on officially reported child abuse and neglect (American Humane Association, 1982, 1983), and the federal government sponsored its own national survey of officially reported child maltreatment (Burgdorf, 1980). Official report data provide information on an extremely large number of cases. But these cases are limited only to those known by service providers. Incidence rates from these data are likely to be lower than the true rates, and the data are biased in a number of ways (Finkelhor and Hotaling, 1984). As with many other types of official records on deviant behavior, the poor are typically overrepresented in official reports, as are ethnic and racial minorities (Gelles, 1975; Newberger et al., 1977).

Random sample surveys. The low base rate of most forms of abuse poses a problem for those who desire to apply standard survey research methods to studying family violence. The low base rate requires investigators to use purposive or nonrepresentative sampling techniques to identify cases (such as drawing samples from social agencies or police reports) or to draw large representative samples. The high costs associated with large samples may, in turn, require that interviews be reduced in length. Some scholars are wary of applying survey research to studying abuse and violence because they assume that subjects will not provide reliable or valid information to interviewers (Pelton, 1979). However, a number of random sample survey studies (Harris, 1979; Straus et al., 1980; U.S. Department of Justice, 1980, 1984) have been conducted. While these studies derive data which are generalizable, the amount of information elicited is frequently limited. Moreover, operationalizing violence and abuse in survey instruments frequently results in compromises. Straus and his colleagues (1980), for example, introduced their violence measure, the Conflict Tactics Scale, by setting the stage in the context of family conflicts. Critics of this form of measurement note that such a procedure limits discussions of violence to conflict situations (Pagelow, 1981; Dobash and Dobash, 1979). Moreover, the Conflict Tactics Scale did not measure the context, consequences, or outcomes of violent acts or whether an injury resulted from the violence.

OPERATIONAL DEFINITIONS

While there is considerable variation in nominal definitions of violence and abuse, the reliance on official statistics and clinical samples has produced surprising similarity in the way that researchers in all disciplines operationally define family violence and especially child abuse. Child abuse, and other forms of family violence (especially abuse of the elderly) are typically defined operationally as those instances in which the victim becomes publicly known and labeled by an official agency.

Researchers have criticized this uniformity of operationalization and claimed that it is biased by the process by which cases come to public attention and are labeled (See Chapter 3). Support for such criticism comes from Turbett and O'Toole's (1980) experiment, which found that physicians are more likely to label minority children and children from lower-class families as abused. Survey research conducted by Giovannoni and Becerra (1979) also found that attitudes and definitions of child abuse vary by professional group and social status.

THE SOCIAL CONSTRUCTION OF FAMILY VIOLENCE

The tendency to operationalize child abuse, wife abuse, and family violence as those cases that come to professional and official attention, or those individuals who choose to seek professional help or flee to a shelter, results in confounding the factors leading people to come forward or be publicly labeled with the factors causing wife abuse, child abuse, and family violence. Because research results are used by clinicians, police, and other labelers to identify suspected cases of family violence, the confounding thus becomes built into the system. Research is based on official reports or cases that come to public attention. Clinicians, agents of social control, and other "gatekeepers" read the literature and use it to diagnose injuries and situations as either instances of abuse or "accidents." Thus, the definition of the situation of violence and abuse is caused and becomes causal. An emergency room physician may treat an injured woman who is reluctant to discuss the nature of her injury. The physician may draw on the literature on wife abuse to see if the woman fits the "profile." If she does, she becomes a case. Later, a researcher may choose to draw cases from the population of the emergency room, and include (or exclude) the woman based on the diagnosis.

The social construction of family violence is consequential for estimating extent, patterns, and causes, and also for studying the impact of intervention and preventions. Researchers may study the impact of interventions and prevention programs on officially known cases and then generalize to the wider population of abuse and violence victims. Obviously, since the wider population is quite distinct from those cases that are publicly identified, the interventions and prevention outcomes may not be generalizable to the undetected or hidden instances of domestic abuse.

The Extent and Nature
of Family Violence

Considerable effort has been expended on discussion, debate, and research concerning the extent of family violence. Part of this effort is aimed at exploding the myth that violence in the home is rare. Another goal has been to convince policymakers, opinion leaders, and the public that child abuse, wife abuse, and other forms of domestic violence are extensive enough to be considered legitimate social problems—especially since one part of the definition of a social problem is that behavior is found harmful to a *significant* number of people (Merton and Nisbet, 1976). Finally, social scientists need data on incidence when they plan social survey research.

Numerous methods have been used to assess the extent of the various forms of family violence. First, scientists employ educated guesses. The majority of estimates that were made about the extent of child abuse were little more than guesstimates (see, for example, Fontana, 1973; U.S. Senate, 1973; Pediatric News, 1975). Others who have tried to base estimates on actual data have used survey data on physical punishment (Erlanger, 1974; Stark and McEvoy, 1970), homicide data (Curtis, 1974; Steinmetz and Straus, 1974), assault (Pittman and Handy, 1964; Boudouris, 1971), and applicants for divorce (Levinger, 1966; O'Brien, 1971), or reports by subjects who know of a case of abuse in their community (Block and Sinnott, 1979; Gil, 1979).

Three national surveys have been conducted with the purpose of assessing the national incidence of domestic violence. Straus et al. (1980) surveyed a representative sample of 2143 couples. Data were collected on violence toward children, violence between spouses, violence between siblings, and violence toward parents. Data on the extent of domestic violence have also been abstracted from the National Crime Survey (U.S. Justice Department, 1980, 1984). These estimates are based on a sample of subjects 12 years of age and older who report crimes against persons or households, whether reported or unreported to the police. The sample includes some 60,000 housing units, and data are available from 1973 to 1981. Finally, the National Center on Child Abuse and Neglect conducted a national incidence survey of child maltreatment (Burgdorf, 1980), and these data include acts of physical maltreatment of children.

Estimates of Incidence and Prevalence

Estimates of incidence range from thousands to millions. Some authors claim that family violence is an epidemic and that perhaps half of all wives are abused.

The survey by Straus and his colleagues yielded an incidence rate of 3.8% of American children aged 3 years to 17 years abused each year (see Table 1). Projected to the 46 million children aged 3 to 17 who lived with both parents during the year of the survey, this meant that between 1.5 and 2 million children were abused by their parents (Gelles, 1978; Straus et al., 1980).

Focusing on violence between marital partners, the investigators report that 16% of those surveyed reported some kind of physical violence between spouses during the year of the survey, while 28% of those interviewed reported marital violence at some point in the marriage (Straus, 1978; Straus et al., 1980).

In terms of acts of violence which could be considered "wife beating," the national study revealed that 3.8% of American women were victims of abusive violence during the 12 months prior to the interview (see Table 2).

The same survey found that 4.6% of the wives admitted or were reported by their husbands as having engaged in violence which was included in the researchers' "Husband Abuse Index." This data, as reported by Steinmetz (1977a) in her article on "battered husbands," set off a major controversy in the study of family violence in the seventies. Steinmetz was accused by her critics (see Pleck et al., 1978) of having misstated and misrepresented the data. While there were significant political overtones to the debate and discussion, it became apparent that the presentation of only the incidence data did not fully represent the different experiences and consequences of violence experienced by men as opposed to women.

The national incidence survey (Straus et al., 1980) found that in one-fourth of the homes where there was couple violence, men were victims but not offenders. In one-fourth of the homes, women were victims but not offenders, and in one-half of the violent homes, both men and women were violent—although the survey could not detect whether the wives' violence was retaliatory or in self-defense.

Despite the clamor about husband abuse data, nominal and operational definitions of violence, and plausible interpretations of the data,

TABLE 1
Frequency of Parental Violence Toward Children

| Violent Behavior | Percentage of Occurrences in Past Year | | | | Percentage of Occurrence Ever Reported |
	Once	Twice	More Than Twice	Total	
Threw something at child	1.3	1.8	2.3	5.4	9.6
Pushed, grabbed, or shoved child	4.3	9.0	18.5	31.8	46.4
Slapped or spanked child	5.2	9.4	43.6	58.2	71.0
Kicked, bit, or hit child with fist	0.7	0.8	1.7	3.2	7.7
Hit child with something	1.0	2.6	9.8	13.4	20.0
Beat up child	0.4	0.3	0.6	1.3	4.2
Threatened child with knife or gun	0.1	0.0	0.0	0.1	2.8
Used a knife or gun on child	0.1	0.0	0.0	0.1	2.9

SOURCE: Adapted from Gelles (1980). Used by permission.

it does seem clear that while women are the most likely victims of spousal violence, there are indeed men who are victimized. Little additional research has been conducted on violence toward husbands.

Sibling violence and abuse were found to be the most common forms of domestic violence in Straus and his colleagues' survey (1980). Finally, the investigators reported that child-to-parent violence was comparable to other forms of family violence—3.5% of teenagers (15-17 years of age) used severe violence toward a parent during the survey year (See Chapter 9).

Data from the National Crime Survey (U.S. Department of Justice, 1984) indicate that the yearly incidence rate of domestic violence (among those 12 years of age and older) was 1.5 per 1000 people in the population.

The incidence survey by the National Center of Child Abuse and Neglect yielded a figure of 10.5 children per 1000 who are known by agencies to be maltreated (Burgdorf, 1980). More than 200,000 children were victims of physical assault.

There are few data on other forms of family violence. There have been some preliminary attempts to assess the extent of the abuse of the elderly (see, for example, Block and Sinnott, 1979, and Chapter 10 for a review

TABLE 2
Frequency of Marital Violence: Comparison of
Husband and Wife Violence Rates (in percentages)

| | Incidence Rate | | Frequency* | | | |
| | | | Mean | | Median | |
	H	W	H	W	H	W
Wife-Beating and Husband Beating (N to R)	3.8	4.6	8.0	8.9	2.4	3.0
Overall Violence Index (K to R)	12.1	11.6	8.8	10.1	2.5	3.0
K. Threw something at spouse	2.8	5.2	5.5	4.5	2.2	2.0
L. Pushed, grabbed, shoved spouse	10.7	8.3	4.2	4.6	2.0	2.1
M. Slapped spouse	5.1	4.6	4.2	3.5	1.6	1.9
N. Kicked, bit, or hit with fist	2.4	3.1	4.8	4.6	1.9	2.3
O. Hit or tried to hit with something	2.2	3.0	4.5	7.4	2.0	3.8
P. Beat up spouse	1.1	0.6	5.5	3.9	1.7	1.4
Q. Threatened with knife or gun	0.4	0.6	4.6	3.1	1.8	2.0
R. Used a knife or gun	0.3	0.2	5.3	1.8	1.5	1.5

SOURCE: From Murray A. Straus, "Wife-Abuse: How Common and Why?" *Victimology*, 1978, 2 (3/4), pp. 499-509. Reprinted by permission. © 1978 Victimology Inc. All rights reserved.

of major studies). Additionally, a number of states have instituted mandatory reporting laws for elder abuse; thus, some official report data on elder abuse are available.

One unintended outcome of the various attempts to measure the incidence of family violence is that the effort has been partially counterproductive. While the use of incidence estimates is partly designed to promote and maintain interest in the problem of family violence, the wide range of estimates has frequently led opinion and policymakers to conclude that the real magnitude of family violence remains unknown (Nelson, 1984).

FACTORS ASSOCIATED WITH FAMILY VIOLENCE

Other reviews have carefully analyzed the factors associated with various forms of family violence (for child abuse, see Maden and Wrench, 1977; Parke and Collmer, 1975; for spouse abuse, see Byrd, 1979. For family violence in general, see Gelles, 1980b; Gelles, 1982; Steinmetz, 1978a).

The last two decades of research on the various aspects of family violence are in agreement on one major point—there are a multitude of factors associated with violence in the home. Nevertheless, the unusual, emotional, and bizarre nature of some instances of family violence has led some researchers, popular writers, and the public alike to grasp at single-factor explanations. Mental illness, character disorders, psychopathology, alcohol and drugs, stress, poverty, growing up in a violent home, and diet have all been pointed to as *the* cause of domestic strife. Social scientists are obviously aware of the drawbacks of single-factor explanations, but they too sometimes select explanations that are single-factor in nature. Dobash and Dobash argue that patriarchy and male domination are the primary causes of violence toward wives (1979).

Among the factors that researchers have consistently found related to various aspects of domestic violence are:

(1) the cycle of violence—the intergenerational transmission of violence;
(2) low socioeconomic status;
(3) social and structural stress;
(4) social isolation and low community embeddedness;
(5) low self-concept; and
(6) personality problems and psychopathology.

It is important to point out that the research that supports the claim for these associations is far from definitive and is often based on empirical research suffering from methodological problems. These include the fact that most studies are based on "caught cases," that is, only cases that come to official attention; studies frequently either do not include comparison groups or have comparison groups that are not equivalent; and studies frequently have small samples and lack generalizability (See Chapter 12).

In addition to the methodological limitations, there are other problems. Associations found tend to be quite modest (perhaps as a result of the low base rate of family violence and the multidimensional nature of the behavior). Frequently, the publicly perceived strength of an association is based on how often the finding is cited, not how strong the statistical association is or how well the research meets the standards of scientific evidence. Houghton (1979) calls this the "Woozle Effect" (based on the Winnie-the-Pooh story—Milne, 1926). In the Woozle Effect, findings are initially stated with a qualification, then repeated in the literature without the qualification. Reviews of the literature cite other reviews, and the strength of a finding grows without the original qualifications or evidence being confirmed through replication. Fortunately, the majority of the factors cited in this section have been found to be associated with family violence by investigators who have used various methods of research and have drawn their data from all three sources of data.

Causal Models

The field of family violence abounds with simplistic theoretical models. In the earliest research reports the model advanced was psychopathology—mental illness caused people to abuse their children, wives, and parents (Steele and Pollock, 1974) (See Chapter 2). Other intraindividual models proposed that family violence is caused by alcohol and drugs.

The major theoretical approaches to family violence have been reviewed extensively elsewhere (Gelles, 1980b, 1982, 1983; Gelles and Straus, 1979). Of interest here is the fact that students of family violence have chosen to view family violence as a *special case* of violence that requires its own body of theory to explain it (Gelles and Straus, 1979). Thus, existing theories of violence and aggression, such as frustration-aggression theory (Berkowitz, 1962; Dollard et al., 1939; Miller, 1941), self-attitude theory (Kaplan, 1962), functional theory (Coser, 1967), and culture of violence theory (Wolfgang and Ferracuti, 1967) have typically not been directly applied to the study of violence in the home. The only existing theoretical model from the general study of violence to be frequently applied to violence in the home has been social learning theory (Bandura et al., 1961; Singer, 1971).

Students of family violence have justified the development of a special body of theory to explain family violence on the basis of the high incidence of violence in the home, because of the unique nature of the family as a small group, and because of the distinctive nature of the family as a social institution (Gelles and Straus, 1979).

While special theories of family violence have been developed, the development has gone in three different directions. Theories have been developed to explain the abuse of children; there are theories that attempt to explain spouse abuse; and there are those theories that are designed to explain family violence in general.

THEORIES OF FAMILY VIOLENCE

Among the special approaches developed to explain family violence are: resource theory (Goode, 1971), general systems theory (Straus, 1973), an ecological model (Garbarino, 1977), an exchange model (Gelles, 1983), a patriarchy explanation (Dobash and Dobash, 1979), a sociobiological perspective; an economic model; and a sociocultural explanation.

Resource theory. A resource theory, the first theoretical approach applied to family violence, proposes that all social systems rest to some degree or force or its threat (Goode, 1971). The use of violence depends on the resources a participant in a system or family member can command. The more resources, the more force can be used, but the less it actually is employed. Those with the fewest resources tend to employ force and violence the most. For instance, husbands tend to resort to violence when they lack the traditional resources associated with the culturally assumed dominant role of the male in the family (Gelles, 1974; O'Brien, 1971).

General systems theory. Straus (1973) and Giles-Sims (1983) use a social system approach to explain family violence. Here, violence is viewed as a system product rather than the result of individual pathology. System operations can maintain, escalate, or reduce levels of violence.

An ecological perspective. Garbarino has proposed an ecological model of child maltreatment. The model rests on three levels of analysis: the relationship between organism and environment; the interacting and overlapping systems in which human development occurs; and environmental quality (Garbarino, 1977). Garbarino proposes that maltreatment arises out of a mismatch of parent, child, and family to neighborhood and community.

Exchange theory. The Exchange Theory approach has been presented in the introduction to this volume. Exchange theory proposes that family violence is governed by the principles of costs and rewards. Violence is used when rewards are higher than costs. The private nature of the family, the reluctance of social institutions and agencies to intervene in violence, and the low risk of other interventions reduce the costs of violence. The cultural approval of violence as both expressive and instrumental behavior raises the potential rewards for violence.

Patriarchy. Dobash and Dobash (1979) see abuse of women as a unique phenomenon that is caused by the social and economic processes that directly and indirectly support a patriarchal social order and family structure. Patriarchy leads to the domination of women by men and explains the historical pattern of systematic violence directed at women.

Sociobiology. One of the newest theoretical models, a sociobiological perspective (or evolutionary perspective), suggests that violence toward human or nonhuman primate offspring is the result of the reproductive success potential of children and parental investment. The theory proposes that parents will not invest in children with low reproductive potential. Thus, children not genetically related to the parent (stepchildren, adopted or foster children), or children with low reproductive potential (handicapped or retarded) are at the highest risk for abuse and infanticide (Hrdy, 1979; Burgess and Garbarino, 1983). It logically follows that the risk is greatest that adoptive parents, foster parents, and caretakers not genetically related to the child (e.g., a boyfriend) will become abusers. Risk of abuse is high where there is lack of bonding between parent and child and where paternity is highly uncertain (Burgess, 1979). Large families can dilute parental energy and lower attachment to children (Burgess, 1979).

An economic model. The economic or social-structural model explains that violence and abuse arise out of socially structured stress. Stress, such as low income, unemployment, and illness, is unevenly distributed in the social structure. When violence is the accepted response or adaptation to stress, stress can lead to violence and abuse (Coser, 1967; Gelles, 1974).

A sociocultural explanation. Finally, students of family violence have explained the occurrence of violence by drawing on sociocultural attitudes and norms concerning violent behavior. Societies, cultures, and subcultures that approve of the use of violence are thought to have the highest rates of domestic violence (Straus et al., 1980).

SUMMARY

The recency of family violence as an area of study for sociologists is best exemplified by the limited level of theoretical development of the field. The field has not developed to the point where theories have actually been subjected to rigorous empirical testing. Individual theories have been tested in limited ways (typically with small, nonrepresentative data sets), and there has yet to be a critical test that pits one theory against another to see which best fits the data. Various criticisms have been leveled against each of the theories. A major limitation of ecological theory is the argument that the theory commits the ecological fallacy by attributing aggregate level demographics to individual level behavior. The patriarchy explanation suffers from being a "single-factor" explanation. Moreover, the variability of the independent variable (patriarchy) has not been adequately specified by the theorists. In its present form, a patriarchy theory is not amenable to an empirical test. This is also the case with sociobiological explanations. Additionally, while sociobiological explanations seem empirically to fit the data on infanticide, the theory does not logically seem to explain nonlethal instances of child maltreatment; nonlethal violence and neglect do not remove the child or increase the inclusive fitness of the other children. Abuse and neglect may actually require a greater parental investment of time and energy in the victimized child. The available data do fit the propositions of resource, exchange, economic, and sociocultural explanations. The next decade of research is likely to be devoted to testing theories and to theoretical integration of the supported theories and propositions.

Other Research Issues

The most recent research on domestic violence has moved beyond the study of incidence and correlations and the proposing of causal models. Researchers have begun to test theories, to study the consequences of family violence, and to examine the impact of interventions on violence in the family. While a full examination of all the developing research issues and questions is beyond the scope of this chapter, this review highlights some of the work that has addressed key questions in the study of domestic violence.

THE CONSEQUENCES OF CHILD MALTREATMENT

Students of child abuse and child maltreatment have begun to turn their attention to the question of the consequences of being an abused child. The clinical literature strongly suggests that abused children have higher rates of developmental delays and difficulties and as adults they have higher rates of drug abuse, alcohol abuse, criminal behavior, and psychiatric disturbances (Smith et al., 1973; Galdston, 1975; Martin, 1972).

Survey data also suggest that abused children have higher rates of juvenile delinquency (Alfaro, 1977; Carr, 1977).

Research on the consequences of abuse and violence typically suffers from numerous methodological flaws (differing definitions, small clinical samples, no comparison groups, and retrospective data— Garbarino and Plantz, 1984). Preliminary data from a prospective study do point to deficits suffered by abused children (Egeland and Jacobvitz, 1984).

PREVENTING AND TREATING FAMILY VIOLENCE

The study of family violence has always had an implicit applied mandate. The search for knowledge has been carried out with the assumption that such knowledge could be useful in designing and implementing prevention and treatment programs. As yet, there are few empirical studies that assess the impact of existing prevention and treatment efforts in the fields of child abuse and domestic violence. An evaluation of child abuse treatment programs was carried out in the late 1970s. The study found that while one-on-one therapy conducted by professional therapists was the most costly treatment, it was the least effective (in terms of recidivism data collected over a very limited time period). The most effective intervention was group counseling provided by lay therapists. This program of intervention was also the least expensive intervention (Berkeley Planning Associates, 1978).

Sherman and Berk (1984) conducted a natural experiment to assess the impact of police interventions in cases of wife abuse. Of three randomly applied interventions—arrest, removing the husband from the home, and trying to cool down the situation—arrest resulted in fewer calls for help and fewer instances of repeated violent behavior.

Conclusion: Future Research

The study of family violence is still relatively new. The psychologist Edward Zigler once claimed that the current knowledge base on child abuse is about equal to what we knew about mental illness in the late 1940s (1976). Zigler could be either too pessimistic about family violence or too optimistic in his assessment of our understanding of mental illness. Nevertheless, it is clear that those who study domestic violence are still struggling with definitional issues, methodological constraints and problems, and have yet to actually test the major theoretical assumptions and models that have been developed.

The study of family violence continues to be an interdisciplinary effort. Psychologists, sociologists, anthropologists, physicians, and social workers frequently share interests, questions, models, and authorship of research reports. In the future, we should expect to see continued efforts to study family violence cross-culturally. Korbin (1981) has already contributed to that effort and her work, and the work of others, is useful in challenging and informing some of the socio-cultural assumptions that developed out of research on violence in the United States (Straus et al., 1980). Research on family violence is examining violence in alternative families (e.g., stepfamilies). Research continues to be conducted by those interested in how professionals label and approach cases of domestic violence (e.g., Hampton and Newberger, 1984). There is considerable interest in the topic of sexual abuse, and marital rape. Researchers have recently begun to try to collect data directly from men who batter, rather than relying only on reports from the victims (e.g., Rouse, 1984). There has also been an expansion of the study of violence between partners by those interested in courtship violence (e.g., Makepeace, 1981, 1983; Cate et al., 1982).

PART II

VIOLENCE TOWARD CHILDREN

Introduction

During the last 20 years there has been a massive growth of attention directed at the problem of abused and neglected children. It seems as if child abuse is a new phenomenon, or if not new, more widespread. Historical evidence suggests that child abuse and violence toward children go back to colonial times in America and Biblical times in human history (Bakan, 1971; DeMause, 1974, 1975; Newberger et al., 1977; Radbill, 1974).

Sociologists who study child abuse and family violence have had a dual mandate. First they have served as debunkers, critiquing medical-model-dominated research and publicly held conventional wisdoms. Sociologists have vigorously attacked the myth that violence and abuse is confined to mentally disturbed people. The second mandate is to use the sociological perspective and research methods to help establish the nature, extent, and dynamics of violence toward women and children. Such information is not only a useful addition to our knowledge base, it has practical value for social service and medical personnel, who need to apply the knowledge base to help deal with the emotionally trying cases of violence they encounter.

The main thrust of research on violence toward children has been to assess the incidence and extent of violence and abuse, to examine the factors associated with abuse, to develop causal models of abuse, and finally to develop and evaluate effective programs of treatment and prevention.

Our first publication on child abuse and the lead chapter in this section, "Child Abuse as Psychopathology: A Sociological Critique and Reformulation," critiques the narrow medical/psychiatric model of child abuse and proposes a theoretical model to explain the abuse of children. This model is useful in understanding abuse and also serves as a guide for the types of programs that are needed to treat and prevent child abuse effectively.

The second chapter focuses on agents and agencies who first come into contact with child abuse and neglect cases. How do these gatekeepers define child abuse? What kinds of people and families are labeled "abusive"? Who is insulated from being labeled an "abuser"? A main point of this essay is to illustrate the social construction of child abuse. Only a fraction of the true number of cases of child abuse come to public attention and are officially labeled "child abuse." The child and families so labeled are a selective sampling of the true population. Low-income families not only are more likely to abuse their children, they are more likely to be labeled as child abusers by official agencies. Higher-income families, while being less likely to abuse, are also insulated from being publicly labeled as abusers. The implications of the social construction of child abuse for both the knowledge base and clinical practice are discussed in Chapter 3, "Community Agencies and Child Abuse."

The two chapters that follow are based on data collected in the First and Second National Family Violence Surveys. The First National Family Violence Survey was designed to measure the extent of family violence, including violence toward children, and examine the factors that are associated with family violence. We measured violence toward children using the Conflict Tactics Scales that were developed by Murray Straus. The data on the incidence of violence toward children have been summarized in Chapter 1.

As we noted earlier, people assume that because there has been more attention focused on violence and abuse, there is more child abuse today than 10, 20, or 50 years ago. One of the goals of the Second National Family Violence Survey was to test whether violence toward children has indeed increased in the last decade. The results of the survey are presented in Chapter 4. They are surprising and challenge commonly held perceptions.

The last chapter, "Maternal Employment and Violence Toward Children" also challenges conventional wisdom about risk factors and abusive violence. It seems almost common sense that a working mother would experience greater stress than a mother who remains at home with her children. Given that stress is associated with increased risk of violence, many researchers and clinicians assumed that children of working mothers are at greater risk of being abused than other children. Again, carefully collected survey data does not bear out conventional wisdom.

CHAPTER 2

CHILD ABUSE AS PSYCHOPATHOLOGY: A SOCIOLOGICAL CRITIQUE AND REFORMULATION

Each year in this country, thousands of children are brutally beaten, abused, and sometimes killed by their mothers and fathers. The dominant theme of research on this problem has been the use of a "psychopathological model" of child abuse—the parent who abuses suffers from a psychological pathology or sickness that accounts for abusing or battering a child.

This essay takes a critical look at the psychopathological theory of child abuse and finds a number of deficiencies with the model. First, this explanation of child abuse is too narrow. It posits a single causal variable (a presumed mental aberration or disease) to account for child abuse, while it ignores other variables that this essay will show are equally or more important causal factors. Second, psychopathology theory is inconsistent in stating that abuse is caused by a pathology, while many of the research reports state that all abusers are not psychopaths. Finally, close examination of the literature on child abuse shows that it is not based on research that meets even the minimal standards of evidence in social science (Spinetta and Rigler, 1972).

The purpose of this essay is to provide a more dimensional analysis of the generative sources of child abuse. The analysis goes beyond the unicausal approach of the psychopathology model; it analyzes socio-cultural features of the abuser such as socioeconomic status, sex,

Author's Note: Reprinted, with permission, from the American Journal of Ortho-psychiatry. Copyright 1973 by the American Orthopsychiatric Association, Inc.

employment status, and previous experience with violence, and it relates these to such factors as the age, temperament, and sib-order of the abused child. In addition, the social context of child abuse is examined.

The essay concludes with a broader, social-psychological model of child abuse and discusses the implications of this approach for strategies of intervention in child abuse.

The Psychopathological Model[1]

THE CHILD ABUSER: A PSYCHOPATHIC PORTRAIT

Essays on child abuse almost invariably open by asserting that a parent who would inflict serious abuse on a child is in some manner sick. This assertion ranges from the point blank statement that the child abusing parent is mentally ill (Coles, 1964) to the indirect statement that the abuser is the patient of the clinician (Bennie and Sclare, 1969). In some cases, the sickness is traced to a flaw in the socialization process, where "something went haywire or was not touched in the humanization process" (Wasserman, 1967). Many essays and books begin with the assumption that the parent abuser is a psychopath. Steele and Pollock (1968) announce that their first parent abuser was a "gold mine of psychopathology"; Kempe et al. (1962) describe the abuser as the "psychopathological member of the family"; while Galdston (1965) mentions parents who "illustrate their psychopathology" when discussing their relations with their children.

The psychopathological model goes on to focus on specific psychological characteristics of the parent. Steele and Pollock (1968) hold that child abusing parents have severe emotional problems, while Kempe et al. (1962) locate the problem in a defect of the character structure. The parent who abuses is described as impulsive, immature, and depressed (Steele and Pollock, 1968; Kempe et al., 1962; Bennie and Sclare, 1969; Zalba, 1971). A link between sex and violence in the abusive parent is shown in the findings that abusive parents are sadomasochistic (Steele and Pollock, 1968) and that they abuse their children to displace aggression and sadism (Bennie and Sclare, 1969). Abusive parents are also described as having poor emotional control (Bennie and Sclare, 1969) and quick to react with poorly controlled agression (Kempe et al., 1962). Some authors describe the child abuser as inadequate (Bennie and Sclare, 1969), having pervasive anger (Zalba, 1971), and dependent, egocentric, narcissistic, demanding, and insecure (Steele and Pollock,

1968). Abusive parents also suffer from some psychosomatic illnesses (Steele and Pollock, 1968) and have a perverse fascination with punishment of children (Young, 1964).

Many other authors (U.S. Department of Health, Education and Welfare, 1969) could be cited as illustration that the psychopathological model views the abusing parent as having abnormal psychological traits. However, those works cited are sufficient to make clear that mental abnormality is viewed as the cause of child abuse.

PARENT AND CHILD: REVEALING THE PSYCHOPATHY

The authors advancing the psychopathological model of child abuse find the disorder manifested in the parent's relationship with his child. One form of this manifestation is the "transference psychosis" (Galdston, 1965). Abusive parents often speak of their child as if he were an adult; they perceive the child as a hostile persecuting adult, and often see former guilt in their own child (Galdston, 1965). As a result of the "transference," the parental distortion of reality causes a misinterpretation of the infant child. The child is perceived as the psychotic portion of the parent, which the parent wishes to destroy (Steele and Pollock, 1968). The child is projected as the cause of the parent's troubles (Steele and Pollock, 1968) and becomes a "hostility sponge" for the parent (Wasserman, 1967).

The psychopathy of the abusive parent is conceived as manifesting itself as a transference and distortion of reality on the part of the parent. In this state, the immature, impulsive, dependent (and the like) individual lashes out at a hostile world. More specifically, he lashes out at what he projects as the source of his troubles—his child.

CAUSE OF THE PSYCHOPATHY

After identifying the abusive parent as sick, listing the traits or symptoms of the sickness, and illustrating how the sickness manifests itself in parent-child relations, the psychopathological model establishes a causal explanation for the presence of the psychopathy. Steele and Pollock (1968) state that one cause is that the parents were raised in the same style (physical punishment and abuse) they re-create in raising their own children. This position is elaborated by Reiner and Kaufman (1959), who find that abusive parents are imbedded depressives because they were emotionally or psychologically abandoned as a child; as a result, violent behavior becomes the child's means of communication.

TABLE 3
Psychopathological Model of Child Abuse

Early Childhood Experience	⟶ Psychopathic States	⟶ Child Abuse
Abused	Personality traits	
Emotionally abandoned	Character traits	
Psychologically abandoned	Poor control	
Physical punishment	Neurological states	

This establishes a life pattern of aggression and violence, which explains both the psychopathy and the abuse (Bennie and Sclare, 1969). Thus, the cause of the pathology is the parent's early childhood experience, which included abuse and abandonment. The assumption is that parents who were abused as children will almost certainly pass this on to their own children.

The resulting psychopathological model is diagrammed in Table 3; it is an elementary linear model. Early childhood experience characterized by abuse creates psychological stress and produces certain psychopathic states. These psychopathic conditions, in turn, cause abusive acts toward the child.

PROBLEMS OF THE PSYCHOPATHOLOGICAL MODEL

A problem of the psychopathological approach is that most of the discussions of the causes of child abuse are clearly inconsistent and contradictory. Some authors contradict themselves by first stating that the abusing parent is a psychopath and then stating that the child abuser is no different from the rest of society. Steele and Pollock (1968) state that their first patient was a "gold mine of psychopathology," and then later state that their patients were a "random cross-section of the general population" who "would not seem much different than a group of people picked by stopping the first several dozen people one would meet on a downtown street." Zalba (1971) states that child abusers do not fit easily into a psychiatric category, while Galdston (1965) maintains that, aside from the transference psychosis, there are no other symptoms of psychotic disorder. Kempe et al. (1962) after describing the psychopathic personality of the child abuser, go on to state that child beating is not confined to people with psychopathic disorders.

A second problem is an inability to pinpoint the personality traits that characterize the pathology. Of 19 traits listed by the authors, there was agreement by two or more authors on only four traits. Each remaining trait was mentioned by only a single author. Thus, there is little agreement as to the makeup of the psychopathy.

A third problem is that few studies attempt to test any hypothesis concerning the phenomenon. A recent comprehensive review of the literature (Spinetta and Rigler, 1972) found that most of the studies start and end with relatively untested common-sense assumptions. This, in turn, is because most of the studies are ex post facto (Spinetta and Rigler, 1972). When the analysis of the behavior takes place after the fact, little analytic understanding of the genesis of the behavior is offered. For instance, authors state that abusive parents have poor emotional control (Bennie and Sclare, 1969), or that they react with poorly controlled aggression (Kempe et al., 1962). Analyzed after the fact, it seems obvious that a parent who beats his child almost to the point of death has poor emotional control and reacts with uncontrolled aggression. This type of analysis does not distinguish the behavior in question from the explanation. The drawbacks of this type of labeling are pointed out by Szasz (1960, 1961, 1970) in his discussion of the myth of mental illness. Szasz argues that people who are labeled mentally ill are *then* thought to be suffering from mental illness. The types of after-the-fact explanations offered by the psychopathologic model offer little predictive power in the study of child abuse.

A final criticism of the psychopathological approach is the sampling technique used to gather the data. Most of the data are gathered from cases that medical or psychiatric practitioners have at hand. Thus, the sample cannot be considered truly representative of child abusers because many or most are not seen in clinics. More importantly, there is no attempt to compare samples of "patients" with any comparative group of nonchild abusers. Without this comparison, we have no way of knowing whether, in fact, child abusers differ from the rest of the population in terms of the causal variables proposed by the psycho-pathological model.[2]

A Sociological Approach to Child Abuse

It should be noted that authors advancing the psychopathological model make a special effort to point out that social variables *do not* enter into the causal scheme of child abuse. Steele and Pollock (1968), for instance, state that social, economic, and demographic factors are irrelevant to the actual act of child beating. Other researchers (Blumberg,

1964; Galdston, 1965; Young, 1964; Zalba, 1971) also argue that their cases of child abuse make up a cross-section of socioeconomic status, ethnicity, age, and education.

In examining the data presented in the research on child abuse it is apparent that, even though the authors deny the relevancy of social factors, there are patterns of sociological and contextual variables that *are* associated with child abuse.[3] This section reexamines the data in terms of three aspects of child abuse; the social characteristics of abusing parents, the social characteristics of the victims, and the situational or contextual properties of the act of child abuse. This section is aimed at broadening our understanding of the causes of child abuse by examining the sociological features of the abusers, abused, and acts of abuse.

THE PARENT WHO ABUSES

Even though the authors note that their case materials evidence a large number of middle-class parents, there is evidence that the working and lower classes are overrepresented among child abusers. The essays that provide data on the socioeconomic class of each abuser show an association between social class and child abuse. Gil (1971) found that, in most of his cases, the perpetrator of the abuse was of low socioeconomic status. Bennie and Sclare (1969) found that 80% of their cases of child abuse (10 cases) were from the lower class (unskilled workers). Factors related to socioeconomic status also support the notion of the low status of the abuser. Gil (1971) reports that education, occupation, and income of child abusers are lower than those of the general population. Galdston (1965) states that battering parents have limited education and financial means.

This evidence lends support to the claims that intrafamily violence occurs more often in the lower class or the working class. Blumberg (1964) points out that the lower class uses "normal violence" more often than do upper classes. Steinmetz and Straus (1971), while arguing that the literature is not conclusive,[4] do concede that intrafamily violence is more common among the working class. In explaining his findings, Gil (1971) argues that the socioeconomic pressures on the lower class weaken the caretakers' psychological mechanisms of self-control; he feels that the poverty of the lower classes produces frustration that is released in a physical attack on the child.

Another finding in the sociological analysis of child abuse is that the sex of the abuser is often female. Resnick's study of child filicide found that mothers kill more often than fathers (1969: 88-43). Of Bennie and Sclare's (1969) 10 cases of abuse, 7 of the abusers were women. Steele and Pollock (1968) report that, of their 57 cases of child abuse, the mother was the abuser 50 times. In Zalba's (1971) study, the sexes split 50-50 in terms of who was the actual abusing parent. Gil's (1971) analysis of cases found that the mother abused children 50% of the time, while the father abused children 40%. (Gil also determined that the reason for this might be the predominance of female-headed households.)

Given the culturally defined male-aggressive/female-passive roles in our society and that men are usually more aggressive than women (Singer, 1971), it might be surprising that females are so highly represented and overrepresented in cases of child abuse. One explanation for this is that the child threatens or interferes with the mother's identity and esteem more than it does the father's. (Except when the father cannot fill the provider role, and the children can be seen as a threat to his identity and esteem [O'Brien, 1971].) An illustration of this hypothesis is a case cited by Galdston (1965), in which a mother had to quit work as a result of a pregnancy and her husband's desire to return to work. Forced into closer contact with her 10-month-old child, she subsequently beat him because she found his cries "so demanding." Other case studies indicate that it is the mother who, through close contact with the child, experiences the frustration of trying to rear and control the child. The child who is perceived by the mother as impinging on her freedom and desires seems to be vulnerable to abuse from the frustrated mother.

THE CHILD WHO IS ABUSED

The most dangerous period for the child is from 3 months of age to 3 years. The abused, battered, or murdered child is most vulnerable during those years when he is most defenseless and least capable of meaningful social interaction. Resnick (1969) found that the first six months were the most dangerous for the child. Bennie and Sclare (1969) report that in their sample, battered children were usually from 2 to 4 months old. Kempe et al. (1962) stated that the "Battered Child Syndrome" was most common in children under 3 years of age, while Galdston (1965) found that the most frequent cases of abuse were from 3 months to 3-and-a-half years. It is entirely possible that these data are somewhat misleading, because the vulnerability of a child to physical damage is greater the younger he is. Older children may also be subject to physical abuse, but they might not appear in medical case studies because their age-produced physical durability makes them less vulnerable to serious physical damage caused by abuse.

There are two analytic directions that can be followed. The first is that there is something about parental relations with young, subsocial children that leads some parents to abuse them; the second is that parental abuse of children is not a function of the child's age and that the data are misleading by nonrepresentative and selective gathering of cases. At this point, I would opt for the first direction. There seem to be three interrelated factors that result in the 3-month to 3-year-old child being particularly vulnerable to parental abuse.

First, the small infant or toddler lacks the physial durability to withstand much physical punishment or force. While an older child might absorb a great deal of physical punishment, the 3-month to 3-year-old is likely to be severely damaged or even killed by the same type of force. Thus, because younger children are more likely to be harmed, they are more easily *abused*. Second, the fact that infants are not capable of much meaningful social interaction may create a great deal of frustration for parents who are trying to interact with infants. The case studies reveal that abusing parents often complain that they hit their children because they could not toilet-train them, get them to stop crying, or get them to obey their commands. Because the parents cannot "reason" with infants, they may feel their only course of action is physical punishment.

Third, the new or infant child may create stress for the parent just by birth alone. The newborn child may create economic hardship for the family, or may interfere with professional, occupational, educational, or other plans of the parents. Thus, the new child may create structural stress for parents which is responded to by abuse.

THE SOCIAL CONTEXT

Perhaps the best example of the narrowness of the psychopathological approach to child abuse is the fact that it does not examine possible social causes of the psychological stress that it sees as leading to child abuse.

One stress-producing condition is unemployment. O'Brien (1971) in his discussion of the causes of intrafamily violence, argues that one should find violence most common in families whose classically dominant member (male-adult-husband) fails to possess the superior skills, talents, or resources on which his preferred superior status is supposed to be based. O'Brien's theory would support the notion that unemployment of the husband would lead to intrafamily violence. This assumption is supported in the child abuse literature. Gil (1971) found that nearly half of the fathers of abused children were not employed at the time of the abusive act. Galdston (1965) also found that, in abusive families, the father of the abused child was unemployed or worked part time while the wife worked part time and cared for the child the rest of the time.

A second contextual factor is that the abused child is usually the product of an unwanted pregnancy. The Massachusetts Society for the Prevention of Cruelty to Children reports that in 50% of 115 families studied, there was premarital conception (Zalba, 1971). Wasserman (1967) found that, in many of the child abuse cases, the child was conceived out of wedlock. Bennie and Sclare (1969) report that the abused child was often the product of an unwanted pregnancy—the pregnancy was unwanted either because it was premarital or inconvenient. In Kempe et al.'s (1962) case #1 the battered child was an unwanted one, born soon after marriage "before the parents were ready for it." One of Resnick's (1969) cases of child murder reveals that a mother killed after she felt "labor pains" and was afraid she was pregnant again. The mother articulated the stress that another baby would cause by stating "how hard it is to raise even two children."

The finding that the abused child is often the product of an unwanted pregnancy ties in with the finding that the abused child is both young and usually the youngest or only child (Bennie and Sclare, 1969), and with Gil's (1971) finding that there is more abuse in families of four or more children. These findings suggest that a newborn, unwanted child may create a tremendous amount of stress in family life. The child may be a financial burden, an emotional burden, or a psychological burden to the parent or parents who did not plan or want the arrival. Thus, the unwanted child can become the receiver of a parent's aggression, not because of some fantasy or transference psychosis, but because the unwanted child is, in fact, a source of stress for the family. The abusive parents are *not* lashing out at a *projected* source of their troubles, they are beating a concrete source of family stress—an unwanted child.

The data about unemployment and unwanted children suggest that economic conditions producing stress and frustration are important factors in explaining parental abuse of children. This is a specific example of Goode's (1971) general proposition that a family that has little prestige, money, and power suffers greater frustration and bitterness and thus may resort to more violence (Goode, 1971).

Economic conditions are not the only source of stress that may lead to child abuse. Bennie and Sclare (1969) found that in four of seven cases of child abuse, women entered into marriage with men of different religions. The authors propose that intermarriage produced prolonged family stress, which eventually was a variable causing child abuse. Bennie and Sclare also found abusive families characterized by disrupted marital relationships. Zalba (1971) also found a great deal of marital and family conflicts in families where there were cases of child abuse.

THE CAUSES OF ABUSE: TOWARD A SOCIAL PSYCHOLOGICAL MODEL

That stress in the family is associated with child abuse is not a sufficient explanation of child abuse. In order to develop a broad causal model of child abuse, one would have to explain why abuse is an adaptation to stress—as opposed to other types of responses (Merton, 1938). This section extends the analysis of the causes of child abuse by examining the experience of parents with violence.

A review of the literature points out that abusive parents were raised in the same style that they have recreated in the pattern of rearing their own children (Steele and Pollock, 1968). Kempe et al. (1962) stated that attacking parents were subject to similar abuse as children, and that this pattern of child rearing is passed on in unchanged form. Gil's (1971) survey found that 11% of parents who abuse their children were victims of abuse during childhood. Granted, as the authors articulating the psychopathological approach argue, that abuse as a child had psychological consequences, it also has sociological consequences. One factor that determines what form of adaptation parents will use in dealing with family stress is their own childhood socialization. An individual who was raised by parents who used physical force to train children and who grows up in a violent household has had as a role model the use of force and violence as a means of family problem-solving. The parents who recreate the pattern of abusive child rearing may be doing this because this is the means of child rearing they learned while growing up. It is the way they know of responding to stress and bringing up their child.

Considering this notion of child socialization and its effect on later patterns of child rearing, we may think of child abuse in terms of a social psychological model such as the one in Figure 1.

Some people would regard this model as the "social origins of psychopathology," and indeed the model does assume that a certain

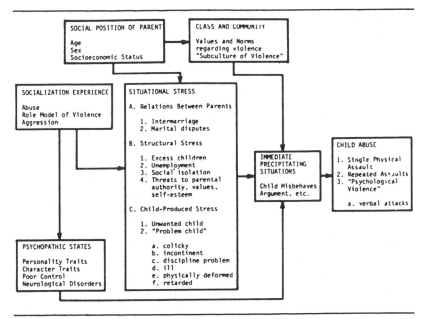

Figure 1: A Social Psychological Model of the Causes of Child Abuse

amount of child abuse is a function of psychopathic states (bottom left box). However, psychopathic states are only a possible, but not necessary, intervening variable in the explanation. The model goes beyond the unicausal approach by analyzing the sociocultural causes of abuse. The model assumes that frustration and stress are important variables associated with child abuse (middle box). Therefore, child abuse can be examined using the frustration-aggression approach (Miller, 1941). Certain structural conditions (Merton, 1938), such as social position, family roles, and unemployment (top left box and middle box) are also associated with abusive behavior toward children. In addition, norms concerning appropriate behavior and levels of physical punishment of children are important considerations (Wolfgang and Ferracuti, 1967) (top right box). Finally, the role of the child is important (middle and middle right box). The disposition of the child, the behavior, and the demands function as both causal factors and precipitating events of child abuse.

The purpose of presenting this model of factors influencing child abuse is not to suggest an exhaustive list of approaches nor to select one that is superior to the others. Instead, the purpose is to illustrate the complexity and the interrelationships of the factors that lead to child abuse.

Conclusion: Implications for Strategies of Intervention and Future Research

When patients are diagnosed as sick, the treatment administered to them is designed to cure their illness. Consequently, when a child abuser is diagnosed as a psychopath, the treatment is designed to cure the disease and prevent future episodes that result from the disease. Basically, the cure prescribed is psychological counseling, psycho-therapy, psychoanalysis, psychiatric aid, and the other psychiatric mechanisms designed to rid the patient of the disorder. So far, the treatment of psychopathic disorders of abusive parents tends to be of limited effectiveness. Psychiatrists feel that treatment of the so-called sociopath or psychopath is rarely successful (Kempe et al., 1962). With this treatment being of limited utility, the only remaining strategy of intervention is to remove the child from the parents. Even this strategy has little success, because the state cannot keep the child from the parent indefinitely. Elmer (1967) reveals the case history of one family in which the child was abused, removed from the family, thrived, returned, and was again beaten.

Thus far, it seems that the existing strategies of intervention in child abuse cases hold little promise for solving the problem. This article suggests that one reason may be that the strategies are based on erroneous diagnoses of the problem. If one steps out of the psycho-pathological framework, it can be seen that the strategies are designed to cure symptoms that in many cases, do not exist. If the parent is not a psychopath in any meaningful sense of the word, then how can treatment aimed at eliminating the psychopathy be of consequence?

As far as developing new strategies of intervention, it is now necessary to stop thinking of child abuse as having a single cause: the mental aberrations of the parents. As Gil (1971) states, physical abuse of children is not a uniform phenomenon with one set of causal factors—but a multidimensional phenomenon. It is time to start thinking about the multiple social factors that influence child abuse. If unemployment and social class are important contextual variables, then strategies to prevent child abuse should aim at alleviating the disastrous effect of being poor in an affluent society. The fact that unwanted pregnancy appears so often in the cases indicates that programs ought to be designed to aid in planned parenthood, birth control devices, and the like. Within this area is also a strong argument for the removal of the legal and social stigma of abortion so that unwanted children do not have to be born. And, finally, because there appears to be an association between child rearing and child abuse, programs should be developed to teach parents alternative means of bringing up their children.

The major flaw that exists in current programs and current strategies of intervention is that they amount to an ambulance service at the bottom of the cliff. Child abuse programs now are after-the-fact treatment of parents and children. What needs to be done is to "fix the road on the cliff that causes the accidents." Strategies should be developed that can deal with the problem before the child is beaten or killed. These programs depend on a predictive theory of child abuse. The social psychological model of child abuse in this essay is a start in that direction.

Notes

1. Not *all* students of child abuse subscribe to or support the psychopathological model. Two notable exceptions, who approach child abuse with a more multidimensional model are David Gil (1971) and Myra Blumberg (1964).

2. Similar problems of the psychopathological approach to child abuse are also articulated in sociological analyses of other forms of deviancy. See, for examples, Dunham (1964); Becker (1963); and Hakeem (1957).

3. This multidimensional approach has been advocated by Gil (1971) in his research on child abuse (see also, Gil, 1970 and Gil, D., 1966, "First steps in a nation-wide study on child abuse," *in* Social Work Practice, Columbia University Press, New York). Much of the material in this section is drawn from Gil's empirical research and theoretical formulations, which focus on social and economic factors related to child abuse.

4. There are a wide range of interpretations that can be applied to statistical data on child abuse (see Steinmetz and Straus, 1973, for detailed discussion of this). One problem in interpreting the data is that middle-class children might be overrepresented in the case literature, because their parents have more resources to draw on in obtaining medical and psychological attention for their children and themselves. On the other hand, middle-class children might be underrepresented because the act of child abuse might be more shocking to middle-class families, and lead them to use their resources to "cover up" the abuse by seeking help from a private physician or clinic.

CHAPTER 3

COMMUNITY AGENCIES AND
CHILD ABUSE:
LABELING AND GATEKEEPING

The traditional ideology employed by the community agencies who come face to face with child abuse is that these agencies are *reactors* to the problem of abuse. This view sees abuse as a personal and family problem which requires individual and family services. As Paulson and Blake state, "The abusive father and mother represent a threat to the community" and it is the task of community agencies to "rehabilitate the parents" (1969: 93).

This essay proposes that agencies are far from simple *reactors* to social problems; rather, they play major and active roles in defining the nature and scope of the problem. Moreover, the definitions of the problem which they employ determine which cases are likely to be processed and which ones will be missed by these agencies.

Child Abuse: Incidence, Cause, and Prevention and Treatment

With the rapid increase in attention focused on the problem of child abuse, community agencies have been under pressure to formulate and institute programs and intervention strategies designed to prevent and treat child abuse. The first effort in developing programs began as a result of the groundbreaking work done by C. Henry Kempe and his

Author's Note: From Richard J. Gelles, "Community Agencies and Child Abuse: Labeling and Gatekeeping." Presented at the Study Group on Recent Research on the Interaction Between the Family and Society, 1975. Ann Arbor: University of Michigan and Society for Research on Child Development.

colleagues. Kempe's article on the battered child syndrome published in 1962 alerted the medical profession to the possibility that a major cause of injuries and deaths in children was willfully inflicted injury administered by a parent or caretaker. The ability to diagnose these injuries was enhanced by technological developments in pediatric radiology which allowed pediatricians to identify previously inflicted injuries (Caffey, 1946, 1957; Silverman, 1953; Woolley and Evans, 1955; Gil, 1970). Once child abuse had captured the attention of a portion of the medical profession it was also identified as a problem by social workers (Elmer, 1967; Young, 1964).

The early works on child abuse focused mainly on estimating the incidence of child abuse and devoting a great deal of time to arguing that abuse was both a widespread and a serious problem in families. Once it had been established that abuse was indeed widespread,[1] the next task was to determine what the etiology of abuse was. The first writings on child abuse (see, for example, Kempe et al., 1962; Steele and Pollock, 1974; Zalba, 1971; Galdston, 1965) proposed a psychological model of the causes of abuse. This position was challenged by authors proposing that the available data was more supportive of a social psychological theory (Gil, 1970; Gelles, 1973). The work (see, for example, Newberger et al., 1975) postulates a multidimensional theory drawing on both psychological and sociological factors to explain the causes of abuse.

Although the question of "cause" of child abuse is still the subject of debate, the recent thrust of work in the area of child abuse has been to design prevention and treatment programs. The Child Abuse Prevention and Treatment Act of 1973 (P.L. 93-237) allocated $60 million for the study of child abuse. The bulk of the money was spent on the development of prevention and treatment programs designed to cut down the estimated high number of cases of abuse per annum.

The effort to develop prevention and treatment modalities has yielded a number of programs which focus on various aspects of the suspected causes of abuse. A sampling of these programs reveals treatment modalities which emphasize behavior modification (Polakow and Peabody, 1975), a combination day-care center and treatment center (Ten Broeck, 1974; Galdston, 1975), hospital programs designed to uncover and treat abuse (Wolkenstein, 1975), a community approach to preventing abuse (Lovens and Rako, 1975), the use of volunteers to treat abusive families (Hinton and Sterling, 1975), and a variety of other personal, familial, and community projects designed either to prevent

the occurrence of abuse or to provide services to families once abuse has occurred.

Although the scope of these projects is quite variable, there is one underlying factor which cuts across all programs established by community agencies to treat abuse—that similarity is the conception that there is some objective category of behavior which we can designate and identify as child abuse. The assumption that there is an objective form of behavior which is abuse makes the role of community agencies a reactive one. By reactive, we mean that if the agency sees abuse as an objective phenomenon, then the agency's mandate is to provide some sort of service to counterbalance the problems which cause abuse to occur.

To accept this view of abuse as being an objective phenomenon and to accept the role of the agency as a reactive role overlooks two important facets of child abuse. In the first place, there is no objective phenomenon which can be automatically recognized as child abuse (Gelles, 1975b). For a child to be diagnosed as abused and for a parent to be accused as an abuser requires someone to observe a behavior or the consequences of a behavior and then categorize that behavior as abusive. The necessity of having someone label a phenomenon "child abuse" means that personal, social, and structural variables impinge on the process by which a suspected case of abuse becomes a confirmed case. There is evidence that selective labeling occurs in the diagnosis of abuse. Newberger and his colleagues state that there is a "preferential susceptibility of poor and minority children to receive the diagnosis child abuse and neglect while children of middle and upper-class families may be more often identified as victims of accidents" (1975). Given the assumption that there is *no* objective phenomenon of abuse, then the role of community agencies and the employees of these agencies becomes far more active. They develop their own operational definition of child abuse, they decide who is and who is not abused, and they prescribe the appropriate treatment or intervention procedure. It is to this point that the balance of the essay is addressed—an examination of the active role played by community agencies in interacting with suspected cases of abuse, and the consequences of the agencies' actions for their clients, for other families who may be abusive, for families who are not abusive, and for our own knowledge of the phenomenon which we call child abuse.

Community Agencies as Gatekeepers

Community agencies such as hospitals, health-care clinics, schools, public social work agencies, private social work agencies, and the police play an active part in diagnosing and then labeling suspected cases of child abuse. Sanders (1972) states that there are still a large number of (abuse) cases that go unreported and it is the responsibility of public and private agencies to develop procedures which ensure that cases will be reported. In Florida this responsibility was carried to its logical conclusion when the state (with federal assistance) instituted a statewide telephone number (using a WATS line which could be used at no charge to the caller) for reporting suspected cases of abuse. In the first two years (1971-1973) 48,814 cases were reported to the Florida Division of Family Services (Hurt, 1975: 13).[2]

In the course of receiving reports of suspected abuse over the telephone or in the course of the work activities of police, physicians, school teachers, and social workers, decisions must be made as to whether an injury or a condition reported or observed in a child is child abuse. The agencies which are confronted with suspected cases of abuse serve as gates and gatekeepers which either admit selected cases as abuse or turn away cases as not being abuse. The actions of people staffing the gates determine who will become a child abuser and an abused child. The implications of these gatekeeping activities go beyond the simple designation of who is or is not an abuser/abused. It is apparent that our current level of knowledge about the causes of child abuse is heavily influenced by the process by which agencies diagnose and label cases child abuse. Throughout the early studies of child abuse (see, for example, Kempe et al., 1962; Galdston, 1965; Steele and Pollock, 1974) the causal analyses of child abuse were based on the at-hand cases in physicians', psychiatrists', or social workers' files. This led to the confounding of those variables which made certain people likely to be labeled child abusers with the variables which were causal factors in the act(s) of child abuse (e.g., Is low socioeconomic status causally related to child abuse, or are people from the lower socioeconomic groups more likely to be labeled child abusers?). Although current researchers have been alerted to the problem of generalizing about the causes of abuse from at-hand case data (see a critique of child abuse research by Spinetta and Rigler, 1972, for a discussion of methodological problems with research on child abuse), the central problem has not been rectified.

For instance, a majority of the research projects on child abuse that were funded by the National Center on Child Abuse and Neglect (under funds provided by P.L. 93-237) chose to operationalize the child abuse concept by using all those cases which are found in the files of state agencies mandated by state laws to be central registries for child abuse (such as the Protective Services Division of state departments of welfare or social and rehabilitative services).

If we operationalize child abuse in this manner, knowledge about the causes of child abuse and suggestions concerning possible intervention strategies are strongly influenced by the actions of those agencies which serve as gatekeepers for suspected cases of child abuse.

Given the fact that agencies and their members are key gatekeepers in determining who is abused and play a major part in the social construction of knowledge about child abuse, it would be beneficial to turn our attention to the various factors and processes which influence the activities of community gatekeepers and determine what is child abuse and who are child abusers.

CHILD ABUSE AND OCCUPATIONAL IDEOLOGY

The subject of community agency gatekeeping and labeling has been partially addressed by Lena and Warkov's (1974) examination of occupational perceptions of child abuse and neglect and Viano's (1974) survey of attitudes toward child abuse among American professionals. Both studies report that the amount of knowledge and interest in the topic of child abuse varies by professional group. Viano found that many professionals were uninterested in the issue of abuse and uncooperative in dealing with the problem (1974:3). Nurses, social workers, clergy, and the police were the only professional groups who stated that they would get personally involved in an abuse case (1974:7). Viano found that educators avoid personal involvement with abuse (1974:7-8). Lena and Warkov's investigation of occupational perceptions focused on how child abuse was defined and the factors which professionals felt were important causal variables in instances of child abuse. Lena and Warkov concluded that there was a fair degree of similarity between occupational groups on what constitutes abuse (1974:7). They went on to propose that professional groups share a perception or "occupational ideology" (Caplow, 1964) of the social problem of child abuse (1974:9).

The similarity of definitions of abuse found by Lena and Warkov is probably due to the fact that they sampled their respondents at seminars on child abuse, and it is likely that only those professionals already interested or informed on the topic of child abuse attended the seminars. Viano's findings that perceptions vary between professional groups probably portrays a more accurate picture of the outlook on child abuse held by community agencies.

Based on the work already done on occupational and professional perceptions of child abuse and on our own research on the social construction of child abuse (Gelles, 1975b, states the basic theoretical position of this research), an initial proposition might be that *the occupational and organizational mandate of a community agency determine how active it will be in identifying cases of child abuse, how likely the employees of the agency are to label particular cases abuse, and the type of cases which are labeled child abuse.*

It is clear that an agency which does not see itself as responsible for providing services to families suspected of child abuse and agencies who do not see it as their responsibility to locate cases of child abuse will simply not locate many cases. They may either overlook cases (i.e., classify a broken arm or leg as an accident), or they may label only those cases which they see as their agency's prime priority. An example of the former strategy of overlooking child abuse was found among physicians. A plastic surgeon who was questioned about his willingness to report suspected child abuse cases stated flatly that "I'm not a detective, that is not my job." It was clear that he meant that he viewed his mandate as being restricted to plastic surgery and that the cause of the condition which required the surgery was not in his occupational or professional domain. In another instance, a physician specializing in internal medicine completely overlooked evidence from an X-ray series that revealed numerous healed fractures of the arms and ribs. He referred the case to another service in the hospital without a mention of the possible causes of the fractures or the likelihood that he was treating a case of child abuse. An example of the latter phenomenon of selective perception of child abuse also is seen in the actions of physicians and hospitals. Research on child abuse done in hospital settings typically reports very few cases of child neglect (nonphysical injury). It is possible that child neglect cases do seek treatment from physicians and emergency rooms in hospitals; however, those physicians who are trained to identify child abuse typically equate abuse to physical injury or trauma (for instance, Kempe et al.'s essay in 1962 which opened up the area of child abuse for the medical profession restricted the definition of child abuse to physical trauma and injury). Social work agencies, by virtue of their training, occupational mandate, and diagnostic equipment and experience, are far more likely to diagnose cases of child neglect than child abuse (e.g., social workers do not have the benefit of X-ray technology to assist their diagnosis).

OCCUPATIONAL POWER AND LABELING

Viano discovered that the professional group which was least likely to become personally involved with child abuse was educators. The clergy was found to be somewhat timid in its willingness to be involved, social workers were split in their opinion, and the professional group which stated they would plunge headlong into the problem was the police (1974:8). Our discussions with educators (teachers and counselors), social workers, and physicians indicated that there were differences in willingness to get involved in reporting cases of child abuse in these professions. Interestingly, educators reported that they suspected large numbers of their pupils as being abused, but they had little desire to report abuse cases (thus, violating state law which mandates reporting). One explanation of why educators are so reluctant to get involved and why police, and to a certain extent physicians, are more likely to report cases of abuse is occupational power.[3] We propose that *the higher the occupational power, the more likely a member of that occupation is to report a suspected case of child abuse.* Physicians possess high occupational power by virtue of their prestigious position in the occupational hierarchy. The police officer's occupational power derives from his or her position as a law enforcer and the fact that he or she is a member of the only profession permitted to carry a weapon and use legitimate violence to enforce laws and rules. At the other end of the continuum, educators have a low degree of power because they are employees of the community who are delegated a narrow jurisdiction over the behavior of children and families. Teachers and counselors are aware of their low power in the community and are quite reluctant to offend the school board or parents by initiating child abuse reports.

PROFESSIONAL-CLIENT RELATIONS

A number of examinations of occupations and professions have focused on the complex relations which occur between client and professional (see Freidson, 1960; Goffman, 1961 for examples). These relationships are crucial in determining the structure and nature of the professional relationship. In the case of child abuse we find that the degree of personal relations between the agency worker and the suspected case of abuse strongly influences how likely the agency is to report a client as an abuser and implement programs designed to treat and prevent abusive acts. Physicians report that they are more likely to report a case of child abuse in the course of their work in clinics or emergency rooms than in their private practice. A House Officer on a pediatrics service stated:

> Given the same condition or injury, a child who is seen in an emergency room is five times more likely to be diagnosed as abused than a child who is seen in a private practice.

Physicians and social workers report that they are much more reluctant to suspect abuse and neglect in families where they have established an enduring relationship. The fact that the more impersonal the relationship, the more chance there is that abuse will be observed and reported may partially explain Viano's finding that police are more likely to become involved in cases of abuse while the clergy and educators are much more timid in their involvement (1974).

The aspect of professional-client relations is evident in the problems encountered by educators in their interaction with suspected cases of child abuse. Educators typically are drawn into suspected cases of abuse either by observing injuries in their students or when the students confide to the educator that their parents or caretakers are abusing them. Teachers, counselors, and principals are thrust into the role of possible "double agents" if they use their observations of the reports they receive from their students as evidence in a reported child abuse case. Educators are torn between their legal responsibility to report abuse and the possibility that if they report a case they will erode the trust that students place in them when they seek counseling or guidance. The more typical resolution of this dilemma is that educators rarely report suspected child abuse cases.

"Normal" Child Abuse

The previous section outlines some factors that influence which agencies are likely to deal with child abuse, what types of child abuse or neglect they focus on, and what factors influence their decision to report a case of child abuse. In this section we would like to explore the types of individuals who are "caught" abusing their children and then examine what factors cause particular individuals and families to be vulnerable to the label of child abuser.

Newberger and his colleagues have pointed out that there is a preferential susceptibility of poor and minority children to receive the diagnosis of child abuse and neglect (1975). We would propose that *given similar conditions of the child, community agencies are more likely to label families with socially marginal status (ethnic outgroups, low socioeconomic status, low power) as child abusers, while labeling families with greater prestige and status as having children who are victims of accidents.* This proposition stands as a plausible rival to the one which states that there is a causal association between social and economic marginality and child abuse. While we tend to agree with the latter hypothesis (see Gelles, 1973), we also are inclined to follow the lead of Horowitz and Liebowitz (1967), who state that social deviance and political marginality are closely associated—in other words, those people who are low in political and social power are most likely to be labeled society's deviants. It appears that the "poor are public" in the sense that their behavior is much more open to public scrutiny and public intervention. Because of this, they may be more vulnerable to the designation of abused/abuser.

DISCOVERING CASES

The literature on child abuse is in almost total agreement on one basic point, the most difficult task facing community agencies is that of uncovering, discovering, and investigating suspected cases of child abuse (Sanders, 1972). This is perhaps due to two facts: first, the family is society's most private institution (Laslett, 1973), thus most abusive behavior occurs in the privacy of the home, and second, the portrait of the child abuser-as-psychopath is so heinous a picture that it may motivate many families to cover up all but lethal instances of abuse.

To reach the population of abusers who are defined as requiring social services, agencies develop a variety of strategies to investigate cases of suspected abuse. These strategies become the standard social screening techniques by which cases of abuse are uncovered.

One technique used by community agencies is to apply their standard of parent-child relations to the behavior they observe between their client and the client's child. We spoke to a pediatrician who informed us that the case she reported as abuse was detected when she noticed that an injured child was quite distant from his mother and quite friendly with the physician. This was in stark contrast to the typical situation pediatricians experience when children resist the doctor and cling to the parent. This pediatrician used her previous experience with children to detect an abnormality which she associated with abuse.

The second example is provided by Paulson and Blake (1969), who advise that effective diagnoses of child abuse can be accomplished if the attending physician looks for discrepancies between the nature and extent of the child's injury and the history of that injury provided by the accompanying person (see also Kempe et al., 1962, for the same advice to physicians). Newberger and Hyde (1975) illustrate this procedure when they describe a case where a massive hematoma overlying the left eye of a 10-month old was accounted for by the parent as being caused by a broom which, almost in defiance of the laws of physics and gravity, was propelled by the mother's foot in the baby's crib where it struck the child.

Thus, the social screening devices used by community agencies makes use of yardsticks of normal parent-child interaction and perceived deviations from these yardsticks as indicators of possible abuse, and the accounts (Lyman and Scott, 1970) used by parents to explain injuries. This indicates that the physical condition of the child is a necessary but not sufficient criterion for the diagnosis.

INVESTIGATING CASES

As in the case of discovering cases of child abuse, certain screening processes are used during the investigation phase of child abuse detection. In most instances where a case of child abuse is suspected, the community agency investigates the case, either by interviewing the suspect or visiting the family. The interviews with suspected abusive parents are typically guided by the agency's knowledge and reading on the subject of child abuse. Many social work agencies make use of Helfer and Kempe's book, *Helping the Battered Child and His Family* (1972). These agencies use the personal interview to screen families for the various social and psychological factors which are considered to be causal factors in acts of child abuse. Other agencies may make use of various writings on child abuse, or may make use of the agency's previous experience with abuse cases.

The most interesting screening devices are employed by agencies in the course of home visits. We have interviewed (informally) a number of private and public social workers and a surprising consistency emerges in their discussion of home visits to suspected cases of child abuse. We learned that the smell of urine and feces are prime indicators of the likelihood of child abuse occurring in a family. Agency workers who have investigated child abuse frequently describe the home as disorganized, with no set time for meals, children running around with tattered or no clothing, and the powerful smell of urine and feces striking the worker as he or she enters the home.

There are a number of other factors, which vary by agency, that are used to identify child abuse. The medical agencies typically screen families by looking for premature births, difficult deliveries, and developmental abnormalities in children. Social work agencies are more keenly aware of familial organization and structural components such as single-parent families and patterns of delivering meals to family members. Educators, unlike other agencies, have to rely on the accounts by the children to learn about child abuse. Thus, teachers, counselors, and school administrators depend on the accounts offered by the alleged victims of child abuse.

"NORMAL" ABUSE

The result of the techniques used to develop screening procedures for discovering and investigating cases of child abuse and the experience gained as a result of these discoveries and investigations produce a normal picture of child abuse in the minds of the workers in community agencies (see Sudnow, 1964, for discussion of the idea of normal deviance as viewed by those individuals who interact with deviants). Each community agency develops a stereotyped or normal portrait of the typical abuser, the typical family in which abuse takes place, the circumstances which produce abuse, the time of day, day of week, and time of the year abuse occurs. These portraits become an occupational shorthand by which agencies can expedite their discovery, investigation, and provision of services to families labeled as abusive. While these techniques are almost inevitable in the course of human interaction, and are often efficient, they have unintended consequences which we shall discuss in the concluding section of this essay.

Community Agency Gatekeeping: Consequences

One of the more obvious consequences of community agency gatekeeping is the fact that whatever screening and investigation devices are used, agencies are going to make mistakes in their diagnoses of abuse. In short, agencies are not only going to discover cases of child abuse, they are also going to have a number of false positives (cases labeled as abuse which are not) and false negatives (cases not labeled as abuse which are). To illustrate this point, let us assume that a screening device was established for use by all community agencies which would diagnose child abuse with a 99% level of accuracy. And, let us assume that this device was used by all community agencies to screen 100 million individuals over the age of 18 for signs of abuse. If there are 10,000 cases of abuse a year in the United States, this technique is going to uncover most of these cases. However, using this technique will also mean that one million families will be labeled abusive by mistake (see Light, 1974, for the statistical procedure used in coming up with these figures).

Thus, using a very precise screening technique we are going to (1) spend a great deal of time and money providing services to families which do not require them, and (2) we are going to subject one million families to the stigma and damage of being falsely labeled child abusers.

The illustration which we provided is not particularly realistic (because neither the screening device, nor the procedure for screening all families exist), but there is a point to be made by this illustration. It articulates the basic problem which must be addressed by community agencies in their interaction with suspected cases of child abuse. Each agency must make the pragmatic and philosophic decision as to how aggressive it will be in seeking cases of child abuse. In other words, what type of "error" does it want to make—missing cases or falsely accusing families. At this point in time, given the social constraints imposed by agency and occupational power and the sensitivity of interpersonal relations, it appears that most agencies are willing to accept false negatives to protect themselves from the consequences of false positive diagnoses.

THE AGENCY "WALTZ"

In the course of interviewing members of 80 families on the subject of intrafamilial violence (Gelles, 1974), we spoke with a number of people who had prolonged interaction with community agencies and who had histories of high physical violence between husband and wife and parent to child. One of the more interesting findings derived from these interviews was that we learned that despite the fact that many of these families could have been reported as abusing their children, none were. The families explained that they really had not made much of an attempt to conceal the fact that they had injured a child with physical punishment. They seemed to be concerned that they had never received much help from the agency, and this was in part due to what one woman called "the agency waltz." The agency waltz was, as our respondent described it, a technique used by agencies to get people the kind of services they desired. What happens is that a parent goes to an agency with a single complaint, but in the course of the intake interview other problems are discussed. The agency then refers the family to another agency more qualified to deal with the total range of problems. This agency refers the family to a third or fourth agency. By this time, only the most persistent families are left in the system, the rest having fallen between the seams of the social service system as a consequence of the agency waltz.

The fact that there are numerous private and public agencies given the task of providing basic and needed services to families is the result of political, economic, and social processes which we are not qualified to discuss. However, we have seen the consequences of this system, and the consequences are that the decentralized system of human services results in many cases of child abuse falling away from the social service system. The newspapers often report cases of fatal incidents of child abuse where the police, courts, and social agencies all knew about the family's history of child abuse, but where no agency had taken the responsibility to do anything.

The gatekeeping process, combined with multiple agencies and multiple agency mandates, means that many if not most cases of child abuse will go undetected and without services.

THE SERVICES PROVIDED

There is little doubt that community agencies do help many or even most of their clients. In the case of child abuse, there are reports of various intervention procedures and strategies working "wonders" with abusive families. Almost every agency and every agency worker can point to particular cases which were aided through community agency intervention. We will not, nor can we, dispute these achievements. But we can point out that the particular ways programs are set up by community agencies, are located in the community, and are staffed determine which type of individual is likely to be identified, treated, and treated successfully. The person who brings a child to a medical center and confides in a doctor is systematically different from an individual who seeks private family counseling for an abuse problem and from an individual who is identified by a social work agency. Thus, in most cases, services provided by agencies are client-specific—they work for particular clients and are dismal failures with others. The clients who do not "thrive" under agency programs either move to another agency (the agency waltz revisited) or drop away from the agency system. Agencies are like social "magnets"; they repel as well as attract cases. This being the case, the services provided are derived as a result of the complex series of interactions between agencies and clients which determine what kinds of problems the agency will deal with and what kinds of clients they will interact with.

Implications for Social Policy

This essay has reviewed the subject of community agency labeling and gatekeeping of cases of child abuse. We have discussed the gatekeeping role played by community agencies and have identified a number of factors which influence the activities of community gate-keepers and determine what cases of child abuse will be diagnosed. Finally, the essay briefly discussed some of the consequences of agency gatekeeping.

The concluding section of the essay focuses on some policy implications which can be inferred from a review of the gatekeeping and labeling activities of community agencies.

WHO SHALL BE PROTECTED?

It is clear that despite good intentions and training, community agencies will make errors of diagnosis in screening children and families for child abuse. As the definition of child abuse is broadened to include such things as "mental injury" and "psychological abuse," the error factor in diagnosing suspected cases will increase. While X-rays can detect current and previous physical abuse, no such technology exists for diagnosing mental or psychological abuse.

Second, as the definition of child abuse is broadened, the cost of screening cases is increased. More attention must be paid to the parents, children, and home environment if the subtle symptoms of nonphysical abuse are to be recognized.

It might be wise for community agencies to determine which children are at greatest risk, and strive to protect them as well as possible. By identifying the most seriously at-risk children, agencies can reduce the error factor in diagnosis to a manageable level, and also provide direct services to children and families within reasonable budgetary constraints. While, in an ideal world, it would be desirable to protect all children and guarantee them the right to a risk-free childhood, it is simply not within our knowledge or resources to protect all children who might be physically, sexually, or psychologically abused.

AGENCY COOPERATION

The idiosyncratic methods used by agencies to diagnose and treat suspected cases of child abuse often put abused children and abusive parents on a never ending merry-go-round of agency visits. Although child abuse research has revealed abuse as a phenomenon with multiple causes, the multidimensional theory has not yet been translated into agency practice. There is a desperate need for more interagency cooperation, both in diagnosing and in treating cases of abuse.

INFORMATION CONTROL

The groundbreaking research on child abuse revealed a problem that went on under the eyes of the medical and social service profession. In many instances, cases of abuse went unnoticed because abusive parents would "hospital-hop" with their children. Thus, each admission of an injured child came with no prior medical or social history. Physicians and hospital social workers were often unable to determine if the injury was the result of an idiosyncratic event, or was part of an ongoing pattern of abuse. To improve on diagnosing cases of abuse, states instituted central clearinghouses for child abuse reports. These clearinghouses offered physicians and social workers information on their clients which they could use to determine if a child had been abused.

Although these clearinghouses are beneficial, they pose a clear and serious danger to the families who have been reported as child abusers. If the clearinghouses do not update and clean their files on confirmed and nonconfirmed cases of abuse, many families run the risk of being permanently falsely identified cases of abuse. The potential for misuse of these clearinghouse files becomes evident when reports are issued that juvenile delinquents are found to have been abused as children. One can easily foresee a situation where child abuse clearinghouse records are used to monitor children from infancy to their teens, looking for the first signs of delinquency. A graver misuse of the records could come if law enforcement agencies could use child abuse records as means of screening suspects for crimes. Clearly, the data which we collect on *suspected* cases of child abuse must be collected, maintained, and used in a manner which protects individuals and families from gross infringements on their personal rights.

Notes

1. "Established" should be interpreted with the caveat that it has not been empirically established exactly what the incidence of child abuse is.

2. The ability to uncover cases of child abuse produced more problems than it solved for the state of Florida. In the first place, the state did not have the financial or programmatic resources to follow up each and every report. Second, the level of knowledge about child abuse, its causes and solutions, was, and is still, not advanced enough for the state to provide ameliorative services to all those callers requesting it for themselves or others.

3. This willingness to get involved varies despite state law which protects all occupations and all individuals reporting child abuse from criminal or civil prosecution.

CHAPTER 4

IS VIOLENCE TOWARD CHILDREN INCREASING? A COMPARISON OF 1975 AND 1985 NATIONAL SURVEY RATES

with Murray A. Straus

Since the early 1960s, when child abuse became an issue of major professional and public concern, there has been a widespread belief that the rates of child abuse and violence toward children have been increasing. This belief has been partially supported by the fact that the number of cases of child abuse that are reported to social service agencies has been rising at a rate of about 10% each year since the mid-1970s (American Humane Association, 1983).

Numerous hypotheses have been put forward to explain the supposed increase; they include greater stress in society, increased unemployment, economic problems, rising divorce rates, increased numbers of single-parent households, and so on. One could also argue, on logical and theoretical grounds, that the opposite is also plausible—that the rates of violence and abuse have gone down. Demographic data indicate that couples are marrying later, having fewer children in general, and having fewer unwanted children in particular (Bane, 1976). Since these factors have all been found to be related to lower rates of domestic assault (Straus, Gelles, & Steinmetz, 1980), these changes may be reducing the risk of violence for family members (Straus, 1981).

Finally, it is possible that the rates of violence and abuse have remained stable.

This chapter presents results from the Second National Family Violence Survey that was designed to provide empirical data on whether the rates of family violence are increasing, decreasing, or stable. The study replicates the First National Family Violence Survey that we carried out in 1976. We were able to compare the rates of reported violence for calendar year 1975 with the violence rates reported for 1985. This chapter examines the rates of violence toward children. A complete analysis of the entire data set and a full theoretical discussion of the results appears in Straus and Gelles, 1986.

Background: Data From Official Reports

There have been no systematic studies conducted with the goal of measuring the changing rates of violence toward children. There are some data that are available, but the limitations of these data preclude using them to answer the question about whether violence in the home is increasing, decreasing, or remaining stable.

OFFICIAL REPORTS OF CHILD ABUSE AND NEGLECT

The National Study of Child Neglect and Abuse Reporting has been conducted by the American Humane Association since 1976. This annual survey measures the number of families, alleged perpetrators, and children involved in official reports of child maltreatment. The information in the study is derived from official reports of child maltreatment that is documented by child protective service agencies in each of the states.

Overall, for all forms of reportable child maltreatment, the American Humane Association study found a 142% increase in child maltreatment reporting from 1976 to 1983 (1983 is the last year of data that have been analyzed to date) (American Association for Protecting Children, 1985). The largest yearly increase was from the first year of the study (1976) to the next—an increase of 24.2%. The actual rate of increase has declined since 1980 and has been stable for the last three years.

A drawback of the American Humane Association tabulations is the between state differences in the method of enumeration. Some states use the *family* as the unit of analysis. This underrepresents the amount of abuse since there may be more than one maltreated child per family. Other states count individual children. Looking at children as the unit of analysis, there has been a 121% increase in the number of children reported as maltreated from 1976 to 1983.

The second drawback to these data is more obvious. Child abuse reports are not the same as incidents of child abuse. Given that so much attention has been focused on child abuse and neglect in the last 2 decades, and that there has been a considerable increase in state and local efforts (and funding) to increase reporting, it would be amazing if the number of reports had not increased since 1976. Laws have been revised in each state, intake systems have been redesigned, 24-hour-a-day WATS hot lines for reporting are now commonplace, and there have been state and national media campaigns (including television docudramas) that have been designed to spur reporting. In short, the increase in official reports can be explained as yet another example of the phenomenon Kai Erikson described in *Wayward Puritans* (1976, p. 24). Erikson theorizes that the number of acts of deviance that come to community attention are a function of the size and complexity of the community's social control apparatus—in this case, the child protection system.

Methods

This section reviews the two surveys of family violence, the First National Family Violence Survey conducted in 1976 and the Second National Family Violence conducted in 1985.

THE 1975 NATIONAL FAMILY VIOLENCE SURVEY

A complete description of the 1975 survey can be found in Straus et al. (1980). Here we briefly review the definition of violence, measurement, and the sample used in the survey.

Defining violence and abuse. Violence was nominally defined as "an act carried out with the intention, or perceived intention of causing physical pain or injury to another person." The injury could range from slight pain, as in a slap, to murder. The motivation might range from a concern for a person's safety (as when a child is spanked for going into the street) to hostility so intense that the death of the person is desired (Gelles & Straus, 1979). Abuse included those acts of violence that had a high proability of causing injury to the person (an injury did not actually have to occur).

Operationalizing violence and abuse. Violence was operationalized through the use of Conflict Tactics Scales (Straus 1979). First developed at the University of New Hampshire in 1971, this technique has been used and modified extensively in numerous studies of family violence

(Allen & Straus, 1980; Cate, Henton, Christopher, & Lloyd, 1982; Henton, Cate, Koval, Lloyd, & Christopher, 1983; Hornung, McCullough, & Sugimoto, 1981; Jorgensen, 1977; Straus, 1974). The Conflict Tactics Scales (CTS) contain items to measure three variables: (1) use of rational discussion and agreement (discussed the issue calmly, got information to back up your side; brought in/tried to bring in someone to help settle things); (2) use of verbal nonverbal expression of hostility (insulted or swore at the other; sulked or refused to talk about it; stomped out of the room or house; did or said something to spite the other; threatened to hit or throw something at the other; threw, smashed, hit, or kicked something); and (3) use of physical force or violence (threw something at the other; pushed, grabbed, or shoved the other; slapped or spanked; kicked, bit, or hit with a fist; hit or tried to hit with something; beat up the other; threatened with knife or gun; used a knife or gun).

The abuse items were those violent acts that had a high probability of causing an injury; kicked, bit, or hit with a fist; beat up; hit or tried to hit with something; threatened with knife or gun; used a knife or gun.[1]

The items of the Conflict Tactics Scales are presented to subjects and the subjects are asked to say how often they used each technique when they had a disagreement or were angry with a family member both in the previous year and in the course of the relationship with the family member. The following relationships were assessed in the 1975 survey—parent to child; child to parent; husband to wife; wife to husband; and sibling.

Reliability and validity. The reliability and validity of the Conflict Tactics Scales have been assessed over the 15 year period of their development. A full discussion of their reliability and validity can be found in Straus (1979) and Straus et al. (1980). There is evidence of adequate internal consistency reliability, concurrent validity, and construct validity.

Sample and administration. A national probability sample of 2,143 households made up the First National Family Violence Survey of 1975. The sample was drawn by Response Analysis and was an area probability sample. In each family where there was at least one child at home between the ages of 3 and 17 years of age, a "referent child" was selected using a random procedure. The lower age limit of 3 years of age was required because one aim of the study was to obtain meaningful data on sibling violence. Also, the study excluded subjects who were not currently living with a partner of the opposite sex. This was done to assure that there would be a sufficient number of couples to conduct an analysis of marital violence.[2]

Interviews, lasting approximately one hour, were conducted in-person by trained interviewers employed by Response Analysis. The completion rate for the entire sample was 65%, varying from a low of 60% for metropolitan areas to a high of 72.3% for other areas.

THE 1985 NATIONAL FAMILY VIOLENCE SURVEY

Modifications to the Conflict Tactics Scales. There were two additions to the Conflict Tactics Scales for the 1985 Second National Family Violence Survey. The 1975 version of the scales omitted items that have been found to be relatively common forms of abusive violence. The item "burned or scalded" was added to the 1985 parent to child version of the scales, while the item "choked" was added to the 1985 marital violence scales.

The 1975 survey focused on behaviors without assessing the consequences or outcomes of acts of violence. In this survey we wanted to obtain a measure of the outcome of violent acts. We added a series of questions that asked whether an act of violence produced an injury that required medical attention—either seeing a doctor or overnight hospitalization.

Sample and administration. A national probability sample of 6,014 households made up the Second National Family Violence Survey. The sample was drawn by Louis Harris Associates using a Random Digit Dial procedure. The sample was made up of four parts. First, 4,032 households were selected in proportion to the distribution of households in the 50 states. Then, 958 households were oversampled in 25 states. This was done to assure that there would be 36 states with at least 100 completed interviews per state.[3] Finally, two additional oversamples were drawn—508 black and 516 Hispanic households.[4]

To be eligible for inclusion in the sample, a household had to include adults 18 years of age or older who were (1) currently married; (2) currently living as a male-female couple; (3) divorced or separated within the last two years; or (4) single parent with a child under 18 years of age and living in a household. When more than one eligible adult was in the household, a random procedure was used to select the gender and marital status of the respondent. When more than one child under the age of 18 was in the household, a random procedure was used to select the "referent child" who would be the focus of the parent to child violence questions.

Interviews were conducted by telephone by trained interviewers employed by Louis Harris and Associates. When telephones were busy or there was no answer, three call backs were made prior to substituting a new household. If contact was madde and subjects refused to be screened or participate, trained "refusal conversion" interviewers were assigned to the household.

The response rate, calculated as "completes as a proportion of eligibles," was 84%. Interviews lasted an average of 35 minutes.[5]

Results

This article reports on the data from the main sample of 4,032 cases. When the data from the over-samples are weighted, they will be included in the analysis.

In order to make the comparison we had to compare the same types of families we surveyed in 1985 to those surveyed in the first study. Thus the comparison is limited to households where there was at least one child between the ages of 3 and 17 years old in the home and where a married couple or a man and a wife living as a couple resided. There were 1,428 such families in the Second National Survey.

Table 4 presents the comparison for each violent act as well as the summary indexes. With the exception of threatening and using guns and knives, *the occurrence of each form of violence toward children declined in the last 10 years.*

The Overall Violence index reports on whether a parent used any one of the eight forms of violence at least once. Here there was essentially no change in the rate of violence between 1975 and 1985.

The most substantial changes were for the use of severe and very severe violence. The rate of severe violence (kicking, biting, punching, hitting or trying to hit with an object, beating, threatening with a gun or knife, or using a gun or knife) declined from 140 cases per 1,000 in 1975 to 107 cases per 1,000 in 1985.

Very severe violence—the index we use to estimate the abuse of children (Gelles, 1978; Straus et al., 1980)—declined from 36 cases per 1,000 to 19 cases per 1,000. This is a decline of 47% from the rate of abusive violence in 1975.

Discussion

Has the rate of severe and abusive violence toward children really dropped? There are three logical explanations for the results we found.

TABLE 4
Parent-to-Child Violence: A Comparison of Rates in 1975 and 1985

Type of Violence	Rate per 1,000 Children Aged 3 through 17[a]		
	1975 (N = 1,146)[b]	1985 (N = 1,428)[c]	t for 1975-1985 Differrences
(1) Threw something	54	27	3.41 ***
(2) Pushed, grabbed, or shoved	318	307	0.54
(3) Slapped or spanked	582	549	1.68
(4) Kicked, bit, or hit with fist	32	13	3.17 **
(5) Hit or tried to hit with something	134	97	2.91 **
(6) Beat up	13	6	0.26
(7) Burned or scalded	N/A	5	N/A
(8) Threatened with gun or knife	1	2	0.69
(9) Used gun or knife	1	2	0.69
Overall violence (1-6; 8-9)	630	620	0.52
Severe violence (4-6; 8-9)	140	107	2.56 **
Very severe violence (4; 6; 8-9)	36	19	4.25 ***

a. For two caretaker households with at least one child 3 to 17 years of age at home.
b. On some items, there were a few responses omitted, but figures for all incidents represent at least 1,140 families.
c. On some items, there were a few responses omitted, but figures for all incidents represent at least 1,148 families.
*p < .05; **p < .01; ***p < .001; two-tailed tests.

First, the change could be the result of parents becoming unwilling to report violence to researchers. Second, the change could be due to some other methodological artifact. Lastly, our findings could reflect an actual change in behavior.

WILLINGNESS TO REPORT

A plausible explanation for the decline in reported severe violence toward children is that respondents may have been more reluctant to report severe violence in 1985 compared to 1975. The last ten years have seen a tremendous increase in public attention to the problem of child abuse. National media campaigns, new child abuse and neglect laws, reporting hot lines, and almost daily media attention have transformed an issue that was ignored for centuries into a major social problem. One consequence of the transformation may be a reluctance to report punching, biting, kicking, beating, and striking children. Our findings may simply be a "social desirability" artifact reflecting a change in social attitudes toward the acceptability of violence, but no real change in behavior.

METHODOLOGICAL ARTIFACTS

Another possibility is that the change is due to the fact that different data collection techniques were used in the two surveys. Data for the 1975 survey were collected by in-person interview, while the 1985 survey was conducted over the telephone. The difference, however, should have produced higher, not lower, rates of reported violence. Although researchers have found no major differences in telephone versus in-person interviewing (Groves & Kahn, 1979), we have found that telephone interviews elicit more valid reporting of sensitive or deviant behaviors. The anonymity offered by the telephone could have led to more truthful, and thus increased reporting of violence. A second difference might have also led to increased reporting. During the in-person interview, respondents were handed cards with the response categories for the Conflict Tactics Scales. All possible answers, including "never," were listed on the cards. For the telephone interviews, "never" was a volunteered response. Interviewers read the response categories, beginning with "once" and continuing to "more than 20 times." Respondents had to volunteer "never" or "don't know" responses. Experience has shown that rates of reported sensitive or deviant behavior are higher if the subject has to volunteer the "no" response (see, for example, Kinsey, Wardell, & Martin, 1948).

Thus the bias in the change of methodologies would have led to higher, not lower, rates of reported violence. Since the rate of severe violence went down, it is unlikely that this change is due to the different methods of data collection.

A CHANGE IN BEHAVIOR

The final explanation is that there has indeed been a decline in severe and abusive violence toward children. As we noted at the beginning of the article, there have been significant changes in family organization since 1975. The average age at first marriage has increased, the average age when having a first child has increased, the number of children per family has gone down, and the number of unwanted children has declined. Parents in 1985 are among the first generation to be able to choose a full range of planned parents options (including abortion) to plan family size. All these factors are related to lower rates of violence and abuse.

The economic climate of the country was better in 1985 than in 1975 (at least for the population we are examining—intact families). The rate of unemployment and inflation is down compared to 10 years ago. The one year referent period that we used for our survey coincided with one of the more prosperous economic periods in the past decade. Thus the lower level of economic stress that families experienced in 1985 may explain the decline in severe violence.

We cannot overlook the massive increase in public awareness of the problem of child abuse. In 1976, polls showed that only about 10% of Americans considered child abuse a serious problem (Magnuson, 1983). A 1982 poll conducted by Louis Harris and Associates found that 90% of those surveyed felt that child abuse was a serious national problem. This is almost an unbelievable increase in public awareness.

Lastly, there have been new and innovative prevention and treatment programs implemented to deal with the problem of child maltreatment. States have enacted reporting laws for abuse and neglect, and public and private social services have been developed to try to treat and prevent abuse. While there have been few rigorous evaluations of the effectiveness of these programs, they do, at the very least, fill the vacuum that existed prior to the 1970s in protective services.

Conclusion

Researchers who study family violence ask questions that no one wants to ask and produce answers that no one wants to believe. This might serve as a good conclusion to a study that had, as one aim, an attempt to determine whether violence toward children has increased, decreased, or stayed the same. No matter what the finding, we could have expected that we would not have been believed.

Our analysis to date indicates that the decrease in the rate of reported severe and very severe violence is probably not due to a methodological artifact. This leaves two plausible explanations for our findings—decreased tendency to report violence or decreased violence toward children.

Even if the change is only one of attitudes, we believe this is a significant change for a ten year period—a change that may well lead to an actual change in behavior. If all we have accomplished in the last 10 years is to raise parents' consciousness about the inappropriateness of violence, then we have begun the process of reducing violence toward children. The first stage of establishing the internal social controls that are necessary to reduce child abuse is to establish a consciousness that violence toward children is inappropriate. Thus if we have measured only an attitude change, a decreased willingness to report violence, we have identified a change that could well lead to reduced risk of physical violence for children.

When we began our research on family violence 15 years ago, we concentrated on developing valid and reliable measures and research designs. We confronted the problems of studying sensitive behavior. We believed that if our measures and designs were the most rigorous and appropriate that we could design, then we should believe our data. Thus we believe that the Second National Family Violence Study has indeed found that the rate of severe violence toward children has declined significantly. The 47% decline in the rate of very severe violence was a greater decline than we had expected. Expressed in other terms it means the following:

(1) The First National Family Violence estimated that 1.5 million children, 3 to 17 years of age, living with two parents, were abused. A decline of 47% means that 705,000 fewer children are the victims of abusive violence in 1985 compared to 1975.

(2) In total, 1 in 25 children, 3 to 17 years of age, living with two parents, was a victim of very severe violence in 1975. In 1985, the figure is 1 in 33 children.

Future papers will report on the changing rates of spousal violence and will further examine the explanations of the changes in severe and very severe violence toward children.

Notes

1. There were two abuse subscales computed for abusive violence toward children—one contained the item, "hit or tried to hit with something"—the other excluded this item.

2. In 1976 we had no idea what the rate of family violence would be. Thus our inclusion criteria for the study (couples, children 3 to 17 years of age) were conservative in order to assure that we would have enough cases of violence for statistical analysis.

3. One objective of the second national survey was to collect data that could be aggregated by state for analysis of state-level trends and relationships.

4. Data were weighted to take into account the state, black, and Hispanic oversamples.

5. A complete description of the sampling and methodology is available from the authors.

References

Allen, C.M., & Straus, M. A. (1980). Resources, power, and husband-wife violence. In M. A. Straus & G. T. Hotaling (Eds.), *The social causes of husband-wife violence* (pp. 188-208). Minneapolis: University of Minnesota Press.

American Association for Protecting Children. (1985). *Highlights of official child neglect and abuse reporting, 1983.* Denver: American Humane Association.

American Humane Association. (1983). *Highlights of official child neglect and abuse reporting.* Denver: Author.

Bane, M. J. (1976). *Here to stay: American families in the twentieth century.* New York: Basic Books.

Cate, R. M., Henton, J. M., Christopher, F. S., & Lloyd, S. (1982, March). Premarital abuse: A social psychological perspective. *Journal of Family Issues, 3,* 79-90.

Erikson, K. (1966). *Wayward Puritans.* New York: John Wiley.

Gelles, R. J. (1978, July.) Violence toward children in the United States. *American Journal of Orthopsychiatry, 48,* 363-371.

Gelles, R. J., & Straus, M. A. (1979). Determinants of violence in the family: Toward a theoretical integration. In W. R. Burr, R. Hill, F. I. Nye, & I. L. & I. L. Reiss (Eds.), *Contemporary theories about the family* (Vol. 1, pp. 549-581). New York: Free Press.

Groves, R. M., & Kahn, R. L. (1979). *Surveys by telephone: A national comparison with personal interviews.* New York: Academic Press.

Henton, J. M., Cate, R., Koval, J., Lloyd, S., & Christopher, S. (1983, September). Romance and violence in dating relationships. *Journal of Family Issues, 4,* 467-482.

Hornung, C. A., McCullough, B. C., & Sugimoto, T. (1981, August). Status relationships in marriage: Risk factors in spouse abuse. *Journal of Marriage and the Family, 43,* 675-692.

Jorgensen, S. R. (1977, August). Societal class heterogamy, status striving, and perception of marital conflict: A partial replication and revision of Perlin's contingency hypothesis. *Journal of Marriage and the Family, 39,* 679-692.

Kinsey, A., Wardell, B., & Martin, C. (1948). *Sexual behavior in the human male.* Philadelphia: W. B. Saunders.

Magnuson, E. (1983, September 5). Child abuse: The ultimate betrayal. *Time,* 20-22.

Straus, M. A. (1974, February). Leveling, civility, and violence in the family. *Journal of Marriage and the Family, 36,* 13-29 (plus addendum in August, 1974 issue).

Straus, M. A. (1979). Measuring intrafamily conflict and violence: The conflict tactics (CT) scales. *Journal of Marriage and the Family, 41,* 75-88.

Straus, M. A. (1981, July). *Societal change and change in family violence.* Paper presented at the National Conference for Family Violence Researchers, University of New Hampshire.

Straus, M. A. (1986). Societal change and change in family violence from 1975 to 1985 as revealed by two national surveys. *Journal of Marriage and the Family, 48,* 465-479.

Straus, M. A., R. J. Gelles, & S. K. Steinmetz (1980) *Behind closed doors: Violence in the American family.* Garden City, NY: Anchor/Doubleday.

CHAPTER 5

MATERNAL EMPLOYMENT AND VIOLENCE TOWARD CHILDREN

with Eileen F. Hargreaves

A number of reports on child abuse have suggested that the risk of child abuse is greater in families where the mother is employed (Mahmood, 1978; Fontana, 1973; Conger, 1978; James, 1975; Delli Quadri, 1978; Galdston, 1965; Justice and Duncan, 1975). Mahmood (1978) captures the essence of the proposal that physical abuse is greater among working mothers by stating that irritation resulting from day-long employment often leads to child abuse. Garbarino (1976) suggests that the demands placed on women by home and work are associated with child abuse and neglect.

Other writers have proposed that nonworking mothers are more likely to be abusive. Korbin (1978), citing from Rohner (1975) and Whiting (1972), notes cross-cultural evidence that indicates that a woman isolated in the child-care role without relief is more likely to treat her child in a negative fashion. Chapa et al. (1978) report on a study of child abuse and neglect which found that abusive mothers were more likely to be unemployed than mothers in the nonabusive comparison group. Steele and Pollock (1968, 1974) imply a "time at risk" explanation of the nonworking mother's risk of abusing her child. When explaining that fathers are less abusive than mothers, Steele and Pollock note the low rate of unemployment of the fathers in their sample and state that there were fewer hours of contact between the fathers and the children. Steele and Pollock go on to hypothesize that in samples where the mothers work and the fathers stay at home, the rate of paternal abuse would be higher. Although they do not explicitly state that "time at risk"

Authors' Note: From Richard J. Gelles and Eileen F. Hargreaves, "Maternal Employment and Violence Toward Children." *Journal of Family Issues*, 1981, 2 (December): 509-530.

explains the higher rate of maternal abuse, this proposition is a logical derivation from their line of reasoning.

Finally, students of child abuse have also found support for the claim that maternal employment is not related to child abuse and neglect. Starr et al. (1978) found no difference between abusers and nonabusers in terms of the current employment of the mothers. Jameson and Schellenbach (1977) studied a sample of 82 perpetrators and concluded that mother's employment status was not an important factor in the female abuser profile. Martin (1970) also reports no differences in employment status of 50 mothers of burned or scalded children and 41 mothers in a comparison group. Oakland and Kane (1973) similarly note no differences in the employment of mothers of neglected Navajo children and the comparison group.

Research on maternal employment also provides varying evidence as to the possible relationship between mother's employment and violence toward children. Hoffman (1961) reported that working mothers were *less likely* to be coercive with their children and that working mothers with positive attitudes toward their employment were less severe in their discipline. On the other hand, Yarrow et al. (1962) concluded that there were no differences in discipline techniques among employed and unemployed women.

When researchers have assessed the relationship between maternal employment and child abuse there have been numerous methodological problems. One problem has been the frequent combination of abuse and neglect into one dependent variable. Some definitions of neglect imply that a mother who works is neglectful simply by the act of leaving home and going to work. Another problem which arises in much of the child abuse literature is the failure to use control or comparison groups (see Chapter 12). Investigators will often report what percentage of abusive mothers in their sample were employed, but fail to provide comparison data from nonabusing families which would indicate whether the employment rate is higher among the abusing families. Some researchers will report the percentage of mothers who worked but fail to cross-tabulate that by whether they abused their children or not. Other times, data on maternal employment are presented with no indication of which parent committed the abusive act. Maternal employment status is frequently confounded with other variables. A finding that working mothers are more likely to abuse their children becomes less clear when the data show that many of the employed mothers were also single parents. Perhaps the most important drawback of the current information on maternal employment and child abuse is that the reports (where there are comparison groups) confine their data analysis to two-by-two tabular presentations of employment status and abuse. Few controls, if any, are introduced in the analyses to explain the relationships.

Sample and Method

This article examines the relationship between maternal employment and violence toward children. The data for this examination come from interviews with a nationally representative sample of 1,146 families who had at least one child age 3 through 17 living at home.[1]

Interviews were conducted with the mother in 623 families and with the father in 523 families. In each family, the data on physical violence were obtained for only one child, and only for the parent who was interviewed. When there was more than one child age 3 to 17 living at home, a "referent child" for this study was selected using a random number table.

One of the major limitations of this sample, both for purposes of estimating the national incidence of violence toward children (Gelles, 1978; Straus, 1979a) and for examining the relationship between maternal employment and violence, is that one- and two-year-olds—a high-risk age group (Fontana, 1975; Galdston, 1965; Kempe et al., 1962)—are omitted.[2] Thus, in this study we have no information on the relationship between employment of the mother and violence toward the high-risk group of the youngest children.

MEASURING VIOLENCE

We measured violence toward children using a series of questions called the "Conflict Tactics Scales" (CTS). The CTS were first developed at the University of New Hampshire in 1971. They have been used and modified in numerous studies of family violence in the United States, Canada, Israel, Japan, Finland, Great Britain, and British Honduras (data on the validity and reliability of the scales are provided in Straus, 1979b).

The CTS generates two measures of violence toward children. The first measure, referred to here as the "Overall Violence Index," includes all acts of physical violence ranging from slapping and spanking to using a knife or a gun. The second measure, referred to as the "Child Abuse Index," includes only those items from the Overall Index where there was a high probability of a violent act causing an injury to the child.

Specifically, the "Child Abuse Index" consists of whether, during the 12 months prior to the interview, the parent has ever kicked, punched, bit, hit with an object, beaten up, threatened with a gun or knife, or actually used a gun or a knife.

The dependent variables in this investigation—violence and child abuse—differ from the dependent variables used in other studies which relate child abuse to maternal employment. First, the measure of child abuse is quite different from that used in other investigations. We rely on a self-report of five violence items from the CTS which we believe place the child at risk of being injured. We have no direct, or even indirect, measure of whether the "referent child" was actually injured as a consequence of any of these acts. For example, a parent may report using a gun or knife, but we do not know if the child was actually stabbed or shot.

Most studies of child abuse operationalize the term *child abuse* as those cases which have been publicly recognized and labeled as children who have been injured by their parents (Gelles, 1975). This creates a systematic bias which insulates some families from being labeled as abusers and increases the chances that other families—especially low-income and racial and ethnic minority families—will be accurately or inaccurately labeled child abusers. Operational definitions of child abuse which rely on publicly labeled cases have been subject to increasing criticism (Gelles, 1975).

A second difference is that rather than confine our investigation to only acts of abusive violence, we also examined a larger range of violent acts.

MATERNAL EMPLOYMENT

Subjects were asked if they were employed at the time of the interview. This produces the disadvantage of having a measure of violence for the previous 12 months, but a measure of employment for only one point in time.

Employed women were asked how many hours a week they were employed, to describe the type of job they held, how many people they supervised, and whether they liked their work.

We also asked about which partner had the greatest say in whether the wife worked. This was accomplished by using the responses to the question, "Who has the final say on what job you should take?" This question was part of a series of items used to measure family power (derived from Blood and Wolfe, 1960).

OTHER VARIABLES

As noted before, one problem with attempts to investigate the relationship between maternal employment and child abuse has been the failure to introduce control variables. Since we were testing three possible directions of a single relationship, we wanted to introduce factors into the analysis which could aid in explaining any of the three possible relationships we could find.

Role strain. Those theorists subscribing to the hypothesis that working mothers are likely perpetrators of child abuse explain the relationship on the basis of stress caused by the work and mother role. We attempted to assess the level of role strain by measuring the disjunction between domestic responsibilities the mother actually had versus the level of responsibilities she desired. The measure, which asked subjects to report on five areas of domestic activity (managing money; cooking, cleaning, or repairing the house; social activities; supervising the children; and disciplining the children), was based on French et al.'s (1974) work on person-environment fit. Subjects were asked how much responsibility they had and how much responsibility they would like to have for each of the five areas. An index was created by subtracting the scores for "responsibility had" from "responsibility desired."

We assessed the level of stress the mothers experienced by administering a modified version of the Holms and Rahe (1967) Stressful Life Events Scale.

Findings

EMPLOYMENT AND VIOLENCE TOWARD CHILDREN

Mothers who did not work and mothers who reported working part-time were the most likely to have used some form of violence toward their children during the previous year.[3]

While there was a relationship between employment and violence for all acts of violence, there was no statistically significant relationship between employment and child abuse (see Table 5).

The rate of child abuse among mothers who held professional, technical, managerial, administrative, sales, clerical, craft, and operative positions was around 15%. The rate for women employed as laborers or in service positions was appreciably higher (27.6%), but not enough to be statistically significant. This difference may, in part, be due to factors such as income, education, and need to work.

TABLE 5
Mother-to-Child Violence by Maternal Employment

		Violence Rate Per 100 Children	
		Overall Violence	Child Abuse
By Mother's Employment			
Full Time	(N=140)	57.6	17.1
Part Time	(N=102)	70.3	19.6
Housewives	(N=373)	71.0	17.4
		$X^2 = 8.684$	$X^2 = 0.303$
		$p \leq .05$	p NS

Most of the women surveyed reported liking their work. There were an insufficient number of women working full- or part-time who disliked their work to allow for a meaningful analysis of work, work satisfaction, and violence toward children.

WORK AND HOUSEHOLD RESPONSIBILITY

The finding that working mothers are not more prone to use violence against their children does not rule out the hypothesis that the dual responsibility of work and home combine to produce violence and abuse. It may be that only a portion of working women feel overwhelmed by their work and family responsibilities (see Table 6).

The relationship between work and violence was examined, controlling for whether or not the mothers felt they had more responsibility for domestic activities than they desired.

In all but two situations (part-time employed mothers with excess responsibility for money and household matters), mothers who reported excess domestic responsibilities had higher rates of violence and abuse than mothers with the same work status who said they had equal or less responsibility than they desired. Women who were employed part-time and also found that they had more domestic responsibilities than they desired had the highest Overall Violence Index rates—nearly 9 out of 10 mothers with part-time jobs who reported an excess of social responsibilities said they had used violence against their children in the previous year. The abuse rate was highest among mothers will full-time jobs who felt excess responsibility for disciplining their children.

TABLE 6

Mother-to-Child Violence by Maternal Employment and Domestic Responsibility

Types of Responsibility		N			Violence Rate per 100 Children					
					Overall Violence			Child Abuse		
		Full Time	Part Time	House-wives	Full Time	Part Time	House-wives	Full Time	Part Time	House-wives
Money:	Excess	41	36	98	72.5	77.1	75.3	17.1	13.9	22.4
	Not Excess	97	48	271	50.5	67.7	69.0	16.5	23.1	15.5
House:	Excess	67	53	164	68.2	75.0	78.7	19.4	18.9	18.3
	Not Excess	72	48	203	47.2	64.6	64.4	13.9	20.8	17.2
Social Activities:	Excess	29	19	85	62.1	89.5	83.5	20.7	21.1	18.8
	Not Excess	109	82	280	56.0	66.7	66.7	14.7	19.5	17.1
Supervising Children:	Excess	47	44	157	71.7	86.0	79.5	21.3	27.3	19.1
	Not Excess	91	58	206	50.5	58.6	64.1	14.3	13.8	16.0
Disciplining Children:	Excess	51	46	156	72.0	86.7	77.4	25.5	21.7	20.5
	Not Excess	86	56	207	50.0	57.1	66.2	11.6	17.9	15.0

STRESS

Since excess responsibility for domestic activities helped explain and specify the relationship between employment and violence, we thought that life stress would also be a relevant variable. Previous analyses of the data from the national survey showed that the families which had experienced the greatest life stress in the previous year had the highest yearly rates of violence and abuse (Gelles, 1980a).

Controlling for whether the families experience less or more than the mean number of stressful events (the mean number of stressful events experienced by the entire sample of 2,143 was 2) did not alter, in any major way, the relationship between mother's work status and violence and abuse toward children (see Table 7).

DECISIONS ABOUT MATERNAL EMPLOYMENT

We would have liked to look deeper into the reasons for the mother's decision to work or not. Specifically, it would have been of great value to compare mothers whose decision to work was motivated by a desire to avoid mothering, or at least to minimize the mothering role, to the mothers whose desire to work was a consequence of economic need, desire for a career, and so on. Hoffman's (1974) research supports the claim that maternal employment, when motivated by noneconomic factors, is not bad for the child.

We were able to glean some information about the decision to work from the series of questions used to measure family power. When the wife or husband has more influence over whether the wife should go to work or quit work, the relationship between employment of the mother and the Overall Violence Index is essentially unchanged from the original relationship. But, when the decision is a joint one, the difference between women with full-time jobs and women without employment is reduced. Children of mothers who work full-time are less likely to be struck if their mothers have at least an equal say in whether they should go to work (see Table 8).

The rate of abuse is highest among housewives whose husbands had the final say on whether the wife should work. The abuse rate is lowest when housewives have the final say on whether they should work.

INCOME

Surveys of violence toward children report an inverse relationship between rates of violence (and abuse) and income (Gelles, 1980a; Gil,

TABLE 7
Mother-to-Child Violence by Employment and Stress

| | | Violence Rate Per 100 Children | |
| | | Overall | Child |
Employment	Stress	Violence	Abuse
Full Time	0 – 2 Stressful Events (N=76)	52.6	13.2
	3+ Stressful Events (N=61)	63.3	21.3
Part Time	0 – 2 Stressful Events (N=61)	71.7	21.3
	3+ Stressful Events (N=35)	71.4	17.1
Housewives	0 – 2 Stressful Events (N=255)	70.1	18.0
	3+ Stressful Events (N=112)	75.9	17.0

TABLE 8
Mother-to-Child Violence by Employment and
Decision Making About Mother's Work

| | | | Violence Rate Per 100 Children | |
| | Final Say on Mother's | | Overall | Child |
Employment	Employment		Violence	Abuse
Full Time	Wife More	(N=79)	57.7	16.5
	Equal	(N=49)	55.1	18.4
	Husband More	(N=11)	63.6	18.2
Part Time	Wife More	(N=50)	73.5	20.0
	Equal	(N=33)	63.6	15.2
	Husband More	(N=18)	72.2	22.2
Housewives	Wife More	(N=136)	72.8	9.6
	Equal	(N=124)	65.3	20.2
	Husband More	(N=103)	77.5	26.2

1970; Parke and Collmer, 1975; Straus et al., 1980). This study found that although there was not a statistically significant relationship between kind of job and violence or child abuse, the rate of violence and abuse was higher in families when women worked as laborers or in service positions. Based on this we expected to find that the income a woman received from her work would affect the relationship between violence and maternal employment (see Table 9).

The relationship between employment and violence was not altered to any important extent when we controlled for the annual income of the woman worker. Housewives still had a higher rate of Overall Violence than women who worked full-time for the least amount of money. In terms of the child abuse rates, women who worked full-time and had incomes in excess of $6,000 had higher rates of abusive violence than housewives.

The total family income did affect the relationship between the rate of Overall Violence and employment. The difference between women with full-time jobs and women who did not work was greater among those in the lower-income groups (income under $12,000), compared to the differences in the zero-order relationship between employment and the rate of Overall Violence. In the lowest income group (under $6,000) the rate of Overall Violence among women who did not work was 50% higher than the rate for women with any type of employment.

The difference between employed women and housewives disappeared in the upper-income groups (income $12,000 or more). One plausible reason for this could be that nonworking women with greater than average family incomes can use their financial resources to insulate themselves from the stress and strain of child rearing and the maternal role.

When we controlled for the income of only the husband, we found that, again, women who reported not working and women who worked had the same rates of Overall Violence in the highest income groups ($20,000 and more) (see Table 10).

AGE OF CHILD

An examination of the age of the "referent child" and the relationship between violence and employment provides some insight into the "time at risk" hypothesis, which proposes that the more time mothers and children spend together, the more opportunities there are for violence or abuse. The "time at risk" hypothesis implies that women who do not work, have preschool children, and thus spend the most time with their children would be the most violent and abusive, while women with full-time positions, who have children in their late teens, and spend the least time with their children would have the lowest rates. (This

TABLE 9
Mother-to-Child Violence by Employment and Wife's Annual Income

| | | | Violence Rate Per 100 Children | |
| | | | Overall Violence | Child Abuse |
Employment	Wife's Annual Income			
Full Time	less than $6,000	(N=70)	59.4	17.1
	$6,000 or more	(N=63)	58.7	19.0
Part Time	less than $6,000	(N=81)	71.6	19.8
	$6,000 or more	(N=8)	62.5	12.5
Housewives	less than $6,000	(N=319)	72.0	18.5
	$6,000 or more	(N=8*)	75.0	12.5

*It is possible to have cases in this cell because women were asked if they worked *at the time of the interview.* The question on income related to *the previous 12 months.* Thus, 8 women who were not employed when the interviews were conducted, apparently had worked in the previous 12 months.

assumption, of course, is speculative and is neither directly nor indirectly testable with the data from the national survey of family violence.) (See Table 11.)

The data partially bear out the "time at risk" hypothesis. The highest rate of child abuse is found among the housewives with children 3 to 4 years of age. These women also had the second highest rate of Overall Violence—exceeded only by women with part-time jobs and referent children 5 to 9 years of age. The lowest rate of abuse was for mothers with full-time jobs and preschool children. Full-time employed mothers with teen-aged children were expected to have the lowest rates of violence and abuse. We found that they had the second lowest rate of child abuse and Overall Violence.

It is risky to infer that age of the child implies how much time a mother spends with the child, especially in light of the finding that violence toward children is generally inversely related to age of the child (Straus et al., 1980). Mothers may be less likely to hit older children, not because they spend less time with them but because other forms of punishment are viewed as more acceptable and effective for children once they are past preschool age. In addition, mothers may be less likely to hit their children as the children grow older because the danger of getting hit back increases. Clearly, though, age of child does make a difference, and we need to know more about the relationship between employment, age of child, and violence.

TABLE 10

Mother-to-Child Violence by Employment,
Family Income, and Husband's Income

Employment	Percent Violent When Income Is:				Percent Abusive When Income Is:			
	less than $6,000	$6,000 to $11,999	$12,000 to $19,999	$20,000 or more	less than $6,000	$6,000 to $11,999	$12,000 to $19,999	$20,000 or more
A. Total Family Income								
Full Time	50.0	48.3	72.3	58.3	0.0	23.3	19.1	16.7
	(2)	(29)	(47)	(48)	(2)	(30)	(47)	(48)
Part Time	50.0	78.6	75.0	64.5	50.0	7.1	20.5	16.1
	(6)	(14)	(44)	(31)	(6)	(14)	(44)	(31)
Housewives	76.7	81.3	72.1	60.0	25.6	21.3	17.7	8.2
	(43)	(80)	(129)	(85)	(43)	(80)	(130)	(85)
B. Husband's Income								
Full Time	55.6	66.1	54.8	59.1	22.2	22.8	9.7	18.2
	(18)	(56)	(31)	(22)	(18)	(57)	(31)	(22)
Part Time	57.1	76.0	78.0	52.9	28.6	8.0	22.0	23.5
	(7)	(25)	(41)	(17)	(7)	(25)	(41)	(17)
Housewives	73.3	81.2	72.9	58.7	24.2	20.0	17.2	9.3
	(45)	(85)	(133)	(75)	(45)	(85)	(134)	(75)

FATHER'S EMPLOYMENT STATUS

If a husband works, even part-time, the original difference between the rate of Overall Violence and maternal employment persists. However, if the husband is out of work, the relationship changes. In this instance, it is the working woman who has a higher rate of Overall Violence than the woman at home. This could be a consequence of resentment over the typical situation of still having to meet domestic and work obligations, even though her husband is available to carry out domestic chores. Or, this could be a consequence of a major status inconsistency between the working wife and the nonworking husband.

**MOTHER'S EMPLOYMENT AND
FATHER'S VIOLENCE**

Mother's employment status is related to use of violence toward children, although whether she works is not related to whether she reports abusing her child. Mother's work is also related to the father's use of violence. Since we asked each respondent only about his or her

TABLE 11
Mother-to-Child Violence by Employment and Age of Child

| | | | Violence Rate Per 100 Children | |
| | | | Overall | Child |
Employment	Age of Referent Child		Violence	Abuse
Full Time	3 – 4	(N=13)	69.2	0.0
	5 – 9	(N=34)	82.4	38.2
	10 – 14	(N=45)	61.4	17.8
	15 – 17	(N=46)	34.8	6.5
Part Time	3 – 4	(N=14)	85.7	14.3
	5 – 9	(N=36)	94.4	19.4
	10 – 14	(N=26)	65.4	30.8
	15 – 17	(N=25)	29.2	8.0
Housewives	3 – 4	(N=71)	90.0	25.4
	5 – 9	(N=129)	83.7	21.7
	10 – 14	(N=110)	58.2	10.9
	15 – 17	(N=55)	41.8	9.1

own violence against his or her children, we had no measure of partner's violence. We did, however, assess the interviews with male subjects in terms of their reports of their wives' employment and their own use of violence.

Fathers who reported that their wives worked had the lowest rates of violence toward children. Even more important, the rate of child abuse among fathers with wives who did not work was 2.5 times greater than the rate for fathers married or living with women who worked full-time. Thus, while maternal employment is not related to the mother's chances of being abusive, it is related to the father's use of abusive violence. It is possible that men whose wives do not work maintain traditional beliefs about the man being the head of the household and believe that it should be the father who takes responsibility for physically punishing the children (e.g., "Wait 'til your father gets home").

Discussion and Conclusions

What do our results say about the claim that maternal employment has negative consequences for the child (Fontana, 1973)? The data on child abuse shows that working mothers are not more likely to be abusive. The data from the Overall Violence Index further undermine the claim that employed mothers are more violent. Women who worked full-time had the *lowest rate* of Overall Violence toward their children, while mothers with part-time jobs and mothers who were not working at the time of our interviews reported higher rates.

Research on child abuse and violence toward children has failed to try to empirically explain any proposed or demonstrated relationship between mothers' work and violence toward their children. Our analysis identified: (1) factors that increase the chances that a working mother will hit her child and (2) situations in which mothers at home were less likely to be violent toward their children.

FACTORS WHICH INCREASE THE CHANCES OF WORKING MOTHERS USING VIOLENCE

One of the factors that was related to the impact of maternal employment on the rate of Overall Violence toward children was perceived excess domestic responsibility. If a working mother felt that she had too much responsibility for financial matters and child care, then her chances of hitting her children rose to the level of violence reported by the nonworking mothers. Excess domestic responsibility had an even greater impact on mothers with part-time jobs. When a woman works part-time and feels she has excessive domestic responsibility, the chances are quite high that she will hit her children.

The likelihood of a mother working full-time and being violent increased slightly if the decisions about her work were made by her husband.

The tendency for mothers at home and mothers employed part-time to hit their children was *increased* if these mothers had preschool children. Working full-time and caring for young school-aged children also increased the chances that a mother would hit her child.

One of the most disadvantageous situations for a mother, in terms of her likelihood of striking her child, is to work full-time and be married to a man who is unemployed. This is the only situation where we found full-time employed mothers exceeded other mothers in their use of violence toward their children.

FACTORS WHICH REDUCE THE LEVEL OF VIOLENCE OF NONWORKING MOTHERS

Mothers who did not work had high rates of violence in nearly all of the situations we analyzed in this study. One factor which lessened the chances of a mother at home being violent was if her husband earned more than $20,000 per year. Another factor which lowered the nonworking mothers' rates of violence toward children was if the decisions about their work (or nonwork) were made jointly by them and their husbands. In addition, nonworking mothers had lower rates of violence toward older children. These findings imply that if mothers can get some relief from the total responsibility of child rearing—either by using financial resources to pay for baby-sitting or day care or by having older children who require less intense supervision—the chances of violence will be reduced. (This interpretation must be read with caution, since we have no direct data on how income was used or whether mothers in these situations actually had less contact with their children.)

POLICY IMPLICATIONS

Earlier research on child abuse which found children with unemployed *fathers* the most likely to be abused has been used to argue for child abuse prevention programs designed to increase employment opportunities for men and thus reduce family stress. Our data on maternal employment and child abuse cannot be used to argue that increased employment opportunities for women are necessary to prevent child abuse—although paternal abuse might be lessened if more mothers worked.

The relationships that we found between maternal employment and the rate of Overall Violence toward children is quite complex. Despite the complexity, our data are useful for formulating policy which could reduce the overall level of violence toward children.

First, the issue of excess domestic responsibility must be met. Women must either be released from the gender-linked burdens of child care and domestic duties or they must be provided with adequate assistance to help them cope with their responsibilities. We suggested that financial resources help in reducing the level of violence among women at home. We believe that women with sufficient financial resources either directly or indirectly use them to insulate themselves from the pressure and responsibility of childrearing. It has previously been argued that gender equality in the home and in society can lessen the level of family violence (Straus et al., 1980), and the results of this study are consistent with that recommendation.

Women need to have a major role in the decisions affecting their employment either in the paid labor force or as housewives. One of the worst situations for a woman who works full-time is to have little or no input in the decision to work.

Last, our data provide additional evidence that unemployment among men has serious noneconomic, negative consequences for their families. One of the major burdens of the father's unemployment falls on the shoulders of the working wife and then, through her violence, onto the children.

Conclusion

While this investigation has supported one of the three alternative directions of a hypothesis about the relationship between maternal employment status and violence toward children, the data from the national survey of family violence do not provide the final word on this issue. The national survey was planned and carried out to ask and answer broad questions about the incidence, nature, and causes of violence in the home. While many facets of family life were explored, many others had to be omitted or given brief coverage due to the limits of time and financial resources. When one considers the constant and detailed attention paid to the relationship between male employment and violence toward children, then it is obvious that we have failed to pay adequate attention to the role of maternal employment in the case of violence toward children. It is necessary and important for the development of knowledge about child abuse and family violence to continue to pursue this issue and to further refine the empirical evidence and theoretical perspectives on this issue.

Notes

1. These 1,146 families are part of a larger sample of 2,143 families who were interviewed as part of a comprehensive study of violence in the family. A national sample of 103 primary areas (counties or groups of counties) stratified by geographic region, type of community, and other population characteristics was generated. Within the primary areas, 300 interview locations (Census districts or block groups) were selected. Each location was divided into 10 to 25 housing units by the trained interviewers. Sample segments from each interviewing location were selected. The final step involved randomly selecting an eligible person to be interviewed in each designated household. For more details on the sample, see Straus et al. (1980).

2. Because the study was a comprehensive study of family violence, including violence between siblings and violence toward parents, we required a sample of referent children who were not younger than 3 years of age.

3. We had great difficulty in choosing the appropriate label for women who reported that they did not work. "Unemployed" does not capture the true nature of their situation—

since many did not choose to work—and using this term would deprecate the occupational functions and value of housework. We finally chose "housewife" because 96.2% of the women who said they were not working at the time of the interview placed themselves into this category (3% said they were unemployed and .8% said they were disabled).

PART III

MARITAL VIOLENCE

Introduction

Throughout history there have been legal and cultural precedents which, to a degree, sanctioned the right of a husband to use violence on his wife. Roman husbands had the right to chastise, divorce, or kill their wives. The expression "rule of thumb" gave legal justification to the common law which allowed a husband to strike his wife with a switch, provided that the stick was no larger than the husband's thumb.

Wife abuse was publicly recognized as a social problem in the early seventies, some ten years after child abuse received widespread public attention. Even though wife abuse has been on the public agenda for over a decade, women are still overlooked as victims of family violence. Worse still, many battered women are blamed for their own victimization. Observers of battered women have been known to comment that the wife's behavior must have been such that she "deserved" her abuse. Others, noting that many battered wives remain with their abusive husbands, have proposed that battered women must like being abused, otherwise they would leave.

Despite the fact that the available evidence on the extent of wife abuse supports the notion that the marriage license is a hitting license (Straus, 1974c), wife abuse still receives less public attention and public concern than the problem of battered children. In large part, this is due to the fact that children (especially young children and infants) are viewed as helpless and innocent victims of parental rage. Battered wives, on the other hand, are frequently viewed with suspicion and contempt.

Nonetheless, the increased attention to battered wives and the creation of more programs and services for battered women appear to have had some effect in the last decade. The results of the Second National Family Violence Survey (Straus and Gelles, 1986) revealed that the rate of wife beating dropped 27% between 1975 and 1985. Whereas 38 husbands per 1,000 were engaged in severe violence in 1975, only 30 husbands per 1,000 were reported engaging in severe violence in 1985. Although this is a significant decline, it hardly points to the elimination of wife abuse.

The explanation for the decline of wife abuse is much the same as our explanation for the drop in rates of child abuse (see Chapter 4). Changes in family structure and economic climate have been in a direction that would have reduced the risk factors for wife abuse. Women have married later, had fewer children, and had fewer unwanted children in the last 10 years. American marriages appear to be becoming a bit more egalitarian (Thornton et al., 1983). Equality and sharing in marriage tends to be related to lower levels of wife abuse (Coleman and Straus, 1985; Straus, 1973; Straus et al., 1980). Another factor is the increase in alternatives for battered women. Many more services and treatment programs are available today for victimized wives than there were 10 years ago. Finally, the criminal justice system has begun to take a firmer stand with battering men.

The chapters in this section on marital violence consider the situation of the woman victim. In "Abused Wives: Why Do They Stay?" we explode the myth that women who remain with assaultive husbands are masochistic. The Update to this chapter reviews some of the developments in the area of treatment and intervention for battered women. In "Violence and Pregnancy: A Note on the Extent of the Problem and Needed Services," we identify one situation in family life which dramatically increases the risk of marital violence. "Power, Sex, and Violence: The Case of Marital Rape" uncovers a topic which few people ever considered—domestic sexual assault.

CHAPTER 6

ABUSED WIVES: WHY DO THEY STAY?

Why would a woman who has been physically abused by her husband remain with him? This question is one of the most frequently asked by both professionals and the lay public in the course of discussions of family violence, and one of the more difficult to adequately answer. The question itself derives from the elementary assumption that any reasonable individual, having been beaten and battered by another person, would avoid being victimized again (or at least avoid the attacker). Unfortunately, the answer to why women remain with their abusive husbands is not nearly as simple as the assumption that underlies the question. In the first place, the decision either to stay with an assaultive spouse or to seek intervention or dissolution of a marriage is not related solely to the extent or severity of the physical assault. Some spouses will suffer repeated severe beatings or even stabbings without so much as calling a neighbor, while others call the police after a coercive gesture from their husbands. Second, the assumption that the victim would flee from a conjugal attacker overlooks the complex subjective meaning of intrafamilial violence, the nature of commitment and entrapment to the family as a social group, and the external constraint which limits a woman's ability to seek outside help. As has been reported elsewhere (Parnas, 1967; Gelles, 1974; Straus, 1974c, 1976), violence between spouses if often viewed as normative and, in fact, mandated in family relations. Wives have reported that they believe that it is acceptable for a husband to beat his wife "every once in a while" (Parnas, 1967: 952; Gelles, 1974: 59-61).

Author's Note: From Richard J. Gelles, "Abused Wives: Why Do They Stay?" *Journal of Marriage and the Family*, 1976, 38 (November): 659-668.

This essay attempts to provide an answer to the question of why victims of conjugal violence stay with their husbands by focusing on various aspects of the family and family experience which distinguish between women who seek intervention or dissolution of a marriage as a response to violence and those women who suffer repeated beatings without seeking outside intervention.[1] We shall specifically analyze how previous experience with family violence affects the decision to seek intervention, and how the extent of violence, educational status, occupational status, number of children, and age of oldest child influence the wife's actions in responding to assaults from her husband. Finally, we shall discuss how external constraints lessen the likelihood of a woman seeking intervention in conjugal assaults.

Victims of Family Violence

Although no one has systematically attempted to answer the question of why an abused wife would stay with her husband, there has been some attention focused on women who attempt to seek intervention after being beaten by their husbands. Snell, Rosenwald, and Robey (1964) examined 12 clinical cases to determine why a wife takes her abusive husband to court. They begin by stating that the question answers itself (because he beats her!), but they go on to explain that the decision to seek legal assistance is the result of a change in the wife's behavior, not the husband's, because many wives report a history of marital violence when they did not seek assistance.

Truninger (1971) found that women attempt to dissolve a violent marriage only after a history of conflict and reconciliation. According to this analysis, a wife makes a decision to obtain a divorce from her abusive husband when she can no longer believe her husband's promises of no more violence or forgive past episodes of violence. Truninger postulates that some of the reasons women *do not* break off relationships with abusive husbands are that: (1) they have negative self-concepts; (2) they believe their husbands will reform; (3) economic hardship; (4) they have children who need a father's economic support; (5) they doubt they can get along alone; (6) they believe divorcees are stigmatized; and (7) it is difficult for women with children to get work. Although this analysis attempts to explain why women remain with abusive husbands, the list does not specify which factors are the most salient in the wife's decision to either stay or seek help.

There are a number of other factors which help explain the wife's decision to stay or get help in cases of violence. Straus (1973) states that self-concept and role expectations of others often influence what is considered to be an intolerable level of violence by family members. Scanzoni's (1972) exchange model of family relations postulates that the ratio of rewards to punishments is defined subjectively by spouses and is the determining factor in deciding whether to stay married or not. The decision of whether or not to seek intervention or dissolution of a marriage may be partly based on the subjective definitions attached to the violence (punishment) and partly on the ratio of this punishment to other marital rewards (security, companionship, and the like).

Additional research on violence between husbands and wives suggests that severity of violence has an influence on the wife's actions (see O'Brien, 1971 and Levinger, 1966 for discussion of petitioners for divorce and their experience with violence). Research on victims of violence sheds little additional light on the actions of abused wives (Straus, 1976).[2]

Methodology

Data for this study were derived from interviews with members of 80 families. An unstructured informal interview procedure was employed to facilitate data collection on the sensitive topic of intrafamilial violence. For this study 20 families suspected of using violence were chosen from the files of a private social service agency. Another 20 families were selected by examining a police "blotter" to locate families in which the police had been summoned to break up violent disputes. An additional 40 families were interviewed by selecting one neighboring family for each "agency" or "police" family.[3]

STRENGTHS AND LIMITATIONS OF THE SAMPLE

The interviews were carried out in two cities in New Hampshire. The sampling procedure employed enhanced the likelihood of locating families in which violence had occurred, but it also meant that this sample was not representative of any larger populations.

Major limitations of this study are that it is exploratory in nature, the sample is small, and the representativeness of the sample is unknown. The small sample, the unknown representativeness, and the possible biases that enter into the study as a result of the sampling procedure all impinge on the generalizability of the findings presented in this essay.

There are, however, strengths in the study which tend to offset the limitations of sample design and sample size. First, this is a unique study. The area of spousal violence has long suffered from selective inattention (Dexter, 1958) on the part of both society and the research community. While some data have been gathered on the topic of family violence, most of the studies focus on one type of population—either petitioners for divorce (O'Brien, 1971; Levinger, 1966), patients of psychiatrists (Snell et al., 1964), or college students (Straus, 1974c; Steinmetz, 1974). This study is one of the few which examines not only those in special circumstances (agency clients or those calling police), but also an equal number of families who had no contact with agencies of social service or control.[4] While the sample is obviously not representative, it is one of the closest yet to a study of violence in a cross-section of families.

A second strength of the methodology is that it yielded a population without working-class, lower-class, or middle-class bias. The sample ranged from families at the lowest regions of socioeconomic status, to middle-class families in which one or both spouses had graduated from college and had a combined family income exceeding $25,000. (For a complete discussion of the social characteristics of the respondents and their families, see Gelles, 1974: 205-215.)

Although the methodology was not designed specifically to address the issue posed in this essay it turned out to be particularly well suited for the proposed analysis. The sampling technique yielded wives who called the police, wives who were clients of a social service agency, and wives who had never sought any outside intervention.

The interviews with the 80 family members yielded 41 women who had been physically struck by their husbands during their marriage. Of these, 9 women had been divorced or separated from their husbands; 13 had called on the police and were still married; 8 sought counseling from a private social service agency (because of violence and other family problems); and 11 had sought no outside intervention.

Findings

We derived some ideas and predictions concerning factors which distinguished between beaten wives who obtained outside intervention and those who did not attempt to bring in outside resources or file for a divorce. These ideas are based on the interviews with the 41 members of violent families and on previous research on family violence. We utilized both quantitative and qualitative data obtained from the interviews to assess the effect of: (1) severity and frequency of violence; (2) experience and exposure to violence in one's family of orientation; (3) education and occupation of the wife, number of children, and age of oldest child; and (4) external constraint on the actions of the victimized wife.

SEVERITY AND FREQUENCY OF VIOLENCE

Common sense suggests that if violence is severe enough or frequent enough, a wife will eventually attempt either to flee from her abusive husband or to bring in some mediator to protect her from violence.

In order to analyze whether severity of violence influenced the reactions of the wife, we constructed a 10-point scale of violence severity (0=no violence; 1=pushed or shoved; 2=threw object; 3=slapped or bit; 4=punched or kicked; 5=pushed down; 6=hit with hard object; 7=choked; 8=stabbed; 9=shot).[5] This scale measured the most severe violence the wife had ever experienced as a victim.

Table 12 indicates that the more severe the violence, the more likely the wife is to seek outside assistance. An examination of wives' reactions to particular instances of violence reveals even more about the impact of violence severity on the actions of abused wives. Of the eight women who were either shot at (one), choked (six), or hit with a hard object (one), five had obtained divorces, two had called the police, and one had sought counseling from a social service agency. At the other extreme, of the nine women who had been pushed or shoved (eight), or had objects thrown at them (one), one had gotten a divorce, one had called the police, and seven had sought no assistance at all.

How frequently a wife is hit also influences her decision whether to remain with her husband, call the police, go to a social worker, or seek dissolution of the marriage. Only 42% of the women who had been struck once in the marriage had sought some type of intervention, while 100% of the women who had been hit at least once in a month and 83% of the women who had been stuck at least once a week had either obtained a divorce or separation, called the police, or gone to a social service agency. Frequency of violence is also related to what type of intervention a wife seeks. Women hit weekly to daily are most likely to call the police, while women hit less often (at least once a month) are more inclined to get a divorce or legal separation.

TABLE 12
Violence Severity by Intervention Mode

Intervention	Mean Violence Severity
No Intervention	2.1
Divorced or Separated	5.1
Called Police	4.0
Went to Agency	4.6
Total for all who sought Intervention	4.6

$F = 5.2$ Statistically significant at the .01 level.

There are a number of plausible explanations as to why frequency of violence influences mode of intervention. Perhaps the more frequent the violence, the more a wife wants immediate protection, whereas victims of monthly violence gradually see less value in staying married to a husband who explodes occasionally. A possible explanation of the findings might be that women who were divorced or separated were ashamed to admit they tolerated violence as long as they did (for fear of being labeled "sadomasochists"). Also, it may be that victims of frequent violence are afraid of seeking a temporary or permanent separation. Victims of weekly violence may be terrorized by their violent husbands and view police intervention as more tolerable to their husbands than a divorce or separation. Finally, women who are struck frequently might feel that a separation or divorce might produce a radical and possibly lethal reaction from an already violent husband.

EXPERIENCE WITH AND EXPOSURE TO VIOLENCE AS A CHILD

Studies of murderers (Gillen, 1946; Guttmacher, 1960; Leon, 1969; Palmer, 1962; Tanay, 1969), child abusers (Bakan, 1971; Gelles, 1973; Gil, 1971; Kempe et al., 1962; Steele and Pollock, 1974), and violent spouses (Gelles, 1974; Owens and Straus, 1975) support the assumption that the more individuals are exposed to violence as children (both as observers and victims), the more they are violent as adults. The explanation offered for this relationship is that the experience with violence as a victim and observer teaches the individual how to be violent and also to approve of the use of violence. In other words, exposure to violence provides a "role model" for violence (Singer, 1971). If experience with violence can provide a role model for the offender, then perhaps it can also provide a role model for the victim.

Women who observed spousal violence in their family of orientation were more likely to be victims of conjugal violence in their family of procreation. Of the 54 women who never saw their parents fight physically, 46% were victims of spousal violence, while 66% of the 12 women who observed their parents exchange blows were later victims of violent attacks. In addition, the more frequently a woman was struck by her parents, the more likely she was to grow up and be struck by her husband.[6]

There are two interrelated reasons why women who were exposed to or were victims of intrafamilial violence would be prone to be the victims of family violence as adults. It is possile that the more experience with violence a woman has, the more she is inclined to approve of the use of violence in the family. She may grow up with the expectation that husbands are "supposed" to hit wives, and this role expectation may in turn become the motivator for her husband to use violence on her. Another explanation of these findings integrates the subculture theory of violence (Wolfgang and Ferracuti, 1967) with the homogamy theory of mate selection (Centers, 1949; Ecklund, 1968; Hollingshead, 1950). Thus, it could be argued that women who grew up in surroundings which included and approved of family violence, are more likely to marry a person who is prone to use violence.

Given the fact that being a victim of violence as a child or seeing one's parents physically fight makes a woman more vulnerable to becoming the victim of conjugal violence, does exposure and experience with violence as a child affect *the actions* of a beaten wife? There are two alternative predictions that could be made. First, the less a woman experienced violence in her family of orientation, the more likely she is to view intrafamilial violence as deviant, and thus, the more she is willing to seek intervention or a divorce when hit by her husband. On the other hand, exposure to violence may provide a role model for the woman as to what to do when attacked. Thus, the *more* violence she was exposed to, the more she will know about how to get outside help, and the more she will seek this help.

Being a victim of parental violence and frequency of victimization appear to have no bearing on the beaten wife's decision whether or not to seek outside intervention[7] (Table 13). Those women who observed their parents engaged in physical fights were slightly more likely to obtain outside intervention after being hit by their husbands. For those women who did see their parents engage in conjugal violence, the predominant mode of intervention in their own family of procreation was a divorce or separation. There is no predominant mode of

TABLE 13
Intervention Mode by Wife's Experience with Violence as a Child

| | Type of Intervention | | | |
Type of Experience as Child	Divorced or Separated	Called Police	Went to Agency	Total Seeking Intervention
A. Parents Violent to Respondent				
None (N=3)	33%	0%	66%	100%
Infrequent* (N=13)	23%	38%	15%	76%
Frequent+ (N=17)	24%	35%	18%	77%
B. Parents Violent to Each Other				
None observed (N=25)	28%	28%	20%	76%
Observed (N=8)	63%	13%	13%	89%

*Less than 6 times a year.
+From monthly to daily.

intervention chosen by those women who did not witness violence in their families of orientation.

Thus, neither of the alternative predictions is strongly supported by the data on experience and exposure to violence. There is the suggestion that exposure to conjugal violence makes women *less tolerant* of family violence and more desirous of ending a violent marriage. Along these lines, some of the women we interviewed stated that after they saw their parents fight they vowed that they would never stand for their own husbands hitting them. However, the data do not support the claim that this position is widespread among wives who witnessed violence as they grew up.

EDUCATION, OCCUPATION, NUMBER OF CHILDREN, AGE OF CHILDREN

Truninger (1971) has proposed that the stronger the commitment to marriage, the less a wife will seek legal action against a violent husband. We have modified this hypothesis by proposing that the fewer resources a wife has in a marriage, the fewer alternatives she has in her marriage; and the more "entrapped" she is in the marriage, the more reluctant she will be to seek outside intervention. Thus, we hypothesize that unemployed wives with low levels of education will not do anything when beaten. It is difficult to predict what influence number of children and age of children have on the actions of the wife. Snell et al. (1964)

state that the presence of an older child motivates women to take their husbands to court.

Looking at the relationship between each variable and intervention, we see that the variable which best distinguishes wives who obtain assistance from those who remain with their husbands is holding a job. While only 25% of those wives who sought no help worked, 50% of the wives who called the police, went to a social service agency, or were separated or divorced from their husbands held jobs. This confirms our hypothesis that the more resources a wife has, the more she is able to support herself and her children, the more she will have a low threshold of violence and call outside agents or agencies to help her. Thus, the less dependent a wife is on her husband, the more likely she is to call for help in instances of violence. In addition to this resource dimension, wives reported that holding a job gave them a view of another world or culture. This new perspective made their own family problems seem less normal and more serious than they had felt when they were at home. This point is illustrated in the following excerpt from one of our interviews with a woman who was the client of a social service agency and who had been beaten by her husband when they were first married.

> Until I started being out in the public, to realize what was going on around me, I was do darned stupid and ignorant. I didn't know how the other half of the world lived. And when I started being a waitress I used to love to sit there—when I wasn't busy—and watch the people—the mother and the father with their children—and see how they acted. And I started to feel like I was cheated . . . and it started to trouble me and I started to envy those people. So I said, "you know . . . am I supposed to live the way I'm living?"

Women who called the police or went to an agency often had teenage children. The data confirm the Snell, Rosenwald, and Robey (1964) finding that women who brought their husbands to court had teenage children. In some of the interviews, wives reported that they started calling the police when their son or daughter was old enough to get embroiled in the physical conflicts. In these cases, the wives wanted to help to protect their children rather than themselves.

Neither education (measured by mean years of school completed and completed high school) nor number of children distinguishes between abused women seeking help and those staying with their husbands (see Table 14).

TABLE 14
Education, Occupation, Number of Children,
Age of Oldest Child by Intervention Mode

	Mean Education	Percent Completed High School	Percent Employed	Mean Number of Children	Mean Age of Oldest Child
No Intervention (N=11)	11.9	63%	25%	2.5	9.3
Divorced or Separated (N=9)	11.7	66%	44% *	3.3	9.3
Called Police (N=13)	11.0	69%	38%	3.0	13.0
Went to Agency (N=8)	11.1	62%	75%	2.6	13.7
All Intervention	11.3	67%	50%	3.0	12.0

*For those wives who are divorced or separated, some may have found employment *after* the divorce or separation. The data did not allow us to determine *when* the wife found employment.

COMBINED EFFECTS OF VARIABLES ON INTERVENTION

Up to this point we have examined the effects of the variables which we believed would be likely determinants of whether or not a wife sought intervention. This analysis, however, does not allow us to assess the effects of all these variables in explaining whether or not a wife would seek outside help in cases of conjugal violence. In order to examine the impact of all the variables together, we employed a step-wise multiple regression procedure which allowed us to see what proportion of the variance of intervention or particular intervention modalities is explained by combinations of the independent variables.[8]

Intervention. Table 15 reveals that the best predictor of whether or not a wife seeks intervention is violence severity in her family of procreation. Thus, women who seek intervention are strongly influenced by the level of violence in their family. The five variables entered into the regression analysis explain 32% of the variance in seeking intervention or not.

Divorced or separated. The best predictor of whether or not a wife obtains a divorce or separation is the level of violence in her family of procreation. The combined effect of all the variables entered into the

TABLE 15
Stepwise Regression of Independent Variables
and Intervention and Intervention Modalities

	Multiple R	R^2	Beta
A. Regression of Intervention on:			
Violence Severity	.434[#]	.189	.365
Completed High School	.488[#]	.238	.331
Parental Violence to Respondent	.530[#]	.280	-.260
Frequency of Violence	.559[#]	.312	.221
Wife's Occupational Status*	.570[#]	.324	-.136
B. Regression of Divorced or Separated on:			
Violence Severity	.281	.080	.211
Wife's Education	.314	.099	.298
Frequency of Violence	.324	.105	.154
Completed High School	.340	.115	-.136
Wife's Occupational Status*	.347	.120	.089
Violence Between Parents	.352	.124	-.027
Number of Children	.355	.126	.261
Age of Oldest Child	.373	.140	.231
C. Regression of Called Police on:			
Wife's Occupational Status*	.195	.038	-.231
Completed High School	.256	.065	.423
Wife's Education	.314	.099	-.245
Parental Violence to Respondent	.319	.101	-.016
Age of Oldest Child	.324	.105	-.233
Number of Children	.340	.115	.233
D. Regression of Went to Agency on:			
Parental Violence to Respondent	.326[+]	.106	-.191
Age of Oldest Child	.350	.122	.480
Number of Children	.425[+]	.180	-.496
Violence Severity	.442	.196	.114

#Statistically significant at the .01 level.
+Statistically significant at the .05 level.
*Occupational Status measured using Bureau of Census status score (see Robinson, Athanasiou, and Head, 1969: 357).

equation is the explanation of 14% of the variance in the dependent variable; however, the multiple Rs are not statistically significant at the .05 level.

Called police. We are able to explain 11% of the variance in this variable, but again, multiple Rs are not statistically significant at the .05 level. Unlike separation or divorce, in which cases severity and extent of violence in her family of procreation played major roles in the wife's actions, the calling of police is associated with the wife's occupational status and her education. Women with less occupational status and lower levels of education are likely to call the police for help. This finding is consistent with the popular assumption that the poor man's social worker is the police officer.

Went to agency. The best predictor of going to a social service agency is how much violence the wife experienced as a child. The less violence, the more likely she is to seek a social worker's help. In contrast to the previous dependent variables, age and number of children play a greater part in influencing a wife's decision to go to a social service agency. Almost 20% of the variance in seeking agency assistance is explained by the four variables in the regression.

EXTERNAL CONSTRAINT

The fact that a woman would call the police or seek agency assistance after repeated incidents of conjugal violence does not necessarily mean that she will call the police again or continue going to an agency. One fact remained quite clear at the end of the 80 interviews: Most agencies and most legal organizations are quite unprepared and unable to provide meaningful assistance to women who have been beaten by their husbands. With minor exceptions such as the work done by Bard (1969) and his colleagues (Bard and Berkowitz, 1969; Bard and Zacker, 1971), little formal training has been given to police in how to intercede in conjugal disputes. Truninger (1971) reports that the courts are often mired in mythology about family violence (e.g., "violence fulfills the masochistic need of women victims") and consequently the justice system is ineffective in dealing with marital violence. Field and Field (1973: 225) echo these sentiments and state that unless the victim dies, the chances that the court system will deal seriously with the offender are slight. Women who are abused by their husbands must suffer grave injury in order to press legal charges. The California Penal Code states that a wife must be more injured than commonly allowed for battery to press charges against her husband (Calvert, 1974: 89). As Field and Field (1973) state, there is an official acceptance of violence between "consenting" adults and the belief that this violence is a private affair. This attitude, held by police, the courts, and the citizenry, constrains many wives from seeking initial help, or once obtaining help, continuing to use it.

Although social work agencies are not as "indifferent" about marital violence as the courts and police are (Field and Field 1973: 236), they are often unable to provide realistic answers for victims of violence because of the rather limited amount of knowledge in this area. The data on marital violence are so scanty that few policy or intervention strategies have been worked out for the use of social workers. Without a good knowledge of the causes and patterns of marital violence, many social workers have had to rely on stop-gap measures which never address the real problem of marital violence.

A final source of external constraint is the wife's fear that the myth of her peaceful family life will be exploded. Many women we spoke to would never think of calling the police, going to a social work agency, or filing for a divorce because those actions would rupture the carefully nurtured myth of their fine family life. One woman, who had been struck often and hard over a 30-year marriage said she would never call the police because she was afraid it would appear in the papers. Truninger (1971: 264) supports these findings by stating that part of the reason why the courts are ineffective in dealing with marital violence is the strong social pressure on individuals to keep marital altercations private.

In summary, even if a woman wants to get help and protection from her husband, she all too frequently finds out that the agents and agencies she calls are ineffective or incapable of providing real assistance. During the course of the interviews, many wives who had sought intervention complained about the futility of such actions. One woman in particular had sought agency help, called the police, and finally filed for a divorce. However, none of these actions actually protected her, and her estranged husband almost strangled her one weekend morning.

The deficiencies of these external agencies and the pressure to cover up family altercations are two powerful forces which keep women with their abusive husbands.

Conclusion

The purpose of this essay has been to address the important question of why victims of conjugal violence stay with their husbands. Our analysis of the variables which affect the decision either to stay with an abusive husband or to seek intervention uncovered three major factors which influence the actions of abused women. First, the less severe and the less frequent the violence, the more a woman will remain with her spouse and not seek outside aid. This finding is almost self-evident in that it posits that women seek intervention when they are severely abused. However, the problem is more complex, because severity and frequency of violence explain only part of the variance in abused wives' behavior. A second factor is how much violence a wife experiences as a child. The more she was struck by her parents, the more inclined she is to stay with her abusive husband. It appears that victimization as a child raises the wife's tolerance for violence as an adult. Finally, educational and occupational factors are associated with staying with an abusive husband. Wives who do not seek intervention are less likely to have completed high school and more likely to be unemployed. We conclude that the fewer resources a woman has, the less power she has, and the more entrapped she is in her marriage, the more she suffers at the hands of her husband without calling for help outside the family.

Another factor which appears to influence the actions of a wife is external constraint in the form of police, agency, and court lack of understanding about marital violence.

Although we have presented some factors which partly explain why abused wives remain with their husbands, we have not provided a complete answer to the question this essay raises. The reason for this is that the factors influencing the reactions of an abused wife are tremendously complex. It is not simply how hard or how often a wife is hit, nor is it how much education or income she has. The decision of whether or not to seek intervention is the result of a complex interrelationship of factors, some of which have been identified in this essay.

Although we have provided tentative answers to the central question of this essay, a main underlying issue of this topic has not been addressed. Even though more than 75% of the women who had been struck had tried to get outside help, the end result of this intervention was not totally satisfactory. The outlook for women who are physically beaten and injured by their husbands is not good. For those who have few resources, no job, and no idea of how to get help, the picture is grim. But even the women who have the resources and desire to seek outside help often find this help of little benefit.

Notes

1. While we would have liked to answer the same question for men who were struck by their wives, we interviewed too few men who had been hit by their wives to conduct any meaningful data analysis.

2. Because we are focusing on the reactions of victims of intrafamilial violence, we had hoped that some insight could be gained from the literature on "victimology." "Victimology" is defined by its proponents (see Drapkin and Viano, 1974; Hentig, 1948;

and Schafer, 1968) as the scientific study of the criminal-victim relationship. However, the current work on these relationships does not focus specifically on factors which lead victims to sever relationships with offenders or to obtain outside intervention. Because victimologists' analyses of marital violence are typically limited to cases of homicide (see Wolfgang, 1957), there are few insights to be gained for the purposes of this essay from the study of the literature on the criminal-victim relationship.

3. For a complete discussion of the methodology, including an evaluation of the sampling procedure and instrument, see Gelles, 1974: 36-43.

4. Another study which examines a cross section of families is Steinmetz's (1975) multimethod examination of 57 families randomly selected from New Castle County, Delaware. The sample size is small, but it is representative, if only of one county in Delaware.

5. For the purposes of this analysis, we viewed each higher point on the scale as more severe than the previous category of violence. In addition, we treated the scale as interval data in order to conduct a one-way Analysis of Variance. The scale was treated as an interval measure because this way the only possible way to assess the impact of violence severity on the wives.

6. Many individuals may find it difficult to label the use of physical force on children as violence. This is because there are many powerful pro-use-of-physical-force-on-children norms in our society (Straus, 1976). If one defines violence as an act with the intent of physically injuring the victim, then physically punishing a child is violent. Note, a complete tabular presentation of these data is available from the author.

7. Although this study deals with 41 families where the wife was a victim of violence, Table 2 presents only 33 wives who were victims of violence. The smaller number of wives occurs because in some of the 41 families we interviewed the husband and have no data on the wife's experience with violence. Some other women reported that they were brought up in foster homes or by one parent, and thus we have no "exposure to violence data" for these women.

8. In order to conduct this analysis the dependent variables (Intervention, Divorce or Separated, Called Police, and Went to an Agency) were transformed into "dummy" variables. Each variable was treated as a dichotomy (e.g., "Sought Intervention" or "Did Not Seek Intervention"). Certain ordinal variables (violence severity, completed high school, violence frequency, parental violence to respondent, and violence between parents) are treated as interval measures.

Update

ADDITIONAL THEORY AND RESEARCH

There has been additional research and discussion of the question of why battered women choose to stay or leave their abusive husbands.

The psychologist Lenore Walker (1979) developed the theory of "learned helplessness" to explain why so many battered women remain with violent men. Walker notes that women who experience repeated physical assaults at the hands of their husbands have much lower self-concepts than women whose marriages are free from violence. Walker postulates that the repeated beatings and lower self-concepts leave women with the feeling that they cannot control what will happen to them. They feel they are unable to protect themselves from further assaults and feel incapable of controlling the events occurring around them. Thus, like laboratory animals, which after experiencing repeated shocks from which there is no escape, battered women eventually learn that they are helpless to prevent violent attacks.

"Learned helplessness" implies a rather passive nature of battered women. It is important not to confuse the situation of trapped laboratory animals (from which the theory of learned helplessness was derived) with battered women. Most battered women are far from passive. Dobash and Dobash (1979) point out that women do not choose just to stay or to leave. Rather, many women stay, leave, and return.

The sociologist Millie Pagelow focused her research on women who sought help from shelters for battered wives. Pagelow (1981) administered questionnaires to 350 women who sought temporary residence in shelters for themselves or their children. Pagelow's findings did not confirm the hypothesis concerning the relationship between frequency and severity of violence and the decision to stay or leave an abusive relationship. Pagelow did find that diminished educational and occupational resources and skills inhibit women from leaving violent relationships.

One reason for the difference between our own findings and those of Pagelow was that different samples were used in each study. We studied women who were not in shelters (there were only one or two shelters for wives in the United States at the time we conducted our research). Pagelow's data were gathered exclusively from shelter residents. Also, Pagelow did not use a comparison group; her study included no women who stayed with their husbands and sought no outside intervention. Thus, while Pagelow can make inferences about women's decisions to leave, she has no data about decisions to remain with violent partners.

Strube and Barbour (1983) studied 98 women and also confirmed that economically dependent women are more likely to remain with their abusive husbands. They also found evidence that *commitment* to the marital relationship was an important and independent factor related to the decision to leave a violent relationship.

In contrast to researchers who focus only on women who leave violent marriages, the sociologist Lee Bowker (1983) examined the

stories and situations of women who chose to stay with their husbands
and were successful in having their husbands stop the violence. Bowker
conducted 136 in-depth interviews over a nine-month period with
women who stayed with their partners and succeeded in getting the
husbands to stop using violence. Bowker reported that the techniques
used by women to get their husbands to stop the violence clustered into
three categories: (1) personal strategies, including talking, promising,
threatening, hiding, passive defense, aggressive defense, and avoidance;
(2) use of informal help sources, including family members, in-laws,
neighbors, friends, and shelters; and (3) formal help sources, including
police, social service agencies, lawyers, and district attorneys. The most
common personal strategy was passive defense—covering one's body
with arms, hands, or feet. The most common informal strategy were
friends. Social services were the leading formal source of help.

Bowker found that no single technique worked best. What mattered
the most was that women showed their determination that the violence
must stop.

CHANGES IN EXTERNAL CONSTRAINTS

There have been changes in the nature and level of external
constraints that limited battered women's ability to seek effective
intervention in 1976.

One significant change has been the increase in alternatives for
battered women over the past 10 years. At the time of our study there
were few shelters for wives in the United States. When the article was
published in 1976 there were six shelters. Today, experts believe that
there are more than 1,000 shelters or refuges for abused wives. Even
1,000 shelters is insufficient to meet the needs of the more than 1½
million battered women in the United States. Yet, the very existence of
shelters provide women with both hope and legitimate threats they can
use to prevent additional violence at home.

New and innovative treatment programs have also been developed.
Whereas no treatment programs for men existed 10 years ago, many
such programs are available today.

Finally, there has been a keener interest shown by the police and
courts to serve as agents of deterrence. Battered women filed numerous
class action suits in the 1970s to force police and the courts to treat wife
assault as they would any other form of stranger assault. The police have
gradually changed their methods of intervening in cases of domestic

assault. In 1975 the training manual for police officers prepared by the International Association of Chiefs of Police recommended separating the warring parties and leaving. The manual now recommends dealing with all assaults—domestic and stranger—on the same basis.

The Minneapolis Police Experiment (Sherman and Berk, 1984—see Chapter 1) found that mandatory arrest resulted in fewer police calls and fewer instances of repeated violent behavior. As a result of this study, a number of police departments have begun to adopt mandatory arrest policies for instances of domestic assault. The United States Attorney General's Task Force on Family Violence also called for stricter criminal justice intervention in cases of wife assault.

CHAPTER 7

VIOLENCE AND PREGNANCY: A NOTE ON THE EXTENT OF THE PROBLEM AND NEEDED SERVICES

In a society which publicly views the birth of a child as a "blessed" event, one does not ordinarily think of pregnancy and interpersonal violence as events which coincide in family life. However, a startling discovery in a study on violence between husbands and wives (Gelles, 1974) was that a number of wives stated that they were physically attacked while they were pregnant. Although there has been research on parenthood as crisis (LeMasters, 1957; Dyer, 1963; Hobbs, 1965), few students of family relations have been aware of the crisis of pregnancy and that this often leads to physical violence. This essay examines the phenomenon of violence toward pregnant wives and posits that it is possible that violence in pregnancy is common enough to be considered an important empirical issue by researchers and practitioners in the field of family relations.

During the conduct of our first study of family violence it became evident that many of the wives who were physically struck by their husbands were hit during the term of their pregnancy. Members of 80 families were interviewed. In more than half of these families (55%) at least one incident of conjugal violence was discussed. In 10 of these 44 families respondents discussed incidents of violence occurring while the wife was pregnant (Gelles, 1974).

Author's Note: From Richard J. Gelles, "Violence and Pregnancy: A Note on the Extent of the Problem and Needed Services," *Family Coordinator*, 1975, 24 (January): 81-86.

Because the sample interviewed was nonrepresentative, it is impossible to generalize the findings beyond these 80 families. However, the fact that violence occurred during pregnancy in almost one-quarter of the families reporting violence indicates that this could be a phenomenon of widespread occurrence. Other sources of information support the notion that physical violence and pregnancy are more highly associated than is commonly realized. For instance, many newspaper accounts of intrafamilial violence and homicide note that the wife/victim was pregnant at the time of the attack. For example:

> A 20-year-old youth accused of strangling his pregnant wife hanged himself last night from a knotted bedsheet in his cell at Clinton County jail [New York Sunday Times, August 26, 1973].

Reports from Britain indicate that beatings during pregnancy are relatively common (Newsweek, 1973: 39; Mindout, 1974).

In addition to these sources of information, evidence comes from a third and more surprising source, contemporary American fiction. Steinmetz and Straus (1974) in an anthology of articles dealing with family violence note that they were unable to locate a single passage in American fiction where a husband or a wife beat each other (with the exception of cases where the protagonist is already labeled a deviant from some other activity—i.e., murderer or criminal, or where the participants are foreign). However, there are three cases in American fiction where violence between spouses is portrayed and the beaten wife is pregnant during the attack. In Puzo's *The Godfather* (1969), the Don's daughter is beaten by her husband while she is pregnant; Rhette Butler throws Scarlette down the stairs while she is pregnant in *Gone With The Wind* (Mitchell, 1936); and in Mary MacCarthy's *The Group*, a pregnant wife is also assaulted by her husband (1963).

Clearly, the exact extent of violence during pregnancy is still an empirical question; however, the examples cited support the tentative hypothesis that violence and pregnancy are somehow associated, such that an important aspect of research and examinations of intrafamily violence ought to focus on violence which occurs during a wife's term of pregnancy.

Why Violence During Pregnancy

The interviews with women who were beaten during their pregnancy give some insight into the causes behind the association between being pregnant and being beaten by one's husband. In addition, research on family transitions and on violence contribute other possible answers to this question. We propose that there are five major factors which contribute to pregnant wives being assaulted by their husbands: (1) sexual frustration, (2) family transition, stress, and strain, (3) biochemical changes in the wife, (4) prenatal child abuse, and (5) defenselessness of the wife.

SEXUAL FRUSTRATION

A number of social workers whom we spoke to in connection with the finding on violence during pregnancy commented that it might well be caused by the sexual frustration which arises during pregnancy. Although doctors now inform prospective parents that there is only a brief period during which couples should abstain from sexual intercourse, pregnancy in many families is taken as the sign that sexual relations must cease. The reasons behind this abstinence range from superstition (a husband was afraid the baby would bite him; Congdon, 1970), to the husband's lack of interest in his physically changing wife. One woman interviewed commented that she was hit during her pregnancy and that her husband's sexual habits at this time were "peculiar":

Interviewer: Did he ever hit you when you were pregnant?
Mrs. (10): Oh yes, this was his pastime. Plus, he's uh, his sex life—I don't know what you would call it a homosexual or what. We would have sex relations and he would have a jar of vaseline. If things weren't going right he would go into the bathroom and masturbate.

Rossi (1968) discussed at length the transition to parenthood and its implications for role relations and role changes in the family. She labels the onset of the pregnancy as the end of the honeymoon stage of the marriage. For many families the transition to parenthood and the resulting effect on family structure create a number of stresses and strains for the husband and wife as the due date approaches.

When a man and woman marry because the woman is pregnant the honeymoon stage ends rather rapidly—if it ever existed. Husbands who marry pregnant wives may feel increasing stress as the baby approaches (or as the wife swells). Mrs. (70), who was beaten often during her pregnancy, discusses the tremendous strain her husband was under because he was forced into the marriage:

> Mrs. (70): Our problem was getting married and having a baby so fast . . .
> that produced a great strain . . . I wasn't ready. I had the baby six months
> after we were married.

A similar problem of a too rapid transition to parenthood occurs if the
baby is conceived shortly after the couple is married.

> Mrs. (59): I think because neither of us were ready to have any children—
> and I got pregnant about three months after I was married. He never
> accepted it really. He loved to ski and hike. We had a place we could go to
> weekends and he didn't want to stop doing anything—and if I couldn't go
> he would go without me.

In Mrs. (59)'s marriage, as in marriages of other women we talked to,
the pregnancy caused a change in the family routine. Often the husband
did not want to change his routine of work and leisure. This led to
conflict, arguments, and in some instances violence.

It is obvious that these women are not the only ones who suffer from
the stress and strain of being pregnant, nor are these the only families for
whom pregnancy brings about a rapid transition and change in family
role relations. The crucial point in bringing about violence was that the
stress of pregnancy was added on to an already high level of structural
stress in these families. Half of the 10 families had less than a $5,000-a-
year income in 1972. Two husbands were unemployed and five more
were seasonally employed (painters, construction work). In addition,
only one husband had a high school diploma. So there is evidence that
these families were already under economic stress when the pregnancy
occurred. The role changes and potential new mouth to feed add to the
stress level.

BIOCHEMICAL CHANGES IN THE WIFE

Another source of stress during this transitional period is the
biochemical changes which are occurring in the wife. Women often
describe the onset of pregnancy as having their heads attached to
another body. Three wives we spoke with said violence grew out of their
irritability which began when they became pregnant.

> Mrs. (19): He hit me one time when I was pregnant—but I was in such a
> nervous condition all the time.

Discussions of pregnancy often indicate that the biochemical changes which women experience cause them to become more critical of their husbands' behavior. For instance, pregnant women become more fearful of being in a car and criticize their husbands' driving more often (Colman and Colman, 1973: 20). Thus, the changes in their bodies often cause pregnant women to "pick on" their husbands, which can lead to conflict. In addition to irritability, these wives mentioned that they became depressed by having to stay home all the time and because they perceived a growing lack of sexual attractiveness.

PRENATAL CHILD ABUSE

Three of the wives who were hit when pregnant reported that the beating was followed by a miscarriage while a fourth wife told that the child born after the beating was handicapped. Whether on a conscious or subconscious level, violence toward a pregnant wife may be a form of prenatal child abuse or filicide. Mrs. (80)'s comments give at least some evidence to support this claim.

> Mrs. (80): Oh yea, he hit me when I was pregnant. It was weird. Usually he hit me in the face with his fist, but when I was pregnant he used to hit me in the belly. It was weird.

It may not have been just weird, it may have been her husband's attempt to terminate the pregnancy and relieve him of the impending stress of yet another child.

Although we may be ascribing more cognitive processes than are actually in play, we believe that for many families violence which brings about a miscarriage is a more acceptable way of terminating an unwanted pregnancy than is abortion. On one hand we know that there is still considerable controversy over the moral and legal aspects of abortion, even after the Supreme Court ruling of 1972, which for all intents and purposes legalized abortion. On the other hand, research on violence indicates violence is typical of family relations and is often normative in family life (Steinmetz and Straus, 1973, 1974; Straus et al., 1973; Gelles, 1974; Schultz, 1969). Consequently, violence which terminates a pregnancy may be more acceptable socially, morally, and even legally than is an abortion.

DEFENSELESSNESS OF THE WIFE

Howard Kaplan's work on aggression points out that aggression is more likely if the other person (the victim) is perceived as unwilling or unable to retaliate (1972: 610). Thus, pregnant wives may be vulnerable to violence because their husbands view them as unable or unwilling to retaliate because of their changed physical condition. Although we cannot know whether this is the case from our limited data, it is possible that just being vulnerable to attack makes the violence a more likely outcome to family conflict than other possible outcomes.

Implications

Our exploratory examination of this issue suggests that violence during pregnancy is much more common than anyone has suspected. There are hints in the findings that violence toward pregnant women is not just an individual aberration of aggressive husbands, but rather grows out of the stress of the situation, and is compounded when the family has other preexisting (i.e., to the pregnancy) stresses.

Furthermore, if we are correct in our assumption about violence toward a pregnant wife being prenatal child abuse, then this violence may serve as an indicator or predictor of future abuse of children in these families. Dr. Eli Newberger of the Children's Hospital Medical Center in Boston has found that child abuse and family stress are highly related. In addition, he has noticed a number of cases of women who were beaten when pregnant showing up in his cases of child abuse. These findings indicate that intrafamily violence arises as a result of stress and severe frustration and that locating a family where a pregnant wife has been assaulted could serve as an indicator of this family's use of physical aggression as a response to stress and the likelihood of future occurrences of violence toward children.

POLICY IMPLICATIONS

If, as we think, the generative sources of violence toward a pregnant spouse are similar to the sources of conjugal violence and child abuse, then the policy implications of this finding are similar to those proposed to deal with husband-wife violence and violence toward children (Gelles, 1973; Newberger et al., 1973). Some suggested strategies of dealing with violence and pregnancy follow:

(1) *Planned Parenthood.* It is a known fact that unwanted children are the most frequently abused children (Gelles, 1973: 617). We have also seen that many wives are battered during their pregnancy because they are carrying unwanted or unplanned-for children. Therefore, one

of the initial steps in formulating a strategy of intervention in cases of violence toward pregnant women is to provide an avenue to prevent or ease the stress of an unwanted pregnancy. Effective planned parenthood programs, dissemination of birth control devices, and the removal of legal and social stigma of abortion are all steps in the direction of reducing the likelihood of stressed pregnancies ending in attacks on the pregnant wife by her husband. This is particularly important because of the danger the assault poses to the unborn fetus. A recent essay published in Britain (Mindout, 1974) discussed the danger of mental retardation in a child due to its mother being beaten when pregnant.

It should be stressed at this point that the problems which are associated with unplanned or unwanted children are serious enough to mandate the inclusion of material on the need for planned parenthood and the alternatives to unwanted children in family life education curricula.

(2) Preparation for Parenthood. As we cited earlier, pregnancy produces a number of chemical and emotional changes in a woman. These come as a surprise to her and a particular surprise to her husband. If neither partner knows about, or understands the origin and nature of these changes, there is the real possibility of severe conflict and stress arising in the family. The preparation for childbirth classes that are held in conjunction with the teaching of natural childbirth serve to teach both potential mothers and fathers about the various aspects and changes that go on in a woman during the term of her pregnancy. Because both spouses are aware of these factors they are likely to be better able to cope with the changes and new irritabilities and stresses posed by pregnancy. One problem is that these classes in prepared childbirth typically do not commence until the seventh month of pregnancy, long after the changes have occurred and had their effect on family life. Thus, it would be helpful, particularly for families already under stress (unemployment, sporadic employment, economic problems, housing difficulties, and so forth) to enter into preparation for childbirth classes early into the pregnancy—as early as possible. Furthermore, these sessions are critically important for the husband, to inform him about what he can expect to occur during the next nine months.

As in the case of planned parenthood, information which prepares men and women for the problems and stresses of pregnancy are of such critical importance to family functioning that they ought to be included in family life education courses. Material which outlines the biological process of pregnancy ought to be supplemented with information which points out the likely problems and social stresses that occur in house-holds during the term of pregnancy. Some of the articles previously cited (Colman and Colman, 1973; Congdon, 1970; LeMasters, 1957: Rossi, 1968) would be most suitable readings in this area.

(3) *Family Crisis Centers.* One major feature which contributes to intrafamily violence is that there typically is no escape from the scene of stress and conflict. Small arguments can escalate into knock-down, drag-out fist fights because there is no place to flee for refuge (Gelles, 1974). In the case of violence toward a pregnant wife, this is an important factor because of the wife's defenselessness. Thus, one policy which can be developed is to establish family crisis centers and crisis telephone numbers. Many wives I talked with said they stayed in the house and were beaten because they had no place to go. If there is some shelter they can go to, they can leave the scene of the conflict in order to let the conflict die down or to be in a neutral setting while others try to intervene with services or through legal means to cope with the situation which led to the potential for violence.

(4) *Basic Needs.* It is obvious to all family practitioners that for a family to function adequately there are certain basic needs which must be fulfilled—medical care, dental care, nutritional needs, housing, and so forth. But in the case of a family where the wife is pregnant, these needs are more critical because of the obvious presence of the potential new member. Thus, a family of two might have certain objective needs during the pregnancy that are being met, but they are more concerned with their future needs because of the addition of the baby. The three-room apartment which is suitable for a two-person family, may be thought by that family to be too small for three. The practitioner or counselor must be aware of and help to provide for a pregnant family's future basic needs as well as their present basic needs.

This topic is too new and I am too inexperienced in the area of family counseling to add further to this preliminary discussion of the policy implications of the findings on violence and pregnancy. But it is important to note that the services needed to deal with this problem will be a synthesis of those services designed for families experiencing conjugal violence, and families where children are abused.

Conclusion

The major contribution of this note has been to alert those involved in providing family services to a previously unrecognized problem in family lives—violence toward pregnant women. In addition this note points out an area which needs more research to provide better data on this issue.

In terms of providing family services and for developing policies of intervention in families where violence occurs, it is important to realize that the crisis and transitions of parenthood begin during the pregnancy and not only after the child is born.

CHAPTER 8

POWER, SEX, AND VIOLENCE: THE CASE OF MARITAL RAPE

The Women's Movement in the 1970s has increased the sensitivity of women and society to two major crimes which women fall victim to: sexual assault and physical assault by their husbands. Victims of rape and battered wives have a great deal in common. For years these two crimes have been the most underreported crimes against persons in the criminal justics system. Additionally, battered wives and rape victims are often accused of "asking for," "deserving," or "enjoying" their victimization. Finally, in most cases of rape or physical assault by their husbands, women who turn to the criminal justice system for assistance or relief are often maltreated or ignored by police, lawyers, and judges.

The purpose of this essay is to examine rape and physical violence together by analyzing the case of marital rape. The entire subject of marital rape, or sexual assault of wives by husbands, opens up a host of controversies. First, the concept of marital rape is one which has not existed legally. By legal tradition, a woman could not be raped by her husband, since the "crime" of rape was ordinarily and legally defined as forcing sexual intercourse on someone other than the wife of the person accused (Brownmiller, 1975; Gallen, 1967; Griffen, 1971; New York Radical Feminists, 1974).[1] Second, labeling sexual intercourse forced on a wife by a husband "marital rape" implies a major value judgment by the labeler concerning appropriate interpersonal relations between family members. Finally, if husbands force wives to have sexual

Author's Note: From Richard J. Gelles, "Power, Sex and Violence: The Case of Marital Rape," *Family Coordinator*, 1977, 26 (October): 339-347.

© 1977 National Council on Family Relations. Reprinted by permission.

relations, even accompanied by physical violence, do the wives or the husbands consider this behavior problematic or "rape"?

The essay begins by examining the controversies surrounding the study of marital rape. Next, the literature on rape is reviewed in order to summarize the facts known about rape which could be applied to the case of marital rape. The third section summarizes two sources of data which we use to shed some light on the incidence and social context of marital rape. The final section discusses further issues in the study of marital rape.

Does Marital Rape Exist?

The major question which must be addressed at the outset is, Can we or should we investigate a phenomenon which, by legal definition, has not even existed? Rape has been defined conceptually as "any sexual intimacy forced on one person by another" (Media and Thompson, 1974: 12). A less objective and more culturally relative definition of rape is provided by Levine in his study of rape in the Gussi tribe. Levine defines rape as "culturally disvalued use of coercion by a male to achieve the submission of a female to sexual intercourse" (1959: 969). The dictionary definition of rape is "sexual intercourse with a woman by a man without her consent and chiefly by force or deception" (Webster's New Collegiate Dictionary, 1975). Thus, by dictionary definition, conceptual definition, and cultural definition, any woman can theoretically be raped by any man. Media and Thompson's definition (1974) implies that a man can also be the victim of rape by a woman, and research on homosexual assault in prison documents that men are raped by men (Davis, 1970). The criminal justice system modifies these definitions by not viewing forced sexual intercourse between husbands and wives as rape. The rationale for this appears to be that the courts view the marriage contract as requiring wives (and husbands) to have sexual relations with their spouses (Cronan, 1969). While the "duty" of sex is, in a legal sense, equally distributed in marriage, the compulsory nature of sexual relations in marriage works chiefly to the advantage of the male (Gillespie, 1971) because men are typically able to muster more physical, social, and material resources in their relations with their wives.

Given that marital rape has not existed legally, should we examine it as part of family behavior and as an aspect of marital violence? We believe that we should. The legal prescriptions which imply that the wife is the "property" of her husband (Griffen, 1971) and which give the husband the permanent right to sexual relations once the wife says "I do" (New York Radical Feminists, 1974) are a reflection of an ideology, not a portrait of reality. The law is a reflection of what behavior ought to be, not what behavior actually is. The fact that the criminal justice system is largely populated by males partially explains the fact that legal statutes reflect a "male dominant" view of family behavior. A case in point is the California Penal Code, which requires that a woman be more injured than is commonly allowed for battery in order to press an assault charge against her husband (Calvert, 1974). The fact that the courts do not accept the concept of marital rape does not, in our opinion, mean that wives are not being raped by their husbands.

Because forced sexual relations between a husband and wife have traditionally not legally been considered cases of rape, the question arises whether or not a wife herself views the incident as a rape. This is an empirical question which we will take up in detail in a later section of the essay, but it is likely that the majority of women who are physically forced into having sexual intercourse with their husbands do not consider this to be an incident of rape, a violent act, or a deviant act. Thus, if the victim herself is unlikely to view the behavior as rape, how can we discuss the phenomenon of marital rape? In order to answer the question it would be wise to briefly analyze why a woman would not view physically coerced sex as rape. Our research on marital violence suggests that many victims of family violence (including abused children) do not view these acts as violence or as problematic. Women who have been beaten severely by their husbands often state that they "deserved to be hit," that they "needed to be hit," or that "husbands are supposed to hit their wives" (see Gelles, 1974; 1976; and Parnas, 1967). The fact that women are socialized to believe that violence between spouses is expected and normative does not diminish the fact that women are often injured by their husbands in trying to redress these acts (see Field and Field, 1973; Truninger, 1971; Gelles, 1976). In analyzing forced sexual relations between spouses, we believe that the pervasive ideology of "women as men's chattel" has served to deny women the opportunity to perceive their own sexual victimization. We have chosen to discuss the issue of marital rape, irrespective of the wife's subjective perceptions of the behavior, because we believe this is a phenomenon which needs to be questioned and studied.

The discussion of the wife's perceptions of forced sexual intercourse and our rationale for choosing to investigate this phenomenon despite the fact that many women do not perceive themselves as rape victims raises the issue of the value implications involved in labeling the phenomenon as rape. Rape is a perjorative term which connotes repulsive and violent deviance. Webster's New Collegiate Dictionary states that rape can also be defined as "an outrageous violation" (Webster's New Collegiate Dictionary, 1975). We have chosen to use the term rape in this essay for the same reasons we have decided to title our investigation "Studies of Violence Between Family Members" and for the same reasons we have chosen to study abused wives. We believe that the area of violence between family members has long suffered from selective inattention (Dexter, 1958) at the hands of both social scientists and society in general. The plight of victims of violence between family members has been overlooked by students of the family, agencies of social control and social services, and the public at large. In order to rectify this situation, it often requires using an emotionally charged word to draw attention to this phenomenon. The history of research on abused children reveals that battered children were largely ignored until Henry Kempe labeled the phenomenon as "The Battered Child Syndrome" (Kempe et al., 1962). We have decided to label this essay as an investigation of marital rape partly as a reaction to the discriminatory practice of not allowing a woman to protect herself from violent or physically coercive sexual intercourse at the hand of her husband, and in an attempt to draw scholarly and public attention to this issue.

Research on Rape

Because the law views rape as an act of sexual penetration of the body of a woman *not one's wife*, there are virtually no official statistics available on the subject of marital rape. Brownmiller alludes to the depiction of a marital rape on a television episode of the series "The Forsythe Saga" (Brownmiller, 1975) and Russell (1975) devotes a chapter of her book to a description of marital rape. Beyond these descriptive data and illustrations, there is little else one can locate which bears directly on the incidence or nature of marital rape. The lack of official statistical data is a direct result of the law not viewing marital rape as a crime. Peters (1975), for example, reports that none of the patients he treated for incestuous rape reported their assaults.[2]

There are two areas of rape research which bear on the case of marital rape. The first area is the study of victim-offender relations and the second considers the element of "power" as a component of sexual assault.

VICTIM-OFFENDER RELATIONS

The conventional wisdom concerning rape suggests that women are typically assaulted in dark alleys by strangers. The research which has been carried out on patterns of rape indicates that this conventional wisdom may be more myth than reality. Amir's research (1971) on patterns of victimization revealed that 48% of the rape victims knew the offender. Pauline Bart's (1975) examination of 1,070 questionnaires filled out by victims of rape found that 5% of the women were raped by relatives, .4% by husbands, 1% by lovers, and 3% by ex-lovers. Thus, a total of 8.4% of the women were raped by men with whom they had intimate relations. Bart's survey also found that 12% of rape victims were raped by dates and 23% were raped by acquaintances. Less than half of the victims (41%) were raped by total strangers.

Additional research on rape also reveals a pattern where victims were likely to know the offender or be related to the offender. Of the 250 victims of rape studied by the Center for Rape Concern at Philadelphia General Hospital, 58% of the rape victims under the age of 18 were assaulted by a relative or acquaintance. When the victim is a child, she is likely to be sexually attacked by her father—six of the 13 children were raped by their fathers (Peters, 1975).

The research on victim-offender relationships dispels the myth that the majority of women are raped by strangers. For the purposes of our focus on marital rape, the research results indicate that intimacy and sexual assault are frequently related. The women who are raped by boyfriends, dates, lovers, ex-lovers, husbands, relatives, and other men that they know *might* represent the tip of an iceberg which reveals a more extensive pattern relating intimacy with forced sexual relations.

POWER AND RAPE

A theme in much of the literature on rape is that rape is less a sexual act and more an act of power in the relations between men and women. Bart concludes, based on her analysis of questionnaires filled out by rape victims, that rape is a power trip, not a passion trip (1975). Brownmiller also perceives rape as a power confrontation. She views rape as an act of hostility toward women by men—rape is an attempt by a man to exercise power over a woman (1975). Seites (1975) agrees that rape is a sexual power confrontation. She postulates that marital rape is an act where a husband can assert his power and control over his wife.

If rape is viewed more as an act of power than a sexual act, then we can examine marital rape by focusing on the power dynamics of the family. Goode (1971) has stated that all social systems depend on force or its threat, and that the family is no exception. Goode goes on to propose that the more resources individuals have, the more force they can command, but the less they will use that force. On the other hand, the fewer resources individuals have, the less force they can command, but the more they will use the force. Goode theorizes that men who lack sufficient resources to hold the socially prescribed dominant role in the family will use physical force to compensate for the lack of resources.

If Goode's resource theory of family violence is correct, then we can predict that men who command limited social/psychological and verbal resources are likely to use more force on their wives than men who are well educated, hold prestigious jobs, and earn a respectable income (see O'Brien, 1971, and Gelles, 1974, for empirical data on this hypothesis). If rape is viewed as an act of violence and an act of power, we could deduce that men who have few social and psychological resources are likely to use an act such as marital rape to intimidate, coerce, and dominate their wives. Rape of wives might grow out of a husband's lack of verbal skills and an inability to argue equally with his wife, or it might be a means of the husband demonstrating how he can dominate his wife despite the fact that he is poorly educated or unemployed. In addition, because rape can be a degrading experience, some husbands may use this act to humiliate their wives and thus gain a degree of power and control over their spouses.

Research on Marital Rape

While the research on victim-offender relationships, on victims of rape, and on family violence allows us to speculate about marital rape, the research carried out to date allows no direct insights into the incidence or nature of the phenomenon. In order to provide some direct information on the topic of marital rape we attempted to gather data which would shed light on this phenomenon. This section reports on two investigations. The first was a survey of Rape-Crisis Centers which asked the centers to provide us information on the number of cases of marital rape they encounter and on specific aspects of these cases. The second investigation was part of a larger study of physical violence between husbands and wives (see Gelles, 1974, 1975c, 1976). The second investigation analyzed transcriptions of interviews with women who had been beaten by their husbands to see what information could be gleaned on the sexual aspects of the beatings.

The increased attention on the plight of victims of sexual assaults led to the establishment of Rape-Crisis Centers throughout the nation which provide legal, medical, and social services to victims of rape. In the spring of 1975 Joan Seites (1975) contacted 40 Rape-Crisis Centers which were chosen from a listing compiled by the Center for Women Policy Studies.[3] From the centers 16 completed questionnaires were returned (one questionnaire was returned because of insufficient address), a response rate of 40%.

The purpose of the survey was to determine whether or not cases of marital rape are reported to Rape-Crisis Centers, and if so, how many cases are reported. Of the 3,709 reported calls dealing with rape and attempted rape received by the 16 centers, 12 calls dealt with marital rape (.3%). This figure is low and comparable with Bart's finding (1975) that .8% of the victims of rape reported being attacked by their husbands.

Because Rape-Crisis Centers do not always record the offender-victim relationship, we cannot be sure that the 12 reported marital rapes fully represent the proportion of husband-wife rapes in the 3,709 calls which were handled. However, the data do reveal that at least some women are reporting instances of marital rape despite the fact that the law does not view forced marital sexual intercourse as rape and despite the fact that few women would view physically coerced sex at the hands of their husbands as requiring a call to a Rape-Crisis Center.

The questionnaires also asked the centers to discuss some of the aspects of the calls they received about marital rape. One agency reported that women complained that their husbands were coming home drunk and hitting them and then raping them. These callers were not asking for rape counseling, they asked for information about divorce. It would appear that because there are few agencies which are capable of providing counseling and assistance to battered wives (there were 6 Battered Wife Centers in the United States as of March 1976), that women who were beaten by their husbands seek help from the best known women's agency—Rape-Crisis Centers. Thus, wives may report rape and battering to centers in order to get some help in solving problems of marital violence.

The agencies which did provide information about cases of marital rape reported that raped wives were likely to be fearful of future assaults and were angry with their husbands. One agency provided a personal account of a woman whose husband attempted to rape her.

> Almost 14 years ago, my first husband attempted to rape me. At the time, we were very close to being separated and I think he wanted to attempt to bring us closer, back together through a sexual act—he always maintained that that was his prime means of communication, how he felt the closest. At first I fought and when he attempted to smother me with a pillow, I panicked and became only concerned with how to get him to stop—I was afraid he was going to kill me. So I became totally unresponsive to him—wouldn't talk or anything and he eventually stopped tearing my clothes and pulling me and there was no intercourse. Because it happened in the context of a whole lot of bad things in our marriage (he had been violent to me once or twice before, but not sexually so), I didn't have any particular feelings at the time except relief that it was over. Very shortly thereafter, I left him. I never thought of the incident as attempted rape until almost 10 years later when I was walking away from a session of a women's group I was in wherein we had been talking about specific rape incidents that had occurred to some of the members. Until that time, I think I felt rape was of the stereotypic type of the stranger leaping out of the bushes and never thought of an incident like that occurring between people who knew each other—especially husband and wife, as rape. I think this is true of many married women—they have accepted society's dictum that a man has sexual access to his wife whenever he wants, whether she does or not. Thus, it never occurs to them that this could be a crime, a felonious assault, that this is, indeed, rape.

The questionnaires from the Rape-Crisis Centers provide some additional information on marital rape. First, although forced sexual intercourse may take place frequently between husbands and wives, most women do not view this as rape.

> I know personally, not professionally, many women who have been raped by their husbands. Some file for divorce. Few consider the act rape, since they themselves consider themselves property.

> Most women probably do not realize, or classify such actions as "rape" because they have been infused with cultural myths surrounding rape.

Many wives view themselves to blame for the incidents of forced sexual intercourse. The woman raped by her husband who was interviewed for Russell's book (1975) indicated that she thought the incident was partially her fault because she should have known not to get into the situation which led to her victimization. This kind of victim-blaming is common in incidents of rape where victims are thought to have brought on the assault through provocative behavior and being "in the wrong place at the wrong time." Victim-blaming by the victim is found in instances of marital rape and marital violence (Gelles, 1974; 1976) as victims of deviance in the family try to neutralize the stigma of the deviance by blaming themselves for their husbands' behavior.

Lastly, as in cases of marital violence, women who are forced into having sexual relations with their husbands are ashamed to tell other people about this problem.

> The biggest issue we've noticed is that married women don't talk to each other about their sex lives to any extent and especially not about rape!

IN-DEPTH INTERVIEWS

Interviews with 80 family members on the subject of violence between husbands and wives elicited some discussions about the relation between sex and violence. A number of wives reported being beaten by their husbands as a result of their husbands becoming jealous over a suspected incident of infidelity. Husbands also reported that their wives struck them over suspicions about extramarital affairs (see Gelles, 1974: 82-85, 147-148).

Although the questions asked in the course of the interviews did not specifically pertain to the subject of marital rape, an analysis of the transcriptions of the interviews identified four women who discussed sex-related violence which could be viewed as instances of marital rape or attempted marital rape. The most consistent pattern found in the interviews with the four women was that they felt that they were coerced or forced into having sex with their husbands and that the husbands criticized the wives for not being affectionate.

> Well, uh, he used to tell everybody that I was cold . . . he (came home) drunk or he had been out half the night. I didn't really feel like it (sexual intercourse). But we never argued about it. Usually he got his way because I wasn't about to go up against it.

> He was one of those—he liked to strike out a lot and hit you and a lot of that was based on sex . . . he thought that I was a cold fish—I wasn't affectionate enough. . . . Sometimes he took a shotgun to me.

He was drinking . . . I know that was the problem—he said as far as he was concerned I wasn't affectionate enough—it (sexual intercourse) was anytime he felt like it—whatever time he came home—it was crazy . . . different hours.

What emerged from the interviews was that wives frequently did not want to have sex with their husbands because of the fact that their husbands were drunk, came home at odd hours, or were critical of their wives' sexual responsiveness. The husbands, however, appeared to believe that their wives should have intercourse with them on demand and that if they refused it was because they (the wives) were frigid. Moreover, husbands seemed to view a refusal of intercourse as grounds for beating or intimidating their wives.

In all four cases, the wives gave in to their husbands' demands rather than be physically forced into having sexual intercourse. Thus, the review of the in-depth interviews did not find an instance of a woman being violently forced into having sex, as in the case discussed previously in this essay or the case discussed by Russell (1975).

We have stated previously that one reason why so little attention has been directed toward forced sexual intercourse in marriage is the theory that this is not viewed as a problem by most wives. One interview indicated that forced sex was, indeed, viewed as problematic by at least one woman in the study. This woman explained that she often provoked her husband into physical fights by verbally taunting him after he came home intoxicated and demanding sex. She went on to state that her husband would beat her after these verbal assaults, she would cry, and he would drop his demands for sex. Thus, she viewed being beaten up as a more acceptable alternative to marital rape.

An analysis of the literature on rape, the survey of Rape-Crisis Centers asking about marital rape, and the examination of transcripts of interviews on marital violence only begins to scratch the surface of the topic of marital rape. There are numerous issues which ought to be considered in detail in further investigations of marital rape. We shall briefly discuss five issues where further consideration is needed.

(1) It is claimed that the family predominates in acts of violence ranging from slaps to murder and torture (Straus, Gelles, and Steinmetz, 1976). Although the official statistics on rape do not bear us out, we believe that a woman is most likely to be physically forced into having sexual intercourse by her own husband. Previous studies of marital violence (Gelles, 1974; Straus, 1974b, 1974c, 1976; Steinmetz, 1975)

have not examined sexual violence in marriage. We think that an important aspect of future research on violence in the family would be a focus on acts of marital rape and acts of violence which involve the sexual suppression of women.

(2) A second issue which we feel needs to be discussed is the nominal and operational definitions of marital rape. The central question which needs elaboration is whether marital rape is an act which must be accompanied by physical force and violence, or whether the act *itself* is violent? Interviews with women who had been victims of violence indicate that most of these women submitted to sexual intercourse without being physically beaten. Because the intercourse was not accompanied by violence, these women did not view the behavior as rape, and instead focused on their husbands' drinking or staying out late as the main problems in the marriage. Because marital rape is technically legal and because women have traditionally been socialized to believe they are the property of their husbands, we would speculate that the only instances of marital rape which would be reported to Rape-Crisis Centers, social service agencies, or social scientists would be those cases where physical violence is involved. Thus, the full extent of how many women are verbally coerced or intimidated into having sex against their wills with their husbands may remain an unknown.

(3) We have been able to glean some insights on marital rape from the research on victim-offender relations in cases of rape. One area where the research on nonmarital rape can provide no help in understanding marital rape is the consequences of the attack. Much of the research on rape goes into great detail on the aftermath of the attack and the affects on the victim. We believe that the consequences of being raped by a stranger or even a boyfriend are far different from being raped by one's husband. Peters (1975) who studied a number of cases of incestuous sexual assault, proposes that rape by a family member or relative produces different emotional consequences than rape by a stranger. Peters states that rape by a stranger might be physically dangerous, but rape by a relative or friend may be more disillusionary. Russell's presentation of a case of marital rape (1975: 71-81) illustrates this point. Mrs. Michel, who was raped by her husband in front of bystanders, stated that she felt the rape was partially her fault. She broke out in hives the next day and felt humiliated by the incident. While we know about the reactions of women who were raped by nonfamily members, and we have some data on battered wives, we know little about women who are sexually assaulted by their husbands. The available data suggest that

raped wives are neither masochists nor do they enjoy being sexually assaulted by their husbands (see Russell, 1975: 75).

(4) A discussion of rape or marital violence almost inevitably raises the question of whether there is an association between acts of violence and acts of sex. Faulk (1977) suggests that marital violence may sometimes be sexually stimulating in itself. He states that some wives report that their husbands want sexual intercourse soon after a violent outburst. Faulk goes on to report that it is uncertain whether the violence itself is sexually stimulating or whether husbands are trying to use sexual intercourse as a means of reconciliation. In addition:

> Some wives report that their clothes were partly torn off during the violence, and a few saw this as sexually motivated. It seems likely, however, that in many cases the clothes were torn off to prevent women from escaping [Faulk, 1977].

The little empirical research and theoretical discussion which focuses on the relationship between sex and violence support Faulk's contention that sex is not an intrinsic component of marital violence. An analysis of TAT responses of college students to ambiguous pictures reveal little association between sexual thema and violent thema in the stories produced (Gelles, 1975a). While women did not associate sex with violence in their fantasy production, there was a slight association in the stories produced by men. Steinmetz and Straus (1974) argue that there is little evidence for a *biological* association between sex and violence and postulate that sex antagonism and sex segregation in this society might explain the tendency to use violence in sexual acts.

The analysis of marital rape suggests that the association of sex and violence are means which husbands can use to dominate and intimidate their wives without fear of outside intervention. Because women cannot legally charge their husbands with marital rape and because acts of marital violence rarely result in successful prosecution of the husband, forced sexual intercourse and marital violence are two unsanctioned methods which husbands can invoke to establish dominance in their families.

(5) The final point for consideration concerns the nature of the law which denies women the right to charge or seek prosecution of their husbands for acts of marital rape. An obvious question which arises is, if marital rape exists, and it is a problem, should the law be changed to provide women avenues of legal recourse for redress in acts of marital

rape? If we argue that yes, the laws should be changed, there are two problems which arise. First, if all wives could take their husbands to court for forcing them into having sexual intercourse, this might flood the court with intrafamily litigations. The already overburdened criminal justice system probably could not handle the large number of cases which it might have to process. Second, arguing for changing the law somehow implies that such a change would provide women with legal rights. The case of marital violence serves as a good reminder that giving a woman the *de jure* legal power to charge her husband with an illegal act does not necessarily mean that the police and courts will provide her with relief and protection. Although women can charge their husbands with physical assault, the chances of the courts intervening and helping them are quite slim (Gelles, 1976; Truninger, 1971; Field and Field, 1973). Any legal change in the area of marital rape would also have to be accompanied by social, attitudinal, and moral changes whereby society views the issue of marital rape seriously, refrains from viewing victimized wives as being masochists or really enjoying the rape, and conveys a willingness to intervene in family matters and provide real protection for victims of marital rape.

Conclusion

The available evidence on marital violence indicates that a number of women are forced into having sexual relations with their husbands through intimidation or physical force. Faulk's research (1977) identified cases where sexual intercourse was forced on a wife after her husband beat her. Other data point to the fact that despite the fact that marital rape is not possible in a strict legal sense, some women are talking about and reporting incidents of marital rape.

From a research point of view, we believe that the topic of marital rape is an important area of investigation for social scientists. Investigations of marital rape and subjective perceptions of forced sexual relations between husbands and wives (including instances where wives are forced into having sexual acts that they find repugnant) will provide valuable insights into the family, power relations in the family, and the range and nature of sexual activities in marriage. A focus on marital rape also tends to move this subject from the taken for granted into the problematic. This transition might serve to call into question the legal position of women and whether women ought to have broader legal rights in terms of dealing with their husbands. We conclude that the head-in-the-sand approach to marital rape is no longer acceptable for social scientists, members of the criminal justice system, or for women in this society.

Notes

1. South Dakota became the first state to eliminate the spousal exclusion from the statute on rape. The 1975 Rape Law reads: "Rape is an act of sexual penetration accomplished by any person." Other states, such as Florida, do not specifically exempt married persons from rape prosecution (Silverman, 1976: 10). NB: As of January 1, 1979, Oregon, Iowa, Delaware, Massachusetts, and New Jersey had removed the spousal exclusion from their Rape Laws. South Dakota placed the spousal exclusion back in the Rape Law in 1977.

2. Incestuous sexual assaults are not reported for other reasons, among which might be the victims' embarrassment.

3. A sample of 40 crisis centers was chosen from the listing. A questionnaire was sent to Rape-Crisis Centers in each state represented in the listing. If more than one Rape-Crisis Center was listed in a state, then a single center was selected based on the degree of professionalism and organization indicated by the name of the center. The sample, while geographically broad, is *not* a representative sample of Rape-Crisis Centers. Each center was sent a questionnaire with a self-addressed, stamped envelope. Only a one-wave mailing was used in this survey.

Update

THE EXTENT OF MARITAL RAPE

Our discovery of marital rape was a serendipitous finding of an exploratory research project aimed at examining violence toward women (Gelles, 1974).

Since the publication of "Power, Sex, and Violence: The Case of Marital Rape," there have been three major research efforts aimed at discovering the extent and patterns of marital rape. The sociologists David Finkelhor and Kersti Yllo interviewed 323 Boston-area women for their book, *License to Rape: Sexual Abuse of Wives* (1985). In their book, 10% of the women said they had been forced to have sex with their husbands or partners. Violence accompanied the rape in about half of the instances. This rate of rape compares to the 3% of the women who reported being raped by strangers. Finkelhor and Yllo conclude that rape by intimates is by far the most common form of rape.

Diana Russell surveyed more than 930 women in San Francisco for her book, *Rape in Marriage* (1982). Of the 644 women who had been married, 14% reported one or more experiences of marital rape.

The sociologists Nancy Shields and Christine Hanneke have also been investigating marital rape and its relation to wife battering (1983). They have found that a significant number of battering victims are also victims of marital rape. Their data suggest that when sexual violence occurs in a marriage it is not an isolated event. Most of the victims in the Shields and Hanneke study were raped more than once or twice.

LEGAL CHANGES

At the time of the initial research on marital rape, there had been little public attention focused on the problem. Only one state had removed the marital exclusion from the rape laws (South Dakota). At the time of the initial publication of "Power, Sex, and Violence: The Case of Marital Rape" the case of John and Greta Rideout was making headlines across the country. Greta Rideout had charged her husband, John, with marital rape; and the case was about to go to trial in Oregon. The case received significant media attention for weeks and ended with John's acquittal and the couple's reconciliation.

There has been a national debate over whether marital rape should be criminalized. Arguments against criminalizing marital rape include the position that outlawing marital rape would lead to frivolous claims, that the private nature of the "crime" would make it impossible to prove, that such a law would have a negative effect on the family and pave the road to divorce, that such a law is a violation of privacy, and that the law is superfluous (Finkelhor and Yllo, 1985).

Nevertheless, those arguing that marital rape is a crime and needs to be outlawed if women are to be protected and the crime is to be deterred have made inroads in nearly every state. At this writing, according to the National Clearinghouse on Marital Rape in Berkeley, California, 28 states and the District of Columbia allow a husband to be prosecuted for rape even while he lives with his partner; 21 states allow prosecution of the partners if they are living apart; and 1 state, Alabama, retains the marital exclusion for married partners, irrespective of where they live.

PART IV

VIOLENCE IN OTHER FAMILY RELATIONSHIPS

Introduction

The first chapter of this volume mentioned that most studies of family violence find a consistent, though not perfect, association between being a victim as a child and using violence in the home as an adult. While some professionals and members of the public interpret these findings to mean that *all* abused children *will* grow up to be abusive adults, and that anyone who was not abused as a child will grow up to be nonviolent, the main body of the research supports a *probabilistic* interpretation that violence does beget violence.

After a decade of research and attention to child abuse and wife abuse, it came as a surprise to many people that parents were being physically attacked by their children. Parent abuse and elder abuse are described as "the newest" and "the most hidden" types of violence in the home. Despite the fact that these forms of violence and abuse may well be more hidden than child or wife abuse, it should not have come as a surprise that parents, young and old, are being assaulted and injured by their children. If, as the research argues, individuals who were treated violently as children are more likely to grow up to be violent adults, why should we be surprised that (a) they wait until they are adults to be violent and (b) they are violent toward their parents?

The learning theory explanation for the intergenerational transmission of family violence (also referred to as the cycle of violence theory), points out that experience and exposure to violence as a child provides a learning experience that teaches children which people are the appropriate victims of family violence, when family violence is appropriate, and how to justify acts of family violence. The exchange theory of family violence presented in the introduction of this volume argues that people will use violence toward family members if they have been taught that this is an appropriate and normative means of dealing with other people *and* if the costs of being violent are lower than the rewards.

While research on elder abuse and violence toward parents is far less advanced than research on the better known forms of family violence, the available evidence indicates that children who assault their parents and adults who abuse their elderly parents are more likely than nonviolent offspring to have experienced and been exposed to severe violence as children. Second, the victims of parental abuse or elder abuse are likely to be individuals who can inflict fewer "costs" on the offender. The first chapter in this section, "Adolescent-to-Parent Violence," reports that the typical case of adolescent violence is that of a son toward his mother. The second chapter, "Elder Abuse: The State of Current Knowledge," finds support for the notion that older, more feeble, and more dependent parents are the most likely victims of elder abuse.

A final note on the state of research on violence in other family relations. Significant public attention was directed toward the problem of elder abuse in the late 1970s. Congressional hearings were held, as were two national conferences. Some states passed legislation calling for mandatory reporting of elder abuse. Considerable media attention was devoted to the subject, and some preliminary research efforts were begun. Somewhat less legislative attention was directed at violence toward nonelderly parents, although the media did devote attention to the issue. Sadly, since 1979 there has really not been the explosion of scientific and public interest that accompanied public attention to child abuse in the 1960s and wife abuse in the early 1970s. A number of plausible explanations exist for the lack of development of knowledge and concern for these topics. One tentative explanation is that parent abuse was not advanced as a social problem by a well-organized constituency. Child abuse was championed by people in the medical profession and social service personnel. Wife abuse was championed by women's groups. Elder abuse seemed to be advanced by those concerned with the general problem of aging; but perhaps that constituency was either less well organized than women's groups or had to divide its attention up among numerous pressing problems (e.g., social security, medical care, nursing-home care, and so on). A second hypothesis is that those advancing the issue of violence toward parents sought national attention at a time when the political climate did not allow for establishing federal agencies, national programs, and funding priorities. Congressional hearings on elder abuse concluded at a time when federal programs for wife abuse were being abandoned and programs for battered children were being cut back. Funding for social research came under considerable attack in 1981 with the advent of the Reagan administration. Thus, agencies might not have been inclined to fund exploratory research as they did a decade or two earlier. A final proposition is that parent victims of family violence are not truly considered appropriate objects for concern. It is possible that many people feel that parents somehow deserve their own victimization and that even if they do not, they can throw the abusive child out of the home. Of course, this explanation does not apply to the helpless elderly victims of abuse and violence. Here the problem might be a general lack of understanding of what to do. Removing a victim from an abusive home does not hold out the same promise for thriving development that the removal of an abused child from a home promises (despite the scientific evidence that such thriving development is rare indeed). Given the suspicion of many people that institutions which care for the elderly also abuse and neglect, removal might be just a move from the frying pan into the fire—without any long-term hope of improvement.

These are rather speculative theories and notions, but they do speak to the lingering question of why recognition of other forms of family violence took so long and why it does not appear that these forms will receive the same concentrated research and social policy attention that child and wife abuse received.

CHAPTER 9

ADOLESCENT-TO-PARENT VIOLENCE

with Claire Pedrick Cornell

Although there has been a considerable growth in professional and public attention to family violence, and a significant knowledge base on child abuse and wife abuse has accumulated over the past twenty years, violence directed at parents by adolescent children has been overlooked and underresearched. Spirited interest and some tentative exploratory studies of one facet of children's violence—the abuse of elderly parents by middle-aged children—is the exception to the rule of scarce attention or research on children's violence toward their parents.

A small number of studies have appeared on violent children, but most of these have focused on the most narrow manifestation of the problem, parricide (Smith, 1965; Sargent, 1962; Bender, 1959). Others examined battering children who have committed homicide (Adelson, 1962). Only a few investigators have studied nonlethal physical assault made by children against their parents (Harbin and Madden, 1979; Straus et al., 1980; Warren, 1978).

Perhaps violence toward parents has been overlooked because few believe that it is an extensive or problematic aspect of family relations. In all likelihood, only the most violent or lethal attacks on parents by children come to public or professional attention. Discussing or reporting parent battering may be "taboo" because parents may assume the blame for their own victimization, or they might fear that others will blame them for their children's violent acts.

Children's violence toward their parents bids for scientific, public, and policy attention for a number of reasons. First, given the known rates of other forms of family violence, including child and wife abuse,

Authors' Note: From Richard J. Gelles and Claire Pedrick Cornell, "Adolescent-to-Parent Violence." *The Urban Social Change Review*, 1982, 15(Winter):8-14.

153

sibling violence, and violence toward the elderly (Straus et al., 1980) it is likely that the rate of children's violence toward their parents is at least as substantial as are the rates of other types of family violence. Second, if the rates are high, but the reporting of the problem low, there are probably numerous victims of violence who desire and require social, medical, and legal assistance and intervention. Third, from a purely scientific point of view, the study of children's violence toward their parents is of interest because it allows for the testing of the hypothesis concerning the intergenerational transmission of violence. Many experts and investigators hold, and find, that violence observed or experienced as a child is related to later expressions of family violence. Such hypotheses are typically tested by questioning a violent spouse or parent about their experience with violence as a child. No studies exist which longitudinally follow children until adulthood to test the hypothesis about the relationship between being abused as a child and the likelihood of being an abusing adult. Violence toward parents is the "missing link" in the study of the intergenerational transmission of violence. If observing and experiencing violence as a child is related to becoming a violent adult, it may well be that evidence for this relationship can be found in the behavior of adolescents. In short, victims of childhood violence may not wait until they are married or have children to express their violence. They may well begin to express it when they learned it, in their families of orientation.

With the exception of the national study of family violence conducted by Straus and his colleagues (1980), what little research has been conducted on violence toward parents has been clinical in nature, with extremely small, nongeneralizable samples (the total number of cases from the Harbin and Madden study, 1979, and the Warren study, 1978, is 30). Little has been learned about the extent, patterns, and causes of parental victimization by adolescent offspring.

Research and Research Questions

Will children, as they grow older and larger, be more inclined to strike out at their parents? According to Harbin and Madden's (1979) clinical investigation of 15 assaultive adolescents and their parents, physical size is often a factor. Abuse of parents occurred in many families where the child was bigger and stronger than the parent. Warren (1978) found dominance over parents by older or stronger children to be nonexistent in her sample of 15 families. The majority of children in her study were females and small boys who relied upon both speed and weapons rather than sheer physical strength. When explaining why child abuse is inversely related to the age of the child, Straus and his colleagues (1980) suggested that parents might not hit older children because they fear that they will be retaliated against by these older and stronger offspring.

Researchers who have examined which parent is most often the victim of parent abuse agree that mothers are abused more often than fathers (Warren, 1978), and they are abused more often by their sons than their daughters (Straus et al., 1980). However, Warren states that her findings may simply reflect the commonness of one-parent families in her sample, while Straus et al.'s findings (1980) are for violence by children 3 to 17 in two-parent households. Shuman (1981) reports that the sons of wife beaters tend to be even more abusive toward their mothers than sons who have not been witnesses to parental violence. She explains that sons, hating their powerlessness in being unable to stop their fathers from abusing their mothers, eventually repeat the pattern of male violence on their mothers and later on their wives. Unfortunately, Shuman fails to reference the data from which she draws this conclusion.

Evidence concerning the intergenerational transmission of violence is inconsistent. Harbin and Madden (1979) report that severe child abuse is rarely related to children abusing their parents and that spouse abuse is only occasionally related to child-to-parent violence. On the other hand, Shuman (1981) reports that wife abuse is often present in homes which report child-to-parent violence. Straus et al. (1980) found that the more often parents hit children aged 3 to 17, the more often these children will hit their parents. Where children are found to be abusing parents, researchers found that these children are abusing a sibling as well (Harbin and Madden, 1979; Warren, 1978).

The intent of this essay is to establish a data base on violence toward parents by adolescent children. The data are derived from a nationally representative sample of 608 two-parent families which had at least one child between the ages of 10 and 17 living at home at the time of the interview. In addition to examining the extent of adolescent-to-parent violence, the chapter also examines the following hypotheses:

(1) Sons will be reported to have been abusive toward their parents more than daughters.
(2) There will be a direct relationship between age of the adolescent and the rate of adolescent-to-parent violence.

(3) Mothers will be hit and abused more often than fathers.
   a. Sons will be violent toward their mothers more than toward their fathers.
   b. Sons from homes where wife abuse occurs will be more likely to be violent and abusive toward their mothers than sons from homes where wife abuse has not occurred.
(4) There will be a direct positive relationship between the rate of violence toward parents and other forms of family violence.
(5) Family stress is directly related to adolescent violence toward parents.

SAMPLE AND METHOD

The data for this examination of adolescent violence toward parents come from interviews with a nationally representative sample of 608 families who had at least one child, age 10 to 17, living at home. This is part of a larger sample of 2,143 families who were interviewed as part of a comprehensive study on violence in the family.[1]

Harbin and Madden (1979) reported that the majority of children who physically attacked their parents were between the ages of 13 and 24. However, they did note extreme cases where such violent behavior was exhibited by children as young as 10 years of age. For this reason, families from the initial sample of 2,143 who had at least one child 10 years of age or older (data obtained only on families with children as old as 17) were examined.

Interviews were conducted with the mother in 315 families and with the father in 293 families. In each family, the data on physical violence were obtained from the parent interviewed for only one child. When there was more than one child age 10 through 17 living at home, a "referent child" for this study was selected by using a random number table.

MEASURING VIOLENCE

Violence toward parents was measured using a series of questions called the "Conflict Tactics Scales" (CTS). The CTS were first developed at the University of New Hampshire in 1971. They have been used and modified over the past eight years in numerous studies of family violence in the United States, Canada, Israel, Japan, Finland, Great Britain, and British Honduras (data on the validity and reliability of the scales are provided by Straus, 1979b).

The CTS generated three measures of violence toward parents. The first measure, referred to in this chapter as "The Overall Violence

Index," includes all acts of physical violence ranging from slapping a parent to "using" a knife or gun. The second measure, which we refer to as the "Severe Violence Index," includes only those items from the Overall Index where there was a high probability of a violent act causing an injury to the parent. Specifically, the Severe Violence Index consists of whether, during the 12 months prior to the interview, the child of the parent interviewed had ever kicked, punched, bit, hit with an object, beaten up, threatened with a gun or knife, or actually used a gun or knife. The third measure referred to in this chapter is the "Violence Severity Index."[2] The Overall Index and the Severe Violence Index reflect only differences in how often *any* act of violence or *severe* act of violence occurred. If it is necessary to take into account different degrees of severity of violence as well as the frequency of violence, one would use the Violence Severity Index. This index multiplies the frequency of each act of violence by the different forms of violence. Each form of violence is weighted according to the severity of the act (see Straus, 1979b, for more information on the index construction).

Our dependent variables, overall violence, severe violence, and violence severity, are different from the dependent variables used in other studies which examine abuse toward parents by adolescents or adult children (Harbin and Madden, 1979; Block and Sinnott, 1979; Douglass et al., 1980). First, our measures are quite different from those used in other investigations. To measure abuse, we rely on a self-report of five violence items from the CTS which we believe place the parent at risk of being injured. While other studies are more concerned with outcome, we have no direct, or even indirect, measure of whether or not the parent was actually injured as a consequence of any of these acts. For example, parents may report that their children used a gun or knife toward them, but we do not know if parents were actually stabbed or shot.

Most studies of parent abuse operationalize the term "parent abuse" as those cases which have been publicly recognized and labeled as parents who have been injured by their children (Harbin and Madden, 1979; Block and Sinnott, 1979; Legal Research and Services for the Elderly, 1980; Douglass et al., 1980; Lau and Kosberg, 1979). This creates a systematic bias since some families, by virtue of social status, are insulated from being labeled as abusers, while other families— especially low-income and racial and ethnic minority families—will be more likely to be accurately or inaccurately labeled as parent abusers.

Another difference is that rather than confine our investigation only to acts of abusive violence, we also examined a fuller range of violent acts. We have three dependent variables—all reported acts of violence, reported acts of severe violence, and severity by frequency of all reported acts of violence. We employed the first two indices when establishing which children were the most frequent users of violence and severe violence. The third index was used when attempting to establish which social factors were related to an increase in severity and frequency of parent abuse.

Findings

Research and public interest concerning child abuse, wife abuse, and the abuse of the elderly all commenced with the question, "How common is this form of abuse?" With but two exploratory studies and a sample of 30, no one has yet ventured even a crude estimate of the extent of violence toward parents.

The Conflict Tactics Scales measure the rates of violence for the preceding 12 months. The national violence study was conducted in 1976. Thus, the rates reported here reflect the rates of violence in 1975.[3] A total of 9% of the parents of adolescents (children 10 to 17 years of age) reported that their children had used one form of violence at least once in 1976. For that same year 3% of the adolescents were reported to have engaged in acts of severe violence, ranging from punching, kicking, or biting, to the use of a knife or gun.

While the actual rates of overall violence and severe violence may seem small, when the percentages are projected to the total population of adolescents aged 10 to 17 years old who lived in two-parent households, the numbers are quite substantial. We estimate that in 1975, more than 2½ million adolescents were reported as having struck a parent at least once. Nearly 900,000 parents of adolescents aged 10 to 17 were either punched, bit, kicked, hit with a hard object, beat up, or were threatened by or had a knife or a gun used on them.

In all likelihood, both the rates and the projection underestimate the true extent of adolescent-to-parent violence. First, the data are limited to two-parent households. Single-parent households, which may have higher rates of adolescent violence, were not part of this study. Second, parents may well have underreported the true extent of their children's violence.

SEX AND AGE OF CHILD

Sons were slightly more likely to be violent (11% versus 7% for daughters) and to use severe violence (3.4% versus 2.8% for daughters) toward their parents, although the differences for both types of violence are not statistically significant. No relatiohship was found between age of the child and either the rates of overall violence or severe violence.

When we examined the rates of violence considering both the age and sex of the child, an interesting pattern emerged. For all types of violence (the overall violence rate), we found that there was no difference in the rates of males and females at age 10 and 11. However, for every age cohort older than 11, sons had higher rates of overall violence (see Figure 2).

Perhaps the most interesting finding was that for severe (or abusive) violence. The rate of son's severe violence increases between the ages of 10 and 17, while the rates of daughters increases from the 10-11 age group to ages 12 and 13. Thereafter, the rate of daughter's violence falls (see Figure 3).

Thus, it may be that boys *do* take advantage of increased size and strength that come with adolescent growth, and become more likely to abuse their parents.

VICTIMS

Mothers were more likely to be struck by their adolescent children than were fathers (11% versus 7%). Mothers were also considerably more likely to be victims of severe violence (5% versus 1% for fathers); thus supporting Warren who reported that mothers were the most likely victims of parent abuse (1978).

Looking at the sex of the adolescent and which parent he or she uses violence against, we find that sons are slightly more likely to engage in some form of overall violence against their mothers than were daughters (11% versus 9%). However, there was a difference of only 1% in the rates of severe violence directed toward mothers—4% of the sons and 5% of the daughters engaged in severe violence.

Violence and severe violence toward fathers is predominantly an act of sons. Sons' rate of overall violence toward their fathers was 8%, compared to 4% for daughter-to-father overall violence. No adolescent daughters in our sample used severe violence toward their fathers, while 2% of the sons were reported as engaging in severe violence toward fathers (see Table 16).

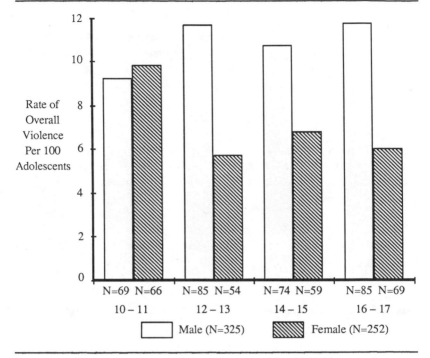

Figure 2: Child-to-Parent Overall Violence by Age and Sex of Child

INTERGENERATIONAL TRANSMISSIONS OF VIOLENCE

In order to examine the hypothesis concerning the intergenerational transmission of violence (the Cycle of Violence Theory—Steinmetz, 1977b), and for the remainder of our analysis of the patterns of adolescent-to-parent violence, we use the third measure of violence, the Violence Severity Index. This index, which is generated by multiplying the frequency of each form of violence by the weight (severity) of the form of violence, allows us to overcome the statistical limitations of using a dichotomous dependent variable (both overall violence and severe violence were coded as 0 = no violence, 1 = any form of violence) with a skewed distribution.

Since students of both child abuse and wife abuse have hypothesized and demonstrated that experience with and exposure to violence as a child is related to being violent toward a child or spouse as an adult, we felt it would be reasonable to assume that children do not wait until they

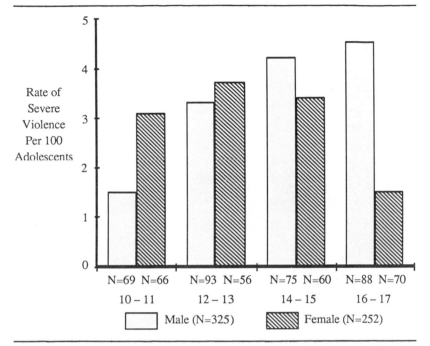

Figure 3: Child-to-Parent Severe Violence by Age and Sex of Child

are adults to begin acting out the violence they have witnessed or experienced. Thus, our hypothesis was that the more violence a child had personally experienced or had possibly observed would be directly related to that child's chances of being violent toward a parent.

As shown in Table 17, the rate of adolescent-to-parent violence severity is directly related to the violence severity that child has experienced as well as directly related to the rates of interspousal violence severity.

Of course, as these are cross-sectional data, a good deal of caution should be used in drawing any causal connections from these data. Obviously, it is just as plausible to assert that violence toward an adolescent led to the adolescent striking the parent as it is to state that adolescents' attacks lead to a retaliation by the victimized parent. And, while children may observe their parents hit one another and then act out the same behavior, our data also could support the claim that adolescent-to-parent violence generates conflict and violence between parents.

TABLE 16
Violence Severity Toward Parents by Sex of Child

Sex of Child	Sex of Parent	Overall Violence		Severe Violence	
Son	Mother	11%	(157)	4%	(166)
	Father	8%	(153)	2%	(159)
Daughter	Mother	9%	(130)	5%	(127)
	Father	4%	(115)	0%	(118)

TABLE 17
Child-to-Parent Violence by Other Forms of Family Violence

Forms of Family Violence	Severity of Violence							
	No Violence		Low Severity		Moderate Severity		High Severity	
Parent-to-Child Violence*								
no violence	97	(300)	2	(5)	1	(3)	4	(5)
low severity	88	(83)	7	(7)	4	(4)	0	(0)
moderate severity	83	(77)	3	(3)	10	(9)	4	(4)
high severity	72	(39)	4	(2)	17	(9)	7	(4)
Husband-to-Wife Violence**								
no violence	92	(456)	3	(14)	2	(22)	1	(6)
low severity	93	(26)	7	(2)	0	(0)	0	(0)
moderate severity	78	(7)	0	(0)	22	(2)	0	(0)
high severity	62	(5)	25	(2)	0	(0)	12	(1)
Wife-to-Husband Violence***								
no violence	92	(469)	3	(15)	4	(19)	1	(6)
low violence	68	(15)	9	(2)	18	(4)	4	(1)
moderate violence	57	(4)	14	(1)	29	(2)	0	(0)
high violence	87	(7)	0	(0)	0	(0)	12	(1)

*$\chi^2 = 67.8060$; $p \leqslant .0001$.
**$\chi^2 = 30.5295$; $p \leqslant .001$.
***$\chi^2 = 34.7965$; $p \leqslant .001$.

SOCIAL INDICATORS

Previous analyses of the data from the national violence survey (Straus et al., 1980) and other research on family violence have found that rates of child and wife abuse vary with social factors such as income, education, occupation, age, race, and family power (see Gelles, 1980b, for a review of factors related to family violence).

While parent-to-child and spouse-to-spouse violence is related to many social factors, adolescent-to-parent violence does not appear to vary in any meaningful way with many family structural variables or social status indicators. No relationship was found between violence severity and mother or father's employment status, mother's occupation, mother or father's age, race, or family power structure. Also, characteristics such as parents' agreement over decisions concerning the children, whether the child had been caught doing something illegal in the previous year, or which parent would hurt the parent-child relationship most if a marital breakup occurred were found to be unrelated to the rate of adolescent-to-parent violence severity.

Father's occupation, total family income, and whether the child had been suspended from school were related to the rate of violence severity (see Table 18). Fathers employed as clerical workers had families with the greatest rates of high violence severity. Moderate violence severity was greatest in homes of blue-collar men. Farmers were the only occupation with no adolescent-to-parent violence.

Income was not as strongly related to adolescent-to-parent violence as it was to parental and interspousal violence. The rate of high violence severity was greatest for middle-income families (between $12,000 to $19,000 income in 1976). Moderate violence severity was highest among the lowest-income families. The highest-income families did conform to the pattern for other types of family violence and report the lowest rate of violence toward parents.

Finally, any child in the home being kicked out or suspended from school was related to the chances of adolescents using violence toward a parent. Regrettably, we had no measure of whether it was the violent adolescent or another child in the home who was kicked out or suspended from school.

STRESS

In addition to experience with violence in childhood and social status, stress has been hypothesized as an important factor related to family violence (Straus et al., 1980; Gelles, 1980b; Gil, 1970; Maden and Wrench, 1977). The measure of stress developed for the national family violence survey contained mostly items which measured the amount of stress experienced by parents, including problems at work, pregnancy or illness, sexual or in-law difficulties, and marital difficulties.

We found no relationship between the stress experienced and reported by the parents and the parents' likelihood of being struck by their adolescent offspring.

TABLE 18

Child-to-Parent Violence Severity by Father's Occupation, Family Income, and Whether the Child Was Kicked Out of School or Suspended

	Severity of Child-to-Parent Violence			
	No Violence	Low Violence	Moderate Violence	High Violence
Father's Occupation				
White Collar	95% (204)	3% (6)	1% (2)	2% (3)
Clerical	77% (17)	14% (3)	0% (0)	9% (2)
Blue Collar	88% (264)	3% (9)	8% (23)	1% (3)
Farmer	100% (14)	0% (0)	0% (0)	0% (0)
$x^2 = 32.8495$ p. $\leq .001$				
Family Income				
$5,999 and under	89% (25)	0% (0)	11% (3)	0% (0)
6,000 – 11,999	84% (79)	6% (6)	8% (8)	1% (1)
12,000 – 19,999	90% (179)	3% (5)	4% (9)	3% (5)
20,000 and over	94% (178)	4% (7)	2% (4)	5% (1)
$x^2 = 15.5251$ p. $\leq .07$				
Any Child at Home Kicked Out or Suspended From School				
Yes	71% (12)	0% (0)	29% (5)	0% (0)
No	91% (442)	3% (5)	4% (20)	1% (6)
$x^2 = 22.5057$ p. $\leq .001$				

Discussion

What do our results tell us about the phenomenon of violence toward parents? First, the lack of attention and research on this aspect of family violence is not the result of there being little or no violence toward parents in American families. While the rate of overall violence directed at parents by children 10 to 17 years of age is lower than the rates of overall violence between other family members, the rate of severe, or what could be called abusive, violence was nearly as high as the rates of child and spouse abuse.

The modal type of adolescent-to-parent violence would appear to be older sons striking and abusing their mothers. Of interest is the finding that the rate of severe violence for sons increases for each age group from 10 to 17, while the rate for girls declines. No doubt hormonal, Freudian, or social explanations of these differences are plausible. A social explanation would concentrate on the cultural norms which reward aggressiveness for teenage boys, but negatively sanction teenage girls' violence.

That mothers are the more likely victims of violence toward parents could be explained by noting that mothers are more likely to spend time with children and be targets for their violence. The time-at-risk line of reasoning is often cited as an explanation for why the rate of violence toward children is higher for mothers than for fathers. However, time at risk may not be the entire story for either form of violence (see Straus et al., 1980, for a discussion of violence toward children). Mothers may be the likely target for adolescent aggression for two main reasons beyond availability. First, mothers typically lack both the physical and the social resources to inflict costly retaliation on their aggressive children. Second, children, especially sons, may *learn* that mothers are an appropriate and acceptable target for intrafamily violence. The low base rates for both wife abuse and severe violence toward parents reduces our sample size so that the findings are suggestive, but Table 19 notes that sons and daughters are more likely to use severe violence toward mothers if their mothers have been abused. Interestingly, in homes where wives are abused, neither sons nor daughters used *any form* of violence against their fathers!

Social, family structural, and situational factors which are associated with adult violence in families are either not or only weakly related to violence by adolescents. Indeed, the only important consistency in the analysis of violence toward parents and other forms of family violence is that the presence in a household of one form of violence is related to the occurrence of other types of violence. That the national violence survey was a cross-sectional survey precludes a definitive conclusion that striking a child will cause that child to grow up and strike his or her parent. However, our analysis does not conflict with the notion that families who socialize their members into viewing violence as a suitable means of resolving conflict run a greater risk of having high rates of all forms of family violence, including violence toward parents.

Our inability to find a relationship between family stress and violence toward parents does not rule out the hypothesis that stress is an important aspect of adolescent violence. The national family violence survey only tapped stress experienced by parents. Had there been a measure of stress experienced by adolescents, we may have found our expected relationship. Although we found that any child in the home being kicked out of or suspended from school increased the likelihood of adolescent-to-parent violence, we do not have a measure of whether the abusive adolescent was the child in the home who was kicked out of or suspended from school. This is unfortunate, since such a measure would have been an indication of the effect of situational stress on adolescent violence.

TABLE 19
Violence Severity Toward Parents by Sex of Child
and Whether Wife Abuse Occurs in the Home

| Sex of Child | Sex of Parent | Severity of Violence | | | N |
		Low Severity	Moderate Severity	High Severity	
Wife Abuse Occurs					
Son	Mother	20% (2)	10% (1)	10% (1)	10
	Father	0% (0)	0% (0)	0% (0)	12
Daughter	Mother	20% (2)	10% (1)	0% (0)	10
	Father	0% (0)	0% (0)	0% (0)	13
(missing observations 8)					
No Wife Abuse					
Son	Mother	1% (2)	8% (11)	3% (4)	142
	Father	5% (7)	4% (5)	0% (0)	139
Daughter	Mother	2% (2)	3% (4)	2% (2)	116
	Father	3% (3)	2% (2)	0% (0)	101
(missing observations 57)					

Conclusions

Our projections of 2½ million parents who are struck each year by their adolescent children and almost 900,000 parents who are victimized by severe violence indicates that violence toward parents is a legitimate problem which should not continue to be ignored by researchers, practitioners, and policymakers.

Clearly, there is a need for social service and criminal justice agencies to take note of the problem of violence toward parents and to take steps which both encourage victims to seek amelioration and discourage victims from blaming themselves for their own victimization. Those in the field of child and wife abuse should take note of data on the relationship between violence toward parents and other forms of family violence and realize that steps to break the "Cycle of Violence" need not wait until children have become adults.

The national family violence survey was not designed for a detailed analysis of violence toward parents, and thus did not contain the proper measures or variables to fully test hypotheses concerning factors related to and causing this form of family violence. Future research on child-to-parent violence needs to explore the social situational aspects of violent children, since social indicators which focus only on parents reveal little about the causes and patterns of violence.

Notes

1. These 608 families are part of a larger sample of 2,143 families who were interviewed as part of a comprehensive study of violence in the family. A national sample of 103 primary areas (counties or groups of counties) stratified by geographic region, type of community, and other population characteristics was generated. Within the primary areas, 300 interview locations (Census districts or block groups) were selected. Each location was divided into 10 to 25 housing units by the trained interviewers. Sample segments from each interviewing location were selected. The last step involved randomly selecting an eligible person to be interviewed in each designated household. For more details on the sample, see Straus et al., 1980.

2. A method of taking into account both the severity and the frequency of violence is possible by constructing a "Violence Severity Index." This index multiplies the frequency of each violent act by the following weights: threw something at other, pushed, grabbed or shoved other, and slapped the other were considered minor acts of violence and were not weighted; kicked, bit, and punched was weighted as a 2; hit with an object was assigned a weight of 3; beat up earned a 5; threatened with a knife or gun equaled a 6; and used a knife or gun was assigned a weight of 8. The frequency of each item was also recoded from the values 1 through 6 in the questionnaire (0 = never, 1 = once, 2 = twice, 3 = 3-5 times, 4 = 6-10 times, 5 = 11-20 times, 6 = more than 20 times) to the approximate midpoints of these categories: 0, 1, 2, 4, 8, 15, and 25, respectively. The scores obtained from multiplying the frequency by severity of each act were then coded into 4 categories (no violence, low violence severity, moderate violence severity, and high violence severity). A score of 0 was accepted as no violence. A score between 1 and 7 was coded as low violence severity. (To be classified as low violence severity a person could never have used a knife or gun against someone but could have committed any of the lower-weighted acts and some of them more than once.) A score of 8 to 17 was classified as moderate violence severity and scores between 18 and 325 were considered high violence severity. All categories were approximately equal in the number of persons per level of violence severity.

3. To calculate a national incidence statistic on the number of children between the ages of 10 and 17 who abused their parents, we first had to calculate the number of children between those specific ages who lived in two-parent households. According to the 1976 population estimates (U.S. Bureau of the Census, 1977), there are 32,498,000 children between the ages of 10 and 17. In 1976, since 80% of all children lived in two-parent households (U.S. Bureau of the Census, 1978), we then estimated that 28,976,000 children between the ages of 10 and 17 lived in two-parent households. To attain the national incidence statistic, we multiplied the abuse rates cited in this chapter by the estimated number of children between those ages living in two-parent households.

CHAPTER 10

ELDER ABUSE: THE STATUS OF CURRENT KNOWLEDGE

with Claire Pedrick Cornell

Two major factors seem to help explain why the abuse of older persons became a focal point of social, scientific, and media attention in the 1980s.

(1) The discovery of a significant number of elderly victims of family violence was a natural outgrowth of intensive research on the extent and patterns of family violence. By conceptualizing the problem as one of "family violence" and not simply "child abuse" or "wife battering," researchers have been able to identify varying patterns and incidence of violence in the family (e.g., Straus et al., 1980).

(2) Major demographic changes have occurred over the last half century which help explain why problems of the elderly and problems of elderly abuse specifically have captured public and scientific attention. First, the life expectancy of the average person has increased by nearly 50% in as many years (U.S. Bureau of Census, 1978). Second, as a consequence of the increased life expectancy (and the population increase in general), there are growing numbers of individuals 60 years of age and older. Third, the proportion of the population 60 years and older also increased (Harris, 1975).

This aging of the population has resulted in an increased need for long-term care of the elderly. Of those between 65 and 72 years of age, only one person in 50 needs long-term care. But of those over 73 years old, the chances increase to one in 15 (Koch & Koch, 1980).

Authors' Note: From Richard J. Gelles and Claire Pedrick Cornell, "Elder Abuse: The Status of Current Knowledge." *Family Relations*, 1982, 31(July): 457-465.

Moreover, as one can see from the changing age distribution, children having the responsibility of caring for their aging parents is also a relatively new and growing aspect of family life (Laslett, 1973). The changing population and a current push toward deinstitutionalization of and home care for the elderly (Maddox, 1975) means that more adult children are providing more home care to a larger number and proportion of the older population. Treas (1977) voices concern about the impact of the increasing burden of home care on the emotional and financial resources of families, especially in light of the increased entry of women into the labor force. This could reduce time and energy for home care for their elderly relatives.

Finally, we are entering a period where the modal family situation is one of fewer children available for sharing the responsibility of providing for and caring for elderly parents. It is against this background of increased research on family violence, demographic changes in the society, and an increased concern for the problems of older persons that elderly abuse became a significant focus.

Most students of child abuse credit Kempe and his colleagues' seminal paper, "The Battered Child Syndrome" (Kempe et al., 1962), as drawing public and scientific attention to the problem of abused children. It was more than a decade from the time that that paper was published until the convening of the first National Conference on Child Abuse, held in Washington, D.C., in 1973. Congressional hearings and congressional legislation on child abuse also did not occur until 1973. While there were scattered investigations and media reports of child abuse in the sixties, concentrated scientific and media attention was not focused on this issue until the seventies.

Prior to 1973 there were but two scientific articles published on wife abuse, and virtually no articles in the popular press. However, the time period from the "discovery" of wife abuse in the early 1970s until there were national conferences, media coverage, and congressional hearings was compressed from 10 years it took for child abuse to be widely discussed to less than 3 years. The time frame from discovery to widespread interest for the topic of elderly abuse was so short that one wonders whether there was any lag at all between discovery, media attention, and legislative initiative at the local, state, and federal level.

While the rapid diffusion of concern for the problem of elderly abuse has been helpful in mobilizing resources to deal with this problem, it has led to some significant problems in terms of identifying what knowledge is available on this subject. In the case of elderly abuse, media interest and concern outpaced the conducting and dissemination of scholarly research.

As scientific information was scarce, journalists tended to locate the same experts, cite the same facts, and advance the same theories. Certain pieces of information, based on tentative research, unpublished reports, or even educated guesses, have been published, republished, cited, and repeated so often that they have taken on the status of "fact" and "conclusive evidence," more because of how often they are reported in newspapers and on television than as a consequence of the data meeting the normal scientific rules of evidence.

This essay examines the scientific status of knowledge about elderly abuse. The first section sets the stage for this review by discussing problems of definition. Next, data and research on the rates of elderly abuse and factors found related to elderly abuse are examined. In the following section theories which have been developed to explain the abuse of the elderly are critiqued. Recommendations for research and practice draw it to a close.

DEFINITIONAL DILEMMAS

Perhaps the most significant impediment in the development of an adequate knowledge base on intrafamily violence and abuse has been the problem of developing a satisfactory and acceptable definition of violence and abuse. Just as confusion about "what is child maltreatment" abounds 20 years after research commenced, there is considerable variation and confusion in the definitions of elder abuse. Students of violence, abuse, and maltreatment of the elderly have stumbled down the same paths tread before by those attempting to study child abuse. The same concerns with intentionality, outcome, physical versus nonphysical maltreatment, acts of omission versus acts of commission, and the range of acts considered abusive have been discussed in the brief period of time during which elderly abuse has been identified and studied as a social problem.

Rathbone-McCuan (1980) restricts the definition of elder abuse to the physical abuse of noninstitutionalized elderly, much in the same way Kempe and his colleagues (1962) 20 years earlier restricted their definition of child abuse to medically diagnosable injury caused by physical attack. Most others in the field of elder abuse use broader definitions which include both passive and active neglect, mental anguish, material abuse, medical abuse, or self-abuse in the definition.

One can plainly see the struggles of defining elder abuse in the recent reports on the problem. Douglass et al. (1980) try to make clear distinctions between passive neglect and active neglect, while also attempting to distinguish between "neglect" and "abuse." Legal Research and Services for the Elderly's (1979) definition included mental abuse as well as physical abuse. Block and Sinnott (1979) added material abuse and medical abuse to acts of abuse and neglect. Lau and Kosberg (1979) included "violation of rights" in their definition of elder abuse, which covered situations where elderly are forced out of their dwelling or into another setting, such as a nursing home.

While few would dispute that any of the acts listed by researchers may be harmful, the problem is that the concept of elder abuse has become a political/journalistic concept, best suited for attracting public attention to the plight of the victims. But while elder abuse may be a fruitful political term, it is fast becoming a useless scientific concept. The variety of definitions of elder abuse in current studies makes the task of comparing the results of the research impossible. Estimates of the extent of elder abuse (as will be discussed in the next section) range from thousands to millions, depending on the definition applied. A more serious problem is that the wide range of behavior lumped into a definition of elder abuse makes it virtually impossible to assess the causal factors related to abuse. By combining behaviors and phenomena which are conceptually distinct, one loses the ability to truly determine what causes elder abuse (e.g., the generative causes of an act of physical violence are different from factors which lead to acts of omission). As long as investigators fail to separate and distinguish between behaviors which are conceptually and etiologically distinct, and as long as definitions vary from narrow to broad, we will be unable to develop an adequate and useful knowledge base in this area of study.

OPERATIONAL DEFINITIONS

While there are various nominal definitions of elder abuse in use, there is nearly overwhelming agreement on operationally defining elder abuse. Nearly all research on elderly abuse has been based on samples drawn from cases officially reported to professionals or paraprofessionals in the field of adult protective services (Lau and Kosberg, 1979; Douglass et al., 1980; Legal Research and Services for the Elderly, 1979; Block and Sinnott, 1979).

Relying exclusively on cases which come to professional attention produces serious problems in assessing the conclusions and generalizability of the data generated by such research. Research on child and wife abuse clearly demonstrates that those cases which come to public attenton represent a skewed and biased portion of the entire population of victims of abuse. Research has also demonstrated that social, racial, and economic factors influence who is labeled "abused" (Newberger et al., 1977; Turbett and O'Toole, 1980). Research which samples *only* from those cases that come to official attention is research which cannot partial out the factors which lead to a case being labeled from factors which caused the person to be abused. A continued reliance on samples drawn *only* from cases which come to professional attention will restrict and limit our ability to learn more about the problem of the abuse of the elderly.

THE EXTENT OF ELDERLY ABUSE

Situations which are viewed by society as legitimate social problems are typically those which are found to be harmful to a significant number of people. There is no question that the abuse of children, women, and the elderly is harmful, but the acceptance of family abuse as a social problem has been dependent on documentation that the problem affects a large number of people. Thus, just as students of child and wife abuse first faced the question, "How common is abuse?" Those who advance the idea of the abuse of older persons as a social problem have asked, "How many elderly are abused?"

The most frequently cited statistics place the range of elder abuse between 500,000 and 2.5 million cases per year (see, for example, Federal Contracts Opportunities, 1980). Four studies are frequently cited by those discussing the extent of elder abuse: (1) Lau and Kosberg's (1979) investigation at the Chronic Illness Center in Cleveland. They reported that 39 of 404 clients, 60 years of age and older, were abused in some manner. They estimated that 1 in 10 elderly persons living with a member of the family are abused each year. (2) A University of Maryland report (Block and Sinnott, 1979) which indicated 4.1% of elderly respondents in the urban areas of Maryland reporting abuse. They believe that if this rate were projected for the national population of elderly, nearly 1 million cases of elderly abuse would occur. (3) An exploratory study of professionals' and paraprofessionals' encounters with elder abuse in Massachusetts (Legal Research and Services for the Elderly, 1979). It was stated that 55% of the respondents (183 out of 322) knew of at least one incident of abuse in an 18-month period. (4) A study in Michigan (Douglass et al., 1980), which was based on recollections of professionals in five study sites in Michigan, concluded that many respondents reported little or no direct, regular experience with verbal or emotional abuse, active neglect, or physical abuse, while 50% reported contact with passive neglect. There was some confusion among respondents as to the exact definition of "passive neglect."

ANALYSIS

It would be necessary, and fair, to say that despite the data presented in available reports, the extent and incidence of the abuse of the elderly is still unknown. There are major problems and limitations with the four major reports on elder abuse. Current estimates of the number and incidence of cases of elder abuse are based on cases which are reported to social service agencies. This is problematic because: (1) instances of child, wife, and elder abuse which are reported to public and private agencies are but a fraction of the total number of cases; (2) mandatory reporting laws for elder abuse exist in only a handful of states; thus, reported cases of elder abuse are probably a smaller proportion of the total number of cases than the fraction of child abuse reports received by agencies (due to the fact that all 50 states have enacted mandatory child abuse reporting laws); (3) the recency of concern and awareness about elder abuse means a low degree of awareness of this problem among professionals, paraprofessionals, the public, and even the victims; and, (4) the number of cases reported to agencies vary by type of agency, location, title, and so on, as demonstrated by the testimony before the House Subcommittee on Aging (U.S. Congress, Select Committee on Aging, Subcommittee on Human Services, 1980).

Current information on the extent of elder abuse is also limited by the fact that the research is based on small, nonrepresentative samples. Any attempt to extrapolate incidence data from such samples to the national population of elderly must be viewed with great caution. For example, Lau and Kosberg's (1979) estimate that 1 in 10 elderly persons residing with caretakers are being abused each year is based on a nonrepresentative sample of 39 persons reported to the Cleveland Chronic Illness Center. This agency cannot be considered representative of other agencies in Cleveland, Ohio, or anywhere else.

Block and Sinnott (1979), who estimated the incidence of elder abuse nationally to be 1 million, conducted a "representative" study of "community dwelling elderly" living in the greater Washington, D.C., SMSA. Although Block and Sinnott state that the elderly they surveyed were "fairly representative" of older persons nationwide, it must be emphasized that *Block and Sinnott's response rate in their interviews was but 16.48%!* This extremely low response rate virtually renders meaningless their claim for representativeness of their sample. Also, there are significant inconsistencies in their printed report, such that it is impossible to determine their exact sample size.[1] Regardless of how large their sample actually was, their estimate of national incidence is based on a total of between *1 and 3 actual reports of elderly abuse.* Even if their sample was representative, the sampling error is such that the lower boundary of the actual range of the incidence of abuse is 0%.

Legal Research and Services for the Elderly (1979) recognized that their nonrepresentative sampling precluded a meaningful attempt to generate a national incidence statistic. Moreover, they note that it is possible that the same case of elderly abuse could have been reported by both a professional and paraprofessional in their study. The possibility of duplication means that 183 reports do not necessarily translate into 183 different cases.

Douglass et al. (1980) also declined to speculate on the national incidence rate. They did report the mean scores for monthly occurrences of cases of neglect and abuse. Nevertheless, the overall response rate to their questions on monthly occurrence was quite low.[2] They note that their findings are not generalizable because (1) they used a purposive sample; (2) the number of respondents in each of the occupational categories was unequal and the categories were not uniformly homogeneous; and, (3) the number of respondents who answered each question was extremely small, and a single respondent with an unusually large caseload could inflate or deflate the mean scores. What was actually found in their investigation was that many respondents (the exact number cannot be determined from their report) reported little or no direct, regular experience with verbal or emotional abuse, active neglect, or physical abuse.

Based upon the methodological problems with the studies, the authors would advise that extreme caution be used when generalizing data from these studies. Due to their exploratory nature, these studies are inappropriate for generating a national incidence statistic.[3]

Factors Associated with Elder Abuse

A first step in unraveling the causes of a phenomenon such as elder abuse is to identify the major social and psychological factors associated with being an abuser or abused. The current research and reports on elder abuse offer some tentative insights into the profile of the abuser, abused, and abusive situation.

AGE AND GENDER

Reports on elder abuse consistently identify females of very advanced age as the most likely victims. The abuser is thought to be middle-aged, female, and typically the offspring (daughter) of the victim (Lau and Kosberg, 1979; Medical News, 1980; Legal Research and Services for the Elderly, 1979; Block and Sinnott, 1979).

PHYSICAL AND MENTAL IMPAIRMENT

Students of child abuse report that children who suffer from physical or mental handicaps are the most likely children to be abused (Friedrich and Boriskin, 1976). Similarly, researchers studying elder abuse are unanimous in agreeing that older individuals with physical or mental impairments run a greater risk of being abused than those of similar age who do not suffer from major impairments (Block and Sinnott, 1979; Burston, 1975; Lau and Kosberg, 1979; Legal Research and Services for the Elderly, 1979; Rathbone-McCuan, 1980).

STRESS

Investigators frequently note that the responsibility for caring for a dependent, aging parent can lead to a stressful situation for the caregiver as well as the entire family (Block and Sinnott, 1979; Legal Research and Service for the Elderly, 1979; Litman, 1971; Rathbone-McCuan, 1980; Steinmetz, 1978a). Legal Research and Services of the Elderly stated that in 65% of the cases of elder abuse, the victim was viewed as a source of stress to the abuser (1978).

Horowitz notes that persons who found the caretaking role the most stressful were often those who were trying to meet the needs of both their spouse and children, while at the same time trying to meet the needs of an older relative.

CYCLE OF ABUSE

While no formal empirical data are presented, researchers believe that the use of violence to resolve conflicts runs in families, and this use of violence is passed on from generation to generation (Briley, 1979;

Rathbone-McCuan, 1980; Steinmetz, 1978a; U.S. Congress, Select Committee on Aging, Subcommittee on Human Services, 1980).

ANALYSIS

Despite the consistency of factors reportedly associated with elderly abuse in the variety of articles and reports written on this subject, it is clear that the support for these claims is intuitive, speculative, and/or based only on findings from studies of other forms of family violence. *There is almost no empirical evidence in the literature which supports the claims made for such associations.*

The major drawback of research to date is that with the exception of the work by Legal Research and Services for the Elderly (1979), *no comparison groups were included in the research designs.* Thus, researchers cannot report whether the factors they found present in their cases of abuse were distinctive of abuse cases, compared to other clients where no abuse was present, or compared to the general population of the elderly. For instance, the finding that abused elderly suffered from mental and physical impairments could simply be a function of the fact that agencies caring for the elderly have many clients who are physically or mentally impaired. The current crop of research reports on elderly abuse cannot answer the question, "Is the stress found in homes where there is elder abuse greater than stress found in homes of similarly aged elderly who are not abused?" Granted the number of very old victims of elder abuse may appear disproportionately high compared to the age distribution of the general population. A question which also must be addressed is, "Is the agency in which the research data have been gathered seeing a disproportionately large population of very old individuals?" The failure to employ comparison groups in the current research means that these questions cannot be answered. Moreover, without comparison groups, it is impossible to establish statistical significance of relationships or magnitude of associations.

As stated earlier, most studies gather data on cases of elder abuse by selecting cases or subjects from elderly seen in agencies which serve the elderly. Because of this procedure, those studies cannot determine if they have discovered factors related to elder abuse or factors related to an individual or family being seen or discovered by an agency.

THEORIES OF ELDERLY ABUSE

Even as there are precious few studies on elder abuse which can meet the minimum standards for empirical evidence, there is a corresponding lack of empirically tested propositions on the generative causes of the abuse of older persons. Much of what is offered as theoretical work on elder abuse are actually propositions and theories which have been developed and applied to other types of intrafamilial abuse.

Working from research on child and wife abuse, researchers have proposed a number of propositions and theoretical explanations of elder abuse. The central problem with these theoretical explanations is that in no case has there been an empirical test of the propositions or explanations. Some propositions are similar to the conventional wisdoms frequently applied to other forms of abuse, and which were subsequently not supported by research (e.g., the claim that abusers of the elderly are psychopaths). Other propositions are borrowed from research on spouse and child abuse (e.g., patterns of violence are passed from one generation to the next), while a third class of propositions is based on assumptions about the status of the elderly in society and the typical family situations of the elderly (e.g., abuse is a consequence of inadequate services available to assist families caring for an aging member). In many instances, these assumptions are of dubious accuracy, and should themselves be subjected to empirical verification or falsification.

The shortcomings in the other areas of study of elder abuse, especially the definitional confusion over what is and is not abuse, come home to roost in the preliminary theoretical work which is available thus far. Clearly, some factors are more likely to be related to acts of overt physical abuse, while other factors may be more closely related to neglect. Such distinctions are not made in the theories since the definitions fail to distinguish between types of abuse.

This critique does not mean that the theoretical propositions which have been proposed are not plausible. Rather, the problem is that there are *innumerable plausible rival explanations for elder abuse.* They will all be plausible until quality empirical data are generated.

Summary

There are three fundamental questions concerning elder abuse (four if one asks, "What is it?"): What is the extent of elderly abuse? Who are the most likely offenders and victims? and, What causes people to abuse elderly relatives? The state of current research on abuse of older persons is such that we can answer all three (four) questions the same way: "We do not really know."

What is truly regrettable about the current state of research on elder abuse is that the lack of quality data has lead to the widespread dissemination of myth, conventional wisdom, and in some cases, falsehood. Statements presented as facts which have no scientific foundations and are then used to frame both policy and programs to treat and prevent the abuse of older persons. Legal changes are proposed, innovative treatment programs are initiated, and recommendations are made by congressional panels, all without so much as one piece of information which can meet normal standards of scientific evidence. Many resulting programs and policies may be misguided. At best, some might even fortuitously prove to be effective. At worst, when we base programs and policies on popularized notions about extent, patterns, and causes, we run the very real risk of doing more harm than good to elderly clients and their families.

The authors believe that programs and policies must be built on a sound knowledge base. Toward this end, the following steps must be accomplished:

(1) *Depoliticizing the definition of elder abuse.* Researchers must carefully construct precise, measurable, and scientifically useful definitions of elder abuse. Acts of commission must be seen as conceptually distinct from acts of omission. Violence must be viewed as different, in kind and cause, from neglect.

(2) *Study more than publicly visible cases.* Research should not be limited to sampling cases of elder abuse from public and private agencies. Prior research on family violence has demonstrated that reliable and valid data can be obtained by utilizing self-reports of abuse from subjects in nonclinical settings.

(3) *A measure of extent must be based on a representative sample.* Multiplying the rate of elder abuse found in a pilot study by the number of persons over 60 years of age yields a large number, but a number which is no way indicative of the incidence of elder abuse. The best way to derive such an estimate is with a representative sample of subjects. The continued reliance on small, nonrepresentative samples will continue to yield unreliable, biased data which cannot be generalized to any population.

(4) *Comparison groups.* This simple issue here is that one cannot identify factors associated with elder abuse without having some kind of comparison group built into the study.

(5) *Theory testing and building.* Finally, researchers need to reject the kind of post hoc analysis which is so evident in current work on elder abuse, and begin to conduct studies which are designed to test theoretical propositions.

Until such a program of serious and adequate research is begun and begins to yield reliable and valid data, those interested in the study of elder abuse should studiously avoid the temptation to further disseminate the current crop of guesses and notions about the extent, patterns, and causes of elder abuse. The truth is that we really do not know very much at this stage, and we need to concentrate our energies on gathering meaningful data on this important topic.

IMPLICATIONS FOR PRACTITIONERS

The implications of the current state about knowledge on abuse of elder persons for practitioners are less clear and direct than the implications for researchers.

While neither definitive nor even tentative answers are available to the major questions concerning elder abuse, it is reasonable to assume that the abuse of elder persons by family members is a significant problem and that clinicians who treat elderly clients could expect to encounter abuse victims. Practitioners face two major problems when treating victims of elder abuse. First, since there is very little in the way of sound scholarly knowledge on this topic, practitioners cannot presently locate quality research knowledge which could be informative for their clinical practice. Second, since elder abuse has only recently been identified as a family and social problem, there are few established resources, services, and treatment programs which can be adopted, copied, or applied to the problem.

Until both knowledge and services are developed, practitioners will have to cope the best they can. Toward that end, a number of steps can be taken.

(1) *Be aware that elderly are abused by family members.* The first step for practitioners is to overcome the selective inattention which has long masked the abuse of elderly from public and professional eyes. Just as pediatricians had to learn not to take patterns of injuries in children for granted, practitioners who service the elderly must be willing to ask difficult and sensitive questions surrounding the appearance of bruises, fractures, or other untoward injuries to an elderly client.

(2) *Use existing domestic violence services.* Fortunately, there has been an intensive and extensive development of services for victims of family violence. Refuges or battered wife shelters have increased from 6 in 1976 to more than 300 today. While there are still an insufficient number of such shelters to meet the needs of battered wives, these shelters do offer potential placements for female victims of elder abuse.

(3) *Support and supporting caretakers.* Clinicians who treat victims of child abuse often find that providing support services to families, such as homemakers, visiting nurses, or home health visitors serves to alleviate family stress and reduce the risk of future abuse. Services which aid and assist those who care for elderly and/or infirm relatives could be an important asset in a treatment program for elder abuse. Just as it is unrealistic to expect that everyone who bears a child has the personal, social, and economic resources to adequately nurture that child, it is equally unrealistic to assume that all those who must care for their elderly relatives have the full resources to do that job with kindness and compassion.

(4) *Avoid applying myths to clinical practice.* Clinical practice with victims of family violence can be emotionally draining and upsetting. To counterbalance these emotions, clinicians often search for simple and direct answers to the problems they must solve. Since the media has milked a few facts for all they are worth, it might be tempting for clinicians to assume that if they read facts about elder abuse often enough in the newspapers, then these are facts which can be applied to clinical practice. This chapter has attempted to show that few facts exist and that clinicians should resist the temptation to apply what they read in the newspapers or magazines to their clinical work.

Notes

1. It cannot be determined if 4.1% of 73 individuals were abused (N = 3), if 4.1% of 48 individuals were abused (N = 2), or if 1 out of 48 individuals (2%) were abused. Block and Sinnott (1979) cited each of these statistics on various pages of their final report.

2. The exact numbers could not be determined because they reported mean scores for many types of abuse and neglect and categories were not mutually exclusive.

3. This section omits reference to, and discussion of, the estimate of 500,000 victims of elder abuse attributed to the second author. The estimate, which has been widely published, is actually a figure arrived at by estimating the number of individuals 65 years old or older who married, had children, and have contact with their children. The 3.5% incidence statistic was based on the percentage of parents who reported being abused by teenage children in a national survey of family violence (Straus et al., 1980). Thus, the estimate has no more empirical standing than a guess, irrespective of how frequently it has been cited in popular and professional literature.

PART V

STUDYING FAMILY VIOLENCE

Introduction

When we began our investigations of the extent, patterns, and causes of violence between family members we were immediately struck by the fact that there was no coherent body of literature which constituted a knowledge base. There were numerous research reports authored by psychiatrists, social workers, and physicians on the subject of child abuse and neglect. There were very few essays on the topic of spouse abuse or the use of violence between marital partners. There were two plausible reasons for the knowledge gap. First, family violence could have been rare and those few cases of violence or abuse could be explained as a function of mental illness. The other plausible hypothesis was that family violence was quite extensive, but social scientists had failed, for various reasons, to investigate it.

The first few tentative probes into the extent of violence between family members (Straus, 1974c; Steinmetz, 1971) cast doubt on the hypothesis that there was no research because there was no violence. After the first few studies it became obvious that one reason why there was little research on family violence was that investigators either did not want to ask questions such as, "Have you stopped beating your wife or child . . ." or felt that they could not obtain reliable and valid answers to such questions.

As we became convinced that the family was a violent institution and as we pushed forward with larger and more ambitious studies, we were continuously told that we could not expect to carry out sound empirical research on family violence because we could not expect people to answer our sensitive questions. But people did answer our questions—

with a startling degree of candor and detail. Whereas we were afraid that people would slam their doors in our faces, we found that many of the subjects we approached would talk to us far beyond the one hour we expected the interviews to run.

The first chapter in this section, "Methods for Studying Sensitive Family Topics," is designed as a road map to provide aid to those who want to study sensitive topics such as family violence. We review the major problems and possible solutions in conducting sensitive topic research, including sampling, rapport, validity, and reliability.

The second chapter is a methodological critique of some of the current forms of research on child abuse and family violence. We argue that some of the methods and some of the data analysis procedures serve to extend rather than explode myths about abuse and violence.

In large part, the chapters in this section are designed to show that sound scientific investigations of family violence can be carried out and researchers need not close down certain research options in advance.

CHAPTER 11

METHODS FOR STUDYING SENSITIVE FAMILY TOPICS

A dilemma confronts social scientists seeking to examine behavior when long-standing taboos exist against discussing such behavior publicly or with one's intimates. Sensitive issues or "taboo topics" (Farberow, 1966) bid for scientific attention for a number of reasons: they are intrinsically interesting, allow scientists to analyze and refute conventional wisdom or myths about human behavior, concern regions of human behavior where knowledge gaps exist, and are fundamentally important for improving our insight and knowledge about less sensitive social phenomena. At the same time, sensitive issues and taboos pose major obstacles for researchers.

Special Problems in Sensitive Area Research

Sensitive issues aside, the family is a complex and difficult social institution to study. For one thing, families are made up of individuals occupying multiple statuses and enacting multiple roles. Thus, a researcher who interviews a family member or requests that a member of a family fill out a questionnaire is collecting data from an individual who is at the intersection of many and varied roles (mother, wife, worker, daughter, sister, and the like). Second, "family" as a group or institution is as much a matter of subjective perception as it is an objective group membership. As Laing (1971) put it, "To be in the same family is to feel the same 'family' inside." And because a number of individuals make up

Author's Note: Reprinted, with permission, from the American Journal of Orthopsychiatry. Copyright 1978 by the American Orthopsychiatric Association, Inc.

a family, there are numerous subjective perceptions of family interactions and individuals. Thus, while there may be a shared "reality" of
family, which can be studied (Berger and Kellner, 1964), there are also
varying subjective perceptions depending on whether the observer is a
"son," "father," "mother," and the like.

The numerous roles, statuses, and shared perceptions complicate
research into the family, but there are two additional facets of the family
that influence the study of sensitive topics. First, the family is essentially
a private institution (Aries, 1962; Laslett, 1973). Second, the family is an
intimate social group.

PRIVACY

A major contingency in the field of family studies is that the family is
a private institution. As such, most relevant family interaction takes
place behind closed doors, out of sight of neighbors, friends, and social
scientists. In order to study the family, most social scientists have made
use of methods and instruments that allow them to penetrate the walls of
the family without actually going into the home. The majority of all
social scientific research on the family involves the use of interviews and
questionnaires. Less than 1% of current research on the family employs
observational techniques (Nye and Bayer, 1963). The reliance on survey
methods rather than field methods in the study of the family also
indicates that the private nature of the family makes it difficult to
employ standard observational or participant observation techniques.
The exceptions are few, and often involve a researcher moving in and
living with a family, as Jules Henry did in his study of families with
psychotic children (Henry, 1971).

While researchers have been allowed entrance into families to study
global family interaction patterns and some researchers have moved in
as boarders in households while pursuing community studies (Whyte,
1955), it would be difficult to gain admittance into a household for the
purposes of observing child beating or varieties of sexual behavior.
Moreover, the private nature of the family also means that certain
rooms are devoted to specific activities. A researcher might be allowed
into a home, but not into the family's bedroom or bathroom for the
purpose of making observations.

In conclusion, the private nature of the family puts a premium on
methods that require the family member to recount previous histories or
events and report them on a questionnaire or in an interview. Even these

methodological approaches encounter the problem of intimacy, which blocks access to certain behavioral and attitudinal domains.

INTIMACY

Unlike other social groups, family structure arises out of intimate interactions. The special nature of intimate relationships tends to produce strong pressures against discussing family matters with outsiders. Parents often reprimand children for discussing their family matters with school counselors, friends, and neighbors. The tendency to view family matters as sacred, private, and intimate leads many individuals to take an adamant stand against uninvited intrusions by social scientists, market researchers, and the like.

Sensitive Topics

One of the most discussed sensitive issues in the past few years has been *child abuse*. This topic became a focal issue in the early sixties—propelled by a groundbreaking essay by Kempe and his associates (Kempe et al., 1962). Today, we still do not have a complete understanding of child abuse. Research which tests hypotheses is rare, causal models are overly simplified, and theory-building research is often inadequately conceptualized.

A related topic is *spouse abuse*. As with child abuse, limited information exists on incidence and causes.

A third issue is *sexual abuse and incest*. Most textbooks on the family devote numerous pages to discussing the extent and nature of incest taboos in various societies and cultures. These discussions attempt to explain why such taboos exist and what form they take. The examination of taboos related to incest masks the fact that exceptions to the rule abound. Huerta (1976) has discussed reasons incest has been a neglected topic for social scientists, and the fact that incest and sexual abuse remain the most underresearched aspects of child abuse and child neglect.

Of the 50 states, many still have laws on the books that prevent a wife from filing a rape charge against her husband (Gelles, 1977); consequently, the issue of *physically coerced sexual relations* between husbands and wives has remained hidden from public view and from the research community. Occasional newspaper accounts of women who have slain their husbands because of demanded sex or sex acts that the wives found repugnant testify to the importance of the issue, but we still have no idea about the incidence and nature of this side of family relations.

While the topic of premarital sex has been reasonably well researched (Hunt, 1973; Kinsey et al., 1948; Reiss, 1960), sexual relations within marriage appear to be underresearched in comparison.

There are numerous other sensitive topics that can provide new and fundamentally important insights into the nature of family relations. In fact, one method of uncovering such sensitive issues is to monitor the popular literature forums in which personal problems are discussed. Columns such as "Dear Abby" and "Ann Landers," along with the personal columns found in magazines such as *Redbook, Good Housekeeping*, and *Woman's Day*, provide informative insights into the backstage areas of the family. An example of how this type of material can stimulate research was related by a colleague who read an article in a women's magazine written by a woman who was married to a homosexual. In discussing this with friends, our colleague learned that the same phenomenon was much more common than he first had realized; he was directed to someone who had experienced it and was willing to talk about it at length.

It would appear that there are many issues that constitute important social problems and provide important insights into the fundamental nature of the family, but have yet to be investigated. Furthermore, there appears to be an abundance of information and data available on these topics once the research community can overcome the major obstacles and hurdles of sensitive topic research in the family.

Methods of Studying Sensitive Issues

SAMPLING

The first problem faced by those who study sensitive family topics is to locate data sources and cooperative subjects. This problem is exacerbated by the low base rate of most sensitive phenomena. If one were to attempt a study of the incidence of child abuse (assuming a base rate of .005) and wanted a confidence level of 95%, the needed sample size would be 76,448 people. At $40 per interview, the cost of the study would exceed $3 million!

Unless a researcher is focusing on an issue with a presumed high base rate, or has unlimited capital, most sensitive issue research on the family will need to employ nonprobability sampling.

When employing nonprobability sampling, researchers require techniques that will produce a sample in which the informational payoff is the highest and in which cooperation is not likely to be a major problem. Some of the sampling techniques used to investigate taboo topics follow.

Group sampling. Group sampling was the technique pioneered by Kinsey and his associates (Kinsey et al., 1948) in their study of sexual behavior. The Kinsey researchers were able to use group sampling because they did not have to concern themselves with the problem of low base rates of the behavior in question. In studying such issues as wife beating, incest, and the like, the use of any functioning group as a sampling unit might not be particularly helpful. However, there are specialized functioning groups where group sampling would be an aid in reaching potential subjects. Self-help groups such as Alcoholics Anonymous, Parents Anonymous (for child beaters), and certain women's groups might provide a number of subjects for research into sensitive issues.

The major drawback of this sampling procedure is that it would identify a particular subportion of the population under study. People who abuse their children and admit to it in a self-help group are thought to be quite different in terms of social and personal characteristics than those individuals who do not admit their abuse of children to others or themselves.

Snowball sampling. Snowball sampling, employed in studies of drug use (Goode, 1969), homosexuality (Humphreys, 1970), and professional gunmen (Polsky, 1969), facilitates research on sensitive issues because it allows the researcher to begin with one or two contacts and branch out to a wider sample of people. For instance, in the marriage of a woman to a homosexual mentioned earlier, the one case was able to identify a number of other women who had similar experiences; in a short time, a number of people were discussed who had experienced this problem. Our research on family violence (Gelles, 1974, which did not employ snowball sampling) often involved interviews with family members who discussed friends and relatives who had experienced violence in their marriages. It is likely that almost any topic is amenable to a form of snowball sampling.

A drawback of snowball sampling is that it taps individuals and families who are immersed in social networks. Some sensitive topics are not particularly suitable for this type of sampling. For instance, the literature on child abuse states that people who abuse their children are often socially isolated from friends and relatives. It would be difficult to use a snowball method of sampling when social isolation is a causal factor of the behavior in question.

Neighbor informant. In 1965 the National Opinion Research Council administered an interview, directed by Gil (1970), which asked subjects if they ever physically injured their children. Of the 1,520 subjects, 6 answered in the affirmative. The survey also asked whether the subjects knew of neighbors who had physically injured their children. Regarding the question, 45 answered in the affirmative, and Gil projected this to an estimate of between 2.53 and 4.07 million children physically abused each year (Gil, 1970). This technique of estimating the incidence of child abuse has become known as the "neighbor informant technique." Basically, the technique acknowledges the problems of reliability and validity in getting people to self-report illegal or deviant behavior. This problem is overcome by getting some outside source who knows the family to report on behavior within the family unit.

While the neighbor informant technique is strong in estimating the incidence or prevalence of certain sensitive issues, it has two major drawbacks. First, it is suitable for particular neighborhoods and subcultures. Where neighborhoods are marked by physical closeness and social openness, the neighborhood informant technique is suitable. However, where physical closeness is low and privacy of family interaction high, neighbors may be able to aid in establishing incidence rates for particular phenomena, but the private and intimate nature of family units makes neighbors poor judges of certain familial qualities such as power or authority. Moreover, many neighbors are probably unable to provide accurate information about important social indicators such as education and age of their neighbor.

Family informant. When a neighbor or someone outside the family has too little knowledge of what goes on in the home to aid the research project, an investigator might make use of an informant *inside* the family. This technique samples family members who provide information about what goes on among the other members of the family. Straus (1974b, 1974c, 1977) and Steinmetz (1974b) surveyed college students and asked them to answer questions about violence in their families during their last year at home (senior year in high school). This technique allowed the investigators to get some insight into the level of intrafamily violence and the causal variables associated with family violence.

While college students are captive audiences and have more knowledge about their own family than do neighbors, there are some limitations to this sampling procedure. First, as Landis (1957) and Berardo (1976) pointed out, there are real problems with the over-reliance on college students as research subjects. College students represent a narrow segment of the population. By using college students to study family life, we restrict our ability to generalize about marriage and family life (Berardo, 1976). Second, family informants might have limited knowledge about their own family life. They are unable to report about their parents' marriage during the early years (before they were born or when they were young), and they may have been sheltered from certain aspects of their family life. Taboo topics, by their very nature and sensitivity, may have been shielded from the children. Nevertheless, family informants are a lot closer to the core of family interaction than are neighbors or others who might be asked for information.

IDENTIFYING SUBJECTS FROM PUBLIC AND PRIVATE RECORDS

When a researcher wishes to investigate an issue in family relations but cannot use any of the previously mentioned methods of identifying and locating subjects, there are other methods that can be employed. Paradoxically, while the family is our society's most private institution, numerous transactions between family members become matters of public record. There are a number of public documents that can be used to identify and locate potential subjects for the study of sensitive issues.

Police records. Most police departments keep logs of all police department activities. These logs, while often crudely kept, are usually open for public inspection (as with most organizations, police departments vary in their desire to cooperate with social scientists wishing to use "public" records). Using the records of one police department to identify families where police officers had intervened in "family disputes," we developed a sample of 20 families who had been visited by police officers (Gelles, 1974, 1975c, 1976). In addition, some families were identified by examining the police log to identify cases where family members filed complaints of assault against another family member. The method of using police records, while allowing for the location of families, has some drawbacks. First, the method depends on the cooperation of the department chief. Second, an officer usually has to be present to assure that no juveniles would be identified in the process of screening families. Finally, police logs are far from the most accurate sources of data—addresses, names, and dates are often in error and a considerable amount of time can be wasted tracking down addresses that are nonexistent or inaccurate.

Police calls. The problem of getting cooperation from police officials often makes using official police records impossible. An alternative, which does not require cooperation, is to monitor the radio calls of police departments. Although this technique is time-consuming, it can yield a sample of families where disputes have taken place, where assaults occur, where child abuse is suspected, and where other matters requiring police attention occur. This method is dependent on being able to secure the operating frequencies of police departments and being able to decipher the codes used. The problem of faulty addresses and inaccurate information still prevails in this technique of locating families or individuals.

Newspapers. Newspapers (depending on region and area served) often provide interesting and informative material on families. We have examined a number of local and regional papers and have found a wealth of information that might be relevant for selecting cases for research on sensitive family topics. Some papers, for instance, list local police activities for the day or week. These listings would aid in locating families in conflict or those with particular attributes (quarrels, violence, and the like). In addition, papers that publish legal notices contain information otf interest to social scientists. Listings of divorces and divorce decrees are published in many papers. A recent issue of the *Providence Journal* published divorce settlements that included statements that restraining orders had been issued against husbands seeing or visiting their families. Our research on family violence indicated that such restraining orders typically grow out of a wife's complaint that she or her children have been physically abused by the husband.

Private agencies. Private agency case files are confidential information. However, if a researcher can work out an agreement with an agency to aid in research, agency records can become sources of subjects. In our own research on family violence, we worked out an arrangement with a private social work agency by which to contact subjects. We told the agency what our research objective was and what type of subjects we needed. The agency then screened their files, and contacted subjects for their permission to be interviewed. When permission was granted, we interviewed families that the agency suspected of using violence on children. Studies of remarriage, multi-problem families, family conflict, child neglect, and the like could all use this method of locating families for research projects.

In addition to helping locate families for research, private agencies can be the primary sources of data on families. During our research on marital violence, we were interested in the topic of marital rape. The problem was that because women cannot file a rape charge against their husbands, data on this issue are nonexistent. Interested in learning about the incidence and nature of physically coerced sex in marriage, we opted for surveying rape-crisis centers and asking them what proportion of their calls came from women claiming to be raped by their husbands. We also asked what the agencies knew about this issue. The data helped us gain some insight into this previously uninvestigated topic (Gelles, 1977).

Advertisements. A final method for locating subjects is to place an advertisement in a magazine, newspaper, or professional journal stating what the research project involves and requesting people who desire to be subjects to contact the investigator. This technique is often facilitated by offering to pay subjects for their time. Prescott and Letko (1977), through an advertisement in *Ms.* magazine, located 40 women who were willing to fill out a questionnaire on wife beating. The drawbacks of this method are obvious, because many people may respond to the advertisement as a lark. The representativeness of subjects located using this procedure is typically unknown.

DATA COLLECTION: AFTER RAPPORT WHAT?

Once a sample of family members has been obtained, the next major problem facing the investigator is to obtain valid and reliable data from the subjects. When the topic under investigation is sensitive and emotionally charged, research subjects may be embarrassed to discuss the issue; they may perceive "demand characteristics" of the instrument or situation (Orne, 1962) and respond in a socially desirable manner; they may be insulted by the researcher's technique, approach, or questions and refuse to continue; or, as was feared by Humphreys (1970), the researcher who asks the wrong question may conclude the research as the target of a series of beatings by subjects.

The literature on research into sensitive issues is limited to discussing the advantages of developing "rapport" with subjects in order to minimize the above-listed risks and to maximize validity and reliability. However, rapport building is such an intricate interpersonal task that many potential researchers are either scared off by the prospect of having to build rapport or proceed willy-nilly into the investigation, overly dependent on their ability to get along with people.

Interviews. Perhaps the most difficult part of any interview on a sensitive topic is the point where the researcher has to ask the respondent the key question or questions under consideration. No matter how much rapport may have been built up in the interview situation, most interviewers are not overly anxious to ask questions on the order of, "Have you stopped beating your wife?" Yet, this type of question is often crucial for the research.

There are a number of techniques for approaching and asking the more sensitive questions in research on the family. The first is a "funneling technique." This approach was employed in an exploratory study of intrafamily violence (Gelles, 1974). The technique was an unstructured interview. However, the flow of the interview was designed to direct the discussion toward the issue of family violence. The interview began with a general discussion of the subject's neighborhood, friends, and their families, and conflict and problems in their neighbor's families. Then the focus of the interview turned to the subject's family. General questions about conflict and problems were channeled toward questions about fights and, ultimately, violence.

The funneling technique allowed the interviewer to establish rapport with the subject, while familiarizing the subject with the basic content of the interview. The discussion gradually was channeled toward the issue of violence, and in many situations the subject began to discuss violence without a direct question. In instances where violence was not discussed spontaneously, the interviewer asked the direct question concerning the occurrence of violence in the family. (The funneling technique is discussed in more detail elsewhere [Gelles, 1974].)

Conflict Tactic Scales. The funneling technique was highly adaptable to an unstructured interview. Such a technique may require modification for use in structured interviews with large samples. An example of a technique used in a sensitive area is the Conflict Tactics Scales developed by Straus (1974c, 1979b) for research on family violence. This technique, designed for and first used with college student subjects, was adapted for and implemented with adults in a national survey of violence in families (Straus et al., 1980). It consists of a list of modes of conflict tactics, ranging from discussing an issue calmly to using a gun or a knife. Each item asks if the mode was *ever employed* in the family and how often the mode was used during the past year.

The advantage of this scale is that it accomplishes in a structured format what the funneling technique accomplishes in an unstructured format—it funnels the interview from the least sensitive to the most sensitive questions. This funneling allows for the building of rapport and has the additional benefit of building the subject's commitment to the interview (e.g., a subject may rationalize: "Well, if I answered that question, I can certainly answer this one.") Although the Conflict Tactic Scales has been used only in family violence research, it is highly adaptable to other sensitive issue research on the family.

Random response technique. No matter how good the rapport between the interviewer and the subject and no matter how successful the funneling technique employed, the researcher will eventually have to ask questions such as, "Have you abused your child?"; "Do you and your wife engage in anal intercourse?"; "Have you ever molested a child?"; "Have you ever used a gun on your wife?" These questions are particularly important and, at the same time, particularly difficult to ask. Interviewers, no matter how well trained, will often balk at asking such questions or ask them in a manner and with an inflection that suggests a "no answer" from the respondent. Subjects, on the other hand, may be embarrassed or afraid of answering the questions.

One manner of dealing with this problem is the random response technique developed by Warner (1965). In the original design a spinner was used to randomly select statements of a sensitive character such as: "I have masturbated . . . " or "I have not masturbated." The subject used the randomizing device out of the researcher's sight to select one statement for response. Responses could only be "yes" or "no." The researcher, not having seen which question was selected, could not interpret the answer, and the respondent's privacy was protected. Because the random response model is based on Bayesian probability theory, the researcher could estimate population parameters from the responses (Fidler and Kleinknecht, 1977; Horvitz et al., 1975; Warner, 1965).

The methodological advantage of the random response technique is that it guarantees confidentiality for the respondent and reduces the amount of response bias due to evasion. The technique has been reviewed and tested by a number of psychologists and they confirm the utility of the technique as a method of collecting accurate confidential information on sensitive issues (Fidler and Kleinknecht, 1977; Horvitz et al., 1975).

The disadvantage of this technique is its conception of the role of an interview subject. An interview subject will have to be extremely trustful of the technique to cooperate. It may be that the technique works only with subjects who are too naive to believe they might be fooled and with subjects who have doctorates in statistics and believe the technique is truly random. All the rest of the subjects in between might be extremely skeptical of how "random" and anonymous the technique is.

Collaborative and conjoint interviews. A fairly common problem in all family research, and particularly important when studying sensitive topics, is the reliance of a large proportion of research enterprises on the information provided by a single family member. Studies of family violence (Gelles, 1974; Straus, 1974c) and studies of child abuse typically gather data by interviewing one member of a family. This technique provides a single perspective on the issue in question. For example, a wife might consider a slap an instance of wife abuse, while to the husband it may have been so insignificant that he would not remember it in an interview. The level and meaning of violence in that family will depend on who is interviewed.

A possible solution to the problem of single perspectives is the conjoint and collaborative interview. Laslett and Rapoport (1975) suggested that conducting repeated interviews with several members of the same family by more than one interviewer increases the internal validity of the research and is particularly appropriate for research on the more private and intimate character of family life. LaRossa (1976) stated that common problems with family research, such as (1) dependence on female subjects, (2) overuse of self-report measures, (3) heavy reliance on "one-shot" data collections, and (4) failure to treat marriage in a holistic manner, can be solved by employing a conjoint interview procedure. This method involves husbands as well as wives, yields behavioral as well as phenomenological data, allows for the in-depth analysis of the marital world, and uses the marriage system level of analysis rather than the individual respondent level.

While LaRossa (1977) was able to employ the conjoint interview fruitfully in his study of first pregnancy, we found that this procedure had serious disadvantages when it came to a study of family violence. Our study of intrafamily violence included four conjoint interviews (Gelles, 1974). During the course of these interviews, issues of conflict and disagreement arose and the couples began to argue and disagree over the "correct" answer to the question. We felt that conjoint interviews sometimes created conflict that might have boiled over into violence after the interviewer had left the house. While we had no evidence that this did or could happen, we felt that it was wiser to conduct interviews with a single family member (Gelles, 1974).

Observations. Direct observation or participant observation in studies of the family is time-consuming, expensive, and rare. In studies that collected data through direct observation in the home the sample size was small and the research focused on global interaction patterns in the family (Henry, 1971).

Research on sensitive family issues involves problems other than those of time, cost, and small sample size. It is unlikely that a family will allow an investigator to make direct observations of sexual relations, violence, incest, or other volatile and private subjects. However, observation can be used to collect some data on households where the behavior in question exists or families who would serve as comparison groups to the others in a sample.

Focused observations in the home enable the investigator to gather valuable behavioral data to complement data that could be obtained through interviews and questionnaires. LaRossa found that the conjoint interview is also an opportunity to collect behavioral data (1976). There are various situations in which focused observation could be employed. For example, if data on how family members cope with stress is desired, an investigator might want to conduct observations of family interaction during dinner time. Bossard and Boll (1966) found that meals in the kitchen or dining room serve as the focal point of family interaction. This is one time of day when most family members are in the same room for a period of time. Additionally, meals are often stressful situations in which conflicts and arguments can erupt and must be dealt with (Gelles, 1974). The disadvantage of this procedure is that families might present a false front during the course of the observation, thus preventing the observer from gaining an insight into the real nature of the family. This problem might be reduced by repeating the observations over time so that the presence of the investigator does not change the fundamental manner in which the family members interact with one another.

Projective techniques. One method that is particularly useful in studying controversial issues is the projective test (Selltiz et al., 1959). Projective techniques such as the Thematic Apperception Test, the Rorschach Test, the draw-a-picture test, and the complete-a-sentence test are presumed to allow the subject to project internal states onto objects and behaviors external to himself (Kerlinger, 1973).

Projective techniques have been used extensively in family research. Numerous studies use them when children are the subjects of research (Haworth, 1966; Kagan, 1958; Radke, 1946). Children's perceptions of their parents have been studied by using line drawings and doll play (Cummings, 1952; Kagan et al., 1961). Projective tests such as the TAT and completion projects have been used with adults to study family-related personality traits (Blum, 1949), attitudes toward family members (Lakin, 1957), and family power (Straus and Cytrynbaum, 1961). Additionally, entire families have been the subjects of projective technique research design to study familial perceptions (Alexander, 1952), and the direction of aggression in families (Morgan and Gaier, 1956).

Other researchers have designed projective tests to test for specific traits in the family. Edith Lord of the University of Miami developed a projective protocol that portrayed misbehaving children. The protocol varied the type of misbehavior and the age of the child (by having size vary). Lord administered the protocol to test for punitiveness in parents to gain some insight into the causes of child abuse. We have used a TAT projective device to test for the association of sex and violence in the fantasy production of college students (Gelles, 1975a).

The obvious advantage of a projective device is that it is a nonreactive method of collecting data. A projective test disguises the true purpose of the research. On the other hand, projective techniques have been criticized for being so ambiguous that they reveal the internal states of the *scorer* rather than those of the subject. In addition, projective techniques concentrate on internal states and it is difficult to argue convincingly that one can predict external behavior from internal states.

Experimental design. Experiments designed to examine sensitive topics in the family are limited by ethical and moral considerations in regard to the types of experimental manipulation the sample can be subjected to. Clearly, a researcher could not ethically design an experiment in which the expected outcome was a parent beating a child. An additional limitation is that experiments using families as subjects typically involve some degree of observation. Because experiments are typically conducted in the controlled setting of the investigator's laboratory, the family members will be interacting in a context quite different from the privacy and familiarity of their homes.

These limitations notwithstanding, there are some experimental designs that are amenable to studying sensitive areas in the family. For instance, if a researcher was testing the hypothesis that stress was causally related to aggression, modes of conflict resolution, or child abuse, the researcher could set up a true experimental design (Campbell and Stanley, 1963) where the variable "stress" was manipulated. The "Simulated Family" or SIMFAM technique, which has been used in studying problem solving (Straus and Tallman, 1971), has been found to be successful in simulating family crisis. By manipulating the "crisis," the investigator might be able to examine the effects of stress on family conflict resolution. Although one could not expect to observe behavioral violence, the investigator could use a projective technique to assess the families' levels of internal aggression in the crisis or "no crisis" situation. The advantage of the experimental design is that it allows for an *explanatory* analysis of the sensitive issues. Although experiments have been criticized for lacking correspondence to the real world, methodologists have argued that a valid experiment can be carried out even when the experimental variable is "phenomenally different" from events in the natural setting, as long as the experimentally produced variable is "conceptually similar" (Rieken et al., 1954; Straus, 1969).

The disadvantages posed by experiments arise when the experimental variables are not truly parallel to the real world. For instance, a researcher studying child abuse would have difficulty arguing convincingly that the experimental condition of depriving a child of candy is conceptually similar to physically abusing that child.

VALIDITY

Perhaps the most persistent question raised in the study of sensitive topics is: "How do you know the subjects told the truth?" Researchers studying sensitive topics tend to assume that few people would respond that they *do* engage in morally or normatively disapproved acts when they actually *do not*. However, there is considerable concern that many people who engage in covert deviance or other emotionally charged behavior will not readily admit it to social scientists. Humphreys, in fact, suggested that covert deviants wear the "breastplate of righteousness" which offers a "holier than thou" presentation of self (1970).

Kinsey and his associates attempted to resolve the threat to validity caused by a "social desirability affect." Kinsey and his colleagues pioneered the "direct approach interview." The Kinsey researchers argued that the burden of denial should be on the respondent, and that the interviewer should not ask questions that make it easy to deny certain behaviors (Kinsey et al., 1948). Thus, the Kinsey group began each interview assuming that every type of sexual activity had been engaged in by the respondent . . . and asked questions such as, "When did you last masturbate?" rather than, "Do you ever masturbate?"

While there is a need for validation studies of the techniques used in research on sensitive topics, to date such studies are rare, and even proposals for validation studies are few and far between. Bulcroft and Straus (1980) carried out a validation study on the use of college students as informants on family conflict tactics. They found that when the same conflict tactics scales were administered separately to students and their parents, there was a high level of agreement on the level of family violence.

The "nomination technique" (discussed in the sampling section of this essay) might be validated by using official records to cross-check whether the neighbor reported for a particular behavior (child abuse, wife abuse) is known to police or social workers in the community. While this method of triangulation (Webb et al., 1966) is applicable to behaviors for which there are legal proscriptions and agents of control delegated the task of dealing with the problem, the cross-check method of validation will be useless for validating results on other behaviors, such as marital rape.

Whatever the method of sampling selected and whatever form of data collection is employed, there will have to be attempts to validate such research if the results of research on sensitive family topics are to be taken seriously.

Additional Constraints

PROTECTION OF HUMAN SUBJECTS

Researchers who engage in studies of sensitive topics that are funded by the federal government encounter additional problems posed by the Department of Health and Human Services guidelines concerning the protection of human subjects.

The purpose of the guidelines is to protect research subjects from physical or psychological injury which might arise as a direct or indirect consequence of the subjects' participation in research. While these guidelines tend to be directed toward medical or drug-related research, they still apply to all federally funded projects that employ humans as subjects.

The major guidelines that influence social science research on the family are the provisions that call for the subjects to give "informed consent" assuring that they have been provided full explanation of the project, a description of the risks involved, if any, a disclosure of alternative procedures that might be used, and an offer to answer any and all questions concerning the project. Additionally, subjects must be informed that they can withdraw from the project at any time (for a detailed definition of informed consent, see *Federal Register*, May 30, 1974: 18917). Researcher proposals must also guarantee that potential risks to the subjects are outweighed by benefits and by the importance of knowledge to be gained from the research.

Earlier versions of the federal guidelines called for informed consent to be obtained, in writing, before data collection began. It is obvious that this poses some problems for research enterprises which depend heavily on the establishment of rapport and trust for valid and reliable evidence to be obtained. It would be difficult for researchers to get a chance to establish rapport if they had to begin the research by stating that they were asking questions to learn about wife abuse, sexual abuse, incest, and the like. Moreover, researchers who vowed that the data collected were to be kept strictly confidential would confront suspicious subjects if they asked them to sign their names to a legal form which might look like a release of information.

The potential problems posed by these guidelines have been alleviated by new interpretations and exceptions made by DHHS officials, which allowed some researchers to obtain complete informed consent at the end of the interview, questionnaire, or observation. In addition, such consent does not always have to be in writing.[1]

A problem with informed consent does arise if the researcher desires to have legal minors (under 18 years of age) as subjects. If children are to be the subjects of sensitive research, informed consent must be obtained from parents or guardians. In addition, the consent must be obtained prior to meeting with the child. This restriction virtually guarantees that children will not be subjects of research on sensitive topics. No researcher could guarantee that a child being asked to report on parents' sexual or violent behavior would not be at risk if the parents knew the content of the research. Parents might give informed consent but still intimidate the child physically or psychologically after the interview. We know of no federally funded research in child abuse that is gathering direct interview or questionnaire data from children, and we conclude that the regulations protecting human subjects have produced this situation.

Thus, researchers seeking federal funding for sensitive research must be aware that the federal guidelines and the disposition of college and university human subjects committees are factors that must be considered in any research design.

"HIRED HAND" RESEARCH

When research projects attempt to investigate emotionally charged issues in the family on a large scale, additional problems are created by virtue of having to employ other staff members for various parts of the project. Roth (1966) has listed and discussed the numerous problems involved in what he called "hired hand" research. He discussed "faking" of observations, collaboration among coders to make their results similar, interviewers completing interview schedules by themselves, and other problems. Large-scale research projects usually develop mechanisms to "catch" the cheaters on their staffs, including call-backs, comparing data of each interviewer to the group average, and reinterviews. Nevertheless, such controls are often absent or are not sufficient to locate instances where interviewers did not take time to develop sufficient rapport, where interviewers used certain intonations when asking questions which assured "socially acceptable" replies, and where research staff members discussed confidential interview material at cocktail parties (Roth, 1966).

Thus, while large research projects can produce larger samples of families with more ability to generalize from the data, the necessary division of labor in these projects and the necessity of using "hired hands" poses serious and often unimaginable risks to the validity, reliability, and ethical conduct of the research.

CONFIDENTIALITY

One of the major steps that must be taken in sensitive topic research is to guarantee to the subjects that all data being collected will be kept confidential. While it is relatively simple to mask the identities of subjects in the write-ups of case studies, and while statistical procedures used in analyzing and presenting data protect the identity of subjects, there is one potential problem that poses risks to the researcher and the subjects.

Although a number of social scientists have discussed problems associated with the right to keep information obtained in academic research confidential, and some researchers (Polsky, 1969) have offered to serve as test cases to determine whether a social scientist could keep his information private despite court orders, no clear precedent exists in this area.[2]

Thus, until the courts decide whether academicians can be granted immunity from having to release confidential data, researchers who engage in research that deals with illegal, sensitive, or taboo topics run the risks of being forced to turn over material they pledged would be kept confidential, of engaging in legal battles, or of spending time in jail for contempt of court.

Conclusion

The purpose of this essay has been to identify the problems associated with carrying out research on sensitive topics in the family and to list and discuss some solutions that can be and have been implemented in the course of research on child abuse, wife abuse, family violence, and sexual behavior. This has not been an exhaustive presentation of all the methodologies that have been employed to study all the taboo topics in the family. Rather, the essay has been largely influenced and confined to methodological insights gained from our own research on family violence (Straus et al., 1973). Nevertheless, many of the issues and methods associated with our research program on family violence are applicable to other types of sensitive research in the family.

A goal of this essay is to aid in moving research on the family into new and unexplored areas of family behavior. We believe that numerous topics of interest and importance have gone uninvestigated because researchers were stumped by the problems of finding subjects, obtaining data, and establishing procedures for producing valid and reliable data.

The final question that arises is whether research on such topics should be done at all—irrespective of whether or not the major hurdles in doing the research can be overcome. Some may argue that the procedures and methods we discuss in this essay border on being unethical invasions of privacy of the family. In addition, some might feel that there are areas in the family that are too private and too sacred and should not be investigated by "snooping" social scientific "voyeurs." Deception, ethics, morality, and the sacred nature of the family as a social institution are often cited as reasons not to carry out research on sensitive topics.

While there are ethical and moral dilemmas involved in the methods discussed in this essay, we would counter the argument that certain topics should not be investigated and that families should not be subjected to the "voyeurism" of family researchers by pointing out that the research community's respect for the privacy of the family and the unwillingness to investigate certain emotional or embarrassing topics did not prevent children from being abused, did not prevent wives from being abused, did not eliminate impotence, and did not enforce the incest taboo. Nor did the perceptual blinders that family researchers wore when viewing the family prevent myths and conventional wisdoms from being accepted as fact when scientific data on sensitive topics was lacking. If we are to learn more about the basic nature of the family and family functioning, and if we are to be capable of dealing with some of the fundamental social problems that exist in the family, we must be prepared to take the risks in the study of sensitive topics and to seek creative and humane solutions to the ethical problems of such research.

Notes

1. The author has had informed consent requirements waived in two research projects. There is no guarantee, however, that such waivers would be granted in all instances of sensitive research.

2. On May 20, 1976, United States District Judge Charles B. Renfrew of California ruled that a Harvard professor did not have to disclose information obtained confidentially in the course of academic research.

CHAPTER 12

ETIOLOGY OF VIOLENCE: OVERCOMING FALLACIOUS REASONING IN UNDERSTANDING FAMILY VIOLENCE AND CHILD ABUSE

Early child abuse researchers were physicians, psychiatrists, social workers, and other clinicians. Their work was based on at-hand cases. Control groups were rarely used. Almost uniformly, the conclusions drawn by these researchers dealt with personality and some social traits, which are said to characterize child abusers. However, lacking control groups, the researchers had no way of knowing whether the traits they felt were causally associated with child abuse were, in fact, overrepresented, underrepresented, or similarly represented in the population at large. Thus, on the basis of the early research, it was impossible to determine whether certain psychological factors were causally associated with child abuse. In fact, as I reread the early essays on child abuse, and even some of the current essays which purport to document numerous psychological traits associated with child abuse, I find profiles of my students, my neighbors, my wife, myself, and my son. It would almost seem that some of these researchers are right when they conclude that child abusers are a random cross-section of the population. However, their research does not tell us anything. Because control groups were not used, there is absolutely no basis upon which to draw any conclusions whatsoever.

Author's Note: From Richard J. Gelles, "Etiology of Violence: Overcoming Fallacious Reasoning in Understanding Family Violence and Child Abuse." Appeared in *Conference Proceedings: Child Abuse: Where Do We Go From Here?* 1978, Washington, D.C.: Children's Hospital National Medical Center.

Let us look at a specific example. Suppose researchers say that 80% of their sample of child abusers have certain neurological impairments. Do they tell us what percentage of the population at large has those same neurological impairments? The Srole (1962) study of mental illness in midtown Manhattan found that as many as 80% of a randomly selected population were physically and/or psychologically impaired by psychological distress. Therefore, to say that 80% of abusers are impaired by psychological distress may in fact mean only that psychological distress is in no way specifically associated with child abusers. In the absence of control groups, many such conclusions about the causes of child abuse are not very meaningful. It has only been in the last three or four years that child abuse research has begun to consider the inclusion of randomly selected or matched control groups in study samples.

A second problem of much research to date has been the use of the medical model. This research paradigm forces a constricted and narrow focus on the study of child abuse. When attempting to explain individual cases of a phenomenon's occurrence, epidemiologists tend to look for commonalities present or factors absent in that phenomenon. An epidemiologist looking for the cause of Legionnaire's disease would examine factors that are common to people who have the disease and absent among people who do not have the disease. Medical researchers are trained to think of behavioral malfunctions or dysfunctions as being caused by one or two germs or toxins in the individual. The problem is that a paradigm of research which explains a phenomenon on the basis of one or two factors, or a combination of a few factors, tends to omit from consideration the complex series of variables and interactions of variables that are part of the causal explanation of social behavior. The medical model, the "search for the germ technique," is inappropriate to the analysis of social phenomena because it uses a biological metaphor for social behavior. Child abuse is a social phenomenon, not a biological or medical phenomenon. It cannot be studied by search for the germ techniques.

The numerous studies of violence and child abuse which have been carried out over the last 20 years are examples of the problems with the medical model explanation of child abuse. Most of these studies are capable of explaining only 4% to 5% of the variance found in the dependent variable because the research is limited to looking at only one or two causal variables. The studies do not consider patterns of variables; they do not consider time order; they do not use multiple regression techniques of analysis or pathanalysis techniques; they do not even consider interaction effects.

The extra y-chromosome argument is another example of the epidemiological approach. It was only a month ago that I heard a prominent director of a social service agency state that one of the causal factors of child abuse and violence in America is the presence of an extra y-chromosome. This individual argued that Richard Speck, the man who murdered nine nurses some years ago, possessed this extra y-chromosome. Well, it so happens Richard Speck did not have an extra y-chromosome (Shah, 1970a, 1970b). In fact, by 1971 the theory of the extra y-chromosome as a viable explanation of violence had been disproven. However, an epidemiological or medical approach tends to encourage notions such as that of the extra y-chromosome because it tends to focus on one fact, one variable, one germ.

Let us look at a more positive example of the research done by sociologist Robert Sokol at Dartmouth College (1976). He found that the variables of social class and social stress were unrelated to child abuse potential, *when examined one at a time*. However, he went on to use more appropriate analytical techniques. He then found that there is a very strong interaction effect such that a combination of certain stresses found among certain people in certain social groups does, in fact, create child abuse potential. Thus, in the area of child abuse, if you look for variables as epidemiologists do—one variable at a time—you are likely to rule out class and stress as causes. The relevancy of class and stress as causal factors is clear only if the interaction effect between the two is examined.

The third problem of much child abuse research, particularly that conducted by those in the fields of medicine, psychiatry, and social work, is the fallacy of false time priority. Many researchers have tended to attribute causal status to variables which may have occurred or arisen *after* the violent or abusive act. For example, abusers have been described as paranoid and depressed. This finding is typically based on an interview with suspected parents after they have brought their children to a clinic or an emergency room. On the basis of such studies we cannot conclude that these psychological states existed before the abusive act took place. It is just as possible that being labeled a child abuser contributes to the creation of these psychological states *after* the violent incident. The same line of reasoning that argues that child abusers are paranoid and that paranoia is a cause of child abuse would lead one to conclude that paranoia is the cause of getting speeding tickets because people who receive tickets tend to act paranoid when the police officer approaches them.

The fourth major problem of many child abuse studies is the fallacy of the search for the perfect association. This fallacious reasoning underlies the argument that because some rich people abuse their children, poverty or low socioeconomic status cannot be a cause of child abuse. Three of the four criteria for demonstrating a causal explanation in the social sciences are (1) that an association be demonstrated to be of a significant magnitude and a consistent pattern; (2) nonspurious; and (3) based on an established time order (that the causal factor precede the caused factor). In order to conclude that socioeconomic status or occupational prestige is a causal factor, it is not necessary to prove that *all poor people* abuse their children and that absolutely no rich people abuse their children. One must simply establish a relationship between a factor and child abuse or violence to support the claim of causality of a factor. *There need not be a perfect association.*

There are those who take the fallacy of perfect association to an even further extreme, saying that factor must explain 100% of the variance and that there may exist no other factors which can explain a phenomenon. Again, a factor does not even have to show a *major* association; it does not have to explain 90%, 80%, or even 75% of the variance. A factor need only (1) have a *significant* association; (2) have taken place before the violent or abusive act; and (3) be nonspurious.

The criterion that an association between variables be nonspurious is very important. Take, for example, the relationship between alcohol and violence. It is commonly held that people who drink excessively tend to be violent, and that people who drink tend to abuse their children. However, the causal relationship implied here between drink and violence tends to disappear when you investigate whether people believe they will or will not be held responsible for their actions when drunk. A story told by Murray Straus illustrates this point well. A counselor was interviewing a couple with a history of wife abuse. The counselor asked the husband, "Why do you beat up your wife?" The husband responded, "I can't control myself. I just lose control." The counselor, being a very wise person, asked, "Well, why don't you shoot her or stab her?" The husband had no response to that because the only answer he could have given would be "I can't stab or shoot my wife, I might hurt her." He knew very well what he was doing.

The research evidence shows that people *do* get drunk and beat their wives and children, but they are fully aware of what they are doing. So aware in fact, that people will drink knowing that their inebriation will give them an excuse for their violence. Thus, the commonly assumed association between alcohol and violence tends to be spurious.

The recent theory that the rising unemployment rates are associated with the rising child abuse statistics exemplifies a fifth problem, that of the "ecological fallacy." Intuitively, the notion that unemployment is causally related to child abuse makes sense, given the fact that research seems to indicate that unemployed people are more likely to abuse their children. However, it is inappropriate to interpret individual behavior on the basis of an examination of aggregate rates. The observation that both unemployment rates and child abuse rates are rising tells us nothing more than that the rates are rising simultaneously. We cannot conclude that unemployed people are abusing their children from these statistics. In fact, even if both the unemployment rates and the rate of child abuse decreased, we would not know if unemployed people who had become employed had stopped abusing their children. There are any number of plausible, if not accurate, hypotheses to explain that relationship. For instance, the simultaneous decrease in unemployment and child abuse rates may mean that hot-line volunteers have found employment, and thus, the recorded rate of child abuse has slowed down. The point is that we must question whether a statistic actually indicates something about individual behavior or whether it is simply an incidental association between rates.

The sixth problem is that our analyses of the causes of child abuse are typically based on at-hand clinical and medical cases, cases that have been officially labeled as child abuse cases. Most of the research to date, and this includes nine of the 11 projects funded by the National Center on Child Abuse and Neglect, define child abuse in terms of the cases which are identified or caught by child protection services, state agencies, local chapters of the Society for the Prevention of Cruelty to Children, and the like. The statistics of such agencies reflect an overrepresentation of poor people, black people, marginal people, and Spanish-speaking people. The conclusion generally drawn from these statistics is that discrimination, or lack of integration into society, is somehow causally related to child abuse. This was a theory which I accepted for a long time until, through my own research, I realized that it is *possible* that the factors associated with being vulnerable to being labeled (caught) a child abuser are confounded with the factors associated with *being* a child abuser. This is a problem of such magnitude that one cannot know for certain whether poverty causes child abuse or whether poverty makes the parents vulnerable to getting caught.

Ned Polsky (1969), who studies criminal and deviant behavior, has argued for years that you cannot try to explain the causes of delinquency, deviancy, and criminal behavior by interviewing inmates in prisons. A study of such a population is a study of the unsuccessful criminals, the ones who have been caught. Similarly, it is the successful child abusers that we do not know about, those who are insulated from the official reporting system. Any explanation of the causes of child abuse must take such individuals into consideration. This means that our research can no longer take a short-cut to defining child abuse by saying that child abuse is represented by all the cases that come to the attention of the authorities. When the three-year funding period of the research projects sponsored by the National Center on Child Abuse and Neglect ends, we are going to know a lot about who gets caught and why they get caught; but ultimately, we will probably know very little about what causes people to abuse their children. This is not to say that this kind of research presents us with no evidence at all—it does and I will present some of that evidence shortly. However, this research presents us with evidence of associations, not causal relationships. It presents possibilities of variables associated with child abuse which should not be considered as causal explanations.

The seventh problem is that causal relationships and/or conclusions tend to result from post hoc examination of data. A very well-known study is a prime example. The researchers constructed the longest interview schedule they thought was tenable, administered it, coded it, put it in a computer, and spent two and one-half years playing with the data to see what things fit together. In my opinion, that is not a test for causal relationships. It is a gold-mining operation which looks for associations and nothing more.

The eighth problem is that of an inappropriate methodological approach to the presentation of tabular data. It is a problem which has plagued even the classic researchers in the field of child abuse. Let us look at Table 20, which presents the relationship between education and child abuse (Table 20 presents data from an actual study of abuse). In this table the independent, or proposed causal, variable is "education." The dependent variable, the factor which we are trying to explain, is

TABLE 20
Education by Child Abuse

Years of Education	Abused Child	Did Not Abuse	Total
0 – 6	24	11	35
7 – 9	42	46	88
10 – 12	140	104	244
some college	13	17	30
college degree	2	6	8
graduate study	2	2	4
Total	223	183	409

TABLE 20a
Education by Child Abuse

Years of Education	Abused Child	Did Not Abuse
0 – 6	11%	6%
7 – 9	19%	25%
10 – 12	63%	56%
some college	6%	9%
college degree	1%	3%
graduate study	1%	2%
Total	100%	100%

TABLE 20b
Education by Child Abuse

Years of Education	Abused Child	Did Not Abuse	Total
0 – 6	69%	31%	100%
7 – 9	48%	52%	100%
10 – 12	57%	43%	100%
some college	43%	57%	100%
college degree	25%	75%	100%
graduate study	50%	50%	100%

"child abuse." In order to standardize the data and interpret the table we must first percentage the raw data. There are three ways to present the percentaged data. The first, which actually reveals nothing, would be to divide the number of cases in each cell by the total number of cases in the table (N = 409). Doing this, however, reveals nothing about the possible association between education and child abuse. The second approach is to percentage in the direction of the dependent variable. In Table 20a we have percentaged in the direction of the dependent variable by dividing the number of cases in each cell by the total number of cases in each category of the dependent variable. The question answered by this approach is "What percent of child abusers have 'x' amount of education?" At first glance it would appear that the most likely abusers are those with 10-12 years of education (69% of the abusers had 10-12 years of schooling). However, this conclusion is misleading. For one, it simply presents the educational distribution of child abusers. One would expect there to be more abusers in the 10-12 years of education category, because most of the population of the United States falls into this range (the median number of years of schooling for the population is between 11 and 12).

What we need to know is not what the education of the child abuser is, but what percentage of child abusers have x years of education and what percentage of people with that level of education do not abuse their children. In other words, are people with one level of education more or less likely to abuse their children? To answer this question, one must percentage the table in the direction of the independent variable as we have done in Table 20b. From this table it can be seen that the greatest difference between abusers and nonabusers is at the lowest and highest ends of the education continuum. In other words, those with the least education are most likely to abuse, while the most educated are the least likely to abuse.

This is a very simple example, but it does demonstrate that different results can be obtained from the same data set, depending on how the data are presented in tabular form.

In the last 10 years, the issue of child abuse has become a priority; the federal government decided that child abuse was an important area; agencies decided that this was a problem they wanted to confront; and we have engaged in a headlong rush to try to understand the causes of child abuse and to solve the problem. A side-effect of this focus of attention has been a tendency to accept and repeat conclusions with little critical awareness. Questionable statistics are cited and recited until they become accepted as fact, until they are accepted as common knowledge. However, many of these statistics are a product of a kind of statistical alchemy. For an example, let us look at the national statistics on the incidence of child abuse. The only reputable figures are those presented by David Gil (1970). Too many other researchers present national statistics which are developed through projections made on the basis of the incidence of child abuse in only one area of the country. For example, Douglas Besharov, the director of the National Center of Child Abuse and Neglect, takes the reported cases from New York state and projects figures for the entire country.

As should be clear from the problems which I have presented, it is incumbent upon those in the field of child abuse not to simply repeat conclusions and associations, not to accept them as fact; but rather, to ask of every citation: What are the rules of evidence that support these conclusions? How viable are these conclusions?

In the future we need research which does not rely on caught or at-hand cases exclusively, we need to use control groups and comparison groups, and we need more studies which are based on representative samples. I think we use at-hand cases because it is convenient, we do not want to get our hands too dirty. It is dirty work to go door to door and try to ferret out the unreported cases. However, it is precisely those unreported cases which are going to provide us with an understanding of what causes child abuse, rather than what causes people to get caught.

I would also recommend that we do research which tests theories. To my knowledge, there are only one or two projects funded by DHSS which actually propose to test a specific theory and either verify it or reject it in terms of the cause of child abuse. The majority of research projects under way are clinical gold-mining operations which hope to come up with a nugget after dredging through thousands upon thousands of responses to inappropriately lengthy interview schedules.

We also need research which has the potential to generate theories. If we cannot test theories, at least we can attempt to generate them. Too many research endeavors stop at the associational level. They present all the material I have presented today, but do not go on to say what the data mean in terms of a theory of child abuse.

Finally, I recommend that we conduct our research about a phenomenon which can be operationalized. I have studied family violence because it can be measured and conceptualized. Child abuse cannot be measured and conceptualized. Child abuse is a political term which was designed to bring attention to an area where children's rights were overlooked. Child abuse is not a specific behavior which can be operationalized and tested. As long as the federal government thinks it can conduct a national incidence study of child abuse, it is doomed to failure.

Child abuse is a nice term to use if you are going to have a conference. It is a nice term to use if you want to convince somebody that you are fundable. But, once you have got the money, forget it. Choose a discrete phenomenon that can be measured and then attempt to explain specific acts of neglect, specific acts of abuse, specific acts against children. This area needs study. It has suffered too long from being overpoliticized and underresearched.

PART VI

APPLYING RESEARCH TO PRACTICE

Introduction

The study of family violence has advanced a great deal in the last decade and a half. Whereas 15 years ago family violence was thought to be rare and confined to people who suffered from mental or psychiatric disorders, today we now have a better understanding of how extensive family violence is and the multiple social and psychological factors which are associated with violence in the home. While no one could, or should, claim that the answers to all of our questions are clear and without contradiction or doubt, we are at least at a point where there are sophisticated theories and empirical data which can be brought to bear on many of the important questions which concern people in the field.

One question which still needs to be addressed is whether this accumulation of knowledge has done any good. If, as some think, we are better able to explain and understand child abuse, wife abuse, and other forms of family violence, does this mean that we are also better able to prevent and treat family violence? At one level, this question could be answered by examining evaluation studies of various prevention and treatment programs to see whether or not a treatment or program succeeded in either preventing family violence or reducing the risk that violence would reoccur in the same household. At another level, however, we could ask if those whose primary work involves prevention and treatment actually make use of the research knowledge that has been accumulated. Are they even aware of the knowledge that is available?

The concluding chapter in this volume is a more personal document than the essays which precede it. Rather than conduct yet another survey to determine whether clinicians and practitioners are aware of research knowledge on family violence and whether they in any way applied this knowledge to their work, I decided that since I knew much about the knowledge, it would be a useful experiment to see whether I could apply it in a clinical capacity.

The chapter describes the clinical experience I undertook and the various successes and failures I encountered in trying to apply my own awareness of the knowledge base to the particular cases of family violence. From the outset, it was apparent that a good number of the variables and concepts that sociologists are familiar with are not directly applicable to clinical work with violent families. One can glibly talk about social structure and family violence when making policy recommendations, but it is certainly another thing to apply these factors to individual cases of child or wife abuse. Irrespective of one's theoretical sophistication, it is typically not possible to change the social class of a violent family. And yet, as the chapter describes, sociologists and students of family violence do have something to offer to clinical practice. The perspectives or conceptual frameworks that sociologists use in the knowledge-generating process do indeed seem to make a contribution to the process of trying to deal with real-world problems and situations.

"Applying Research on Family Violence to Clinical Practice" is not the definitive manual on how to link research and practice, but it does provide an opening or window through which the transfer could begin.

CHAPTER 13

APPLYING RESEARCH ON FAMILY
VIOLENCE TO CLINICAL PRACTICE

An assumption held by a number of researchers and clinicians is that research on family relations can inform clinical practice (Sprenkle, 1976; Framo, 1972; Hurvitz, 1979; Glassner and Freedman, 1979; Kargman, 1957). This can be seen in the frequent use of research findings and theories by clinicians in their publications, and can be found increasingly in the writings of researchers when they direct their comments and suggestions to clinical audiences.[1]

The assumed relevancy of research for clinical practice is quite strong among those who study and/or treat family violence, wife abuse, child abuse, abuse of the elderly, and sexual abuse.

The recency of family violence as a research and clinical issue, the paucity of research reports on the causes of family violence and effective treatment modalities, and the intense emotions which cases of family violence arouse in clinicians may partially explain the interest in applying research to clinical practice in this area. In the emotionally trying context of clinical practice with victims of abuse and their abusers, and with the absence of an extensive knowledge base, clinicians may assume that their social scientist colleagues have gained new and useful insights and knowledge.

Thus, while clinicians who specialize in divorce counseling or other family issues may not be as willing or interested in turning to research

Author's Note: From Richard J. Gelles, "Applying Reseach on Family Violence to Clinical Practice." *Journal of Marriage and the Family,* 1982, 44 (February): 9-20.

for guidance, clinicians who deal with violence and abuse have literally flocked to researchers for scientifically generated knowledge which can hopefully support, change, or improve clinical practice. Researchers, flattered by attention, are often more than willing to accommodate their clinical colleagues.

The transfer of research knowledge from researcher to clinician is typically accomplished in one of two ways. The first and perhaps most common method is for researchers to recommend that interested and inquiring clinicians read specific books or scholarly articles. An occasional researcher might even author an article to be published either in a clinically focused journal or in a book which will be marketed to a clinical audience. A second common means of transferring research knowledge is through a seminar, workshop, or conference where clinicians attend and listen to presentations made by researchers. Whether the conference is organized and run by researchers or clinicians is immaterial to the final forum, which typically has the researcher setting the agenda.

The presentation is made in the researcher's language, with the researcher selecting the issues, theories, concepts, and data which will be presented. After the researcher's didactic presentation, the audience (clinicians) then has an opportunity to ask questions, challenge statements, or perhaps even compliment the presenter. A considerable number of questions involve clinicians stating the facts about a specific case and asking the speaker what should be done, based on what the research says. Another version of this type of question is when clinicians ask, "What type of treatment works?" or, "What can we *do* based on what we *know*?" The typical researcher might answer the question, in mostly general or stochastic terms, or turn to the moderator, hoping that the question and answer session will mercifully be brought to a close.

The two common methods of transferring research knowledge to those in clinical practice most often fail. Despite the fact that researchers and clinicians share a common subject matter and concern for the well-being of individuals and families, they share little else. Their language is different. They may use the same words, but hold different meanings for the concepts. Rarely do they share the same concern for the issues, and they infrequently agree on what are the important questions which require answering.

The transfer is incomplete. Researchers and clinicians often leave interactions feeling inadequate—researchers feeling that they did not communicate well, clinicians feeling that they were not intelligent enough to understand what was said. Or, researchers might sneer at the clinicians who "can't see the forest for the trees"; while clinicians sneer back, holding that researchers are hopelessly tangled in the ivy wrapped around their ivory towers. In the end both might end up agreeing that perhaps research is better suited for addressing policy rather than practice issues.

Case Study in Applying Research to Clinical Practice

This chapter reports on an attempt to apply research on family violence to clinical practice. I was trained as a traditional sociologist and engaged in eight years of research on family violence prior to accepting a position as a fellow in the Family Violence Training Program at the Children's Hospital Medical Center, Boston. In this position I engaged in supervised diagnostic work and therapy in the Department of Psychiatry, Children's Hospital Medical Center and in the Family Development Clinic, an outpatient clinic of the same hospital. (The activities will be described in detail below.)

Both this report and the attempt of a researcher actually to engage in clinical practice and apply knowledge gained from research to that practice are unconventional. As stated previously, nearly all attempts by researchers to apply their knowledge to practice have either been in the course of didactic presentations or have been attempted by persons who were trained as clinicians and in research. Those who have written the most on applying research to practice were themselves trained in both areas (e.g., Sprenkle, 1976; Hurvitz, 1979; Kargman, 1957). I was not trained, schooled, or otherwise acquainted with the theories or nature of clinical practice prior to my commencing work at Children's Hospital. I entered this experience with *only* my training as a "pure" researcher and my interest in attempting to apply this experience to clinical work.

This chapter is unconventional, especially for someone trained as a researcher, because the data, analysis, and conclusions are based on an N of 1, with no comparison group. This is exactly the type of research report which pure researchers (including myself—Gelles, 1973, 1978) are so inclined to criticize savagely. As a means of accounting for this anomaly, both in the course of my clinical work and in authoring this chapter, I have comforted myself in viewing this enterprise as a form of participant observational research which employs the case study method.

RESEARCH BACKGROUND

I came to my experience in hospital-based clinical practice with a standard and traditional research background. Armed with the normal sequence of research methods courses, statistical training, and orientation to theoretical frameworks, my first article on family violence was a critique of existing research and theory on child abuse (Gelles, 1973). This was followed by an in-depth study of 80 families, with the focus on violence between husbands and wives (Gelles, 1974, 1975c, 1976). An additional theoretical concern which developed from the early research concerned the social construction of child abuse (Gelles, 1975b). This work analyzed how clinicians identified cases of child abuse, attached the label "child abuse," and which characteristics of victims, family, situation, and clinician influenced the labeling process. Last, I spent five years working with Murray Straus and Suzanne Steinmetz on a national survey of violence in families (Straus et al., 1980; Straus, 1978; Gelles, 1978; Steinmetz, 1977b). Among the contributions of the national study was a profile focusing on the factors related to various types of intrafamily violence without confounding with factors which led families to be labeled as "abusive."[2]

CLINICAL BACKGROUND

My exposure to clinical practice up to the point of my year at Children's Hospital was nonexistent, as either student, clinician, or patient. I had interviewed a number of social workers, physicians, police officers, and school personnel as part of my research on the processes of identifying and labeling child abuse. But my primary contact with clinicians in the field of family violence was through participation in workshops and conferences on child abuse, wife abuse, and family violence. Both as presenter and as a member of the audience I gained considerable experience with the difficulties of translating research theory and data into answers to questions posed by clinicians, as well as with the other side of the coin—the frustration of clinicians attempting to state their concerns clearly for researchers.

CLINICAL ACTIVITIES AT CHILDREN'S HOSPITAL MEDICAL CENTER

My clinical activities at Children's Hospital Medical Center began September 1979 and continued until July 1980. There were three main areas of clinical work, as well as one consulting role.

Diagnostic assessments. I conducted diagnostic assessments in the Department of Psychiatry. Diagnostic assessments are carried out by two clinicians (male and female).[3] The team sees a family for an initial 50-minute session (the 50-minute clinical hour). This is followed by a second 50-minute session the following week. A final diagnostic report is written by the team after the two sessions. Generally, the team is given a brief referral prior to the first session. This typically provides the names of the parent and child, address, and presenting problem. One clinician sees the child for both visits, while the second sees the parents. During the week between sessions, the clinicians typically obtain additional diagnostic materials from others, for example school counselors, mental health workers, social workers, physicians, and those who may have seen the child or parents in relation to the presenting problem. As I was matched with another intern, we also met with a supervisor for one hour before and after each session with the patients.

Psychotherapy. Therapy patients are assigned by the Department of Psychiatry to a team of clinicians. Clinicians see the patients under the child guidance model (child sees one therapist, adult(s) see second therapist). Occasional family meetings and family sessions may be scheduled during the course of the therapy. I saw late-latency-aged male child and a 65-year-old Hispanic woman once a week for eight months. A preschool male who had also been assigned to me dropped out of therapy after our second visit.[4]

Interdisciplinary outpatient clinic. The remainder of my active clinical work took place with the Family Development Clinic (Newberger and McAnulty, 1976). The Family Development Clinic is an interdisciplinary clinic consisting of medical providers (pediatricians and a nurse practitioner), social workers, and psychologists (and one sociologist). The clinic holds an organizational meeting for 90 minutes per week, and sees patients one afternoon a week. Children and families are referred to the clinic by a variety of sources, including juvenile court, social workers with the state department of social services, legal counsel, and some self-referrals (few in number). Referrals typically request that the children and their families be assessed in terms of psychosocial-medical factors. The clinic primarily deals with children who are suspected of being physically abused, neglected, or sexually abused. Teams of clinicians conduct these assessments through medical examinations, psychological testing, and diagnostic interviews. Additional information is also obtained from other clinicians in and outside of the medical center (similar to the procedures used in the diagnostic assessments). The activities of the clinic differ from diagnostic work in the Department of Psychiatry. The clinic is interdisciplinary and typically makes its report and recommendations to an outside agency (a court) and not the family. The clinic also provides some primary medical care to children. Also, the clinic may see the same families for long periods of time. It is not unusual for each clinic meeting to include a child and family who have been coming to the clinic for diagnosis and medical care from four to six years.

Trauma X. My last activity was as consultant to the hospital Trauma X Team (Newberger et al., 1973). The Trauma X Team is similar to other hospital Child Abuse Teams: it is a case management team which advises units in the hospital regarding cases of suspected child abuse and neglect. The team provides consultation surrounding issues of reporting of cases, assessment of needs, and disposition of cases. Because my work with this group was as a consultant, I will not include any thoughts or observations on this work in my assessments of the link between research and clinical practice.

Research Available for
Application to Clinical Practice

Before assessing how well research on family violence can be applied to clinical practice, it is a good idea to review briefly what research knowledge and theory is actually available for application.

As recently as 1962 there was but a limited knowledge base on the subject of child abuse. Prior to 1970 only two scholarly articles on wife abuse had been published. And there has been almost nothing published on elderly abuse as of 1981.

While there has been an explosion of interest concerning the subjects of child and wife abuse and family violence, the present knowledge base is limited and immature (Gelles, 1980b). This is especially so when compared to the accumulated knowledge in the fields of schizophrenia, suicide, and divorce. There is still confusion and debate over nominal and operational definitions of child abuse, wife abuse, and elderly abuse. There is heated debate over whether child and wife abuse are conceptually and empirically linked or whether they are and should be treated as distinct research and clinical issues (see, for example, Dobash and Dobash, 1979).

Limitations. There are six major limitations to current research and theory in the field of family violence.

(1) *Most studies based on caught cases.* As many as 90% of all studies of child and wife abuse are based on small, nonrepresentative samples of women and children who have either been labeled as victims of abuse or who have sought public assistance by seeking refuge in a battered wife shelter or filing a child abuse report. The drawbacks of basing generalizations on small, nonrepresentative cases are reviewed by others (Bolton et al., 1981; Gelles, 1973; Spinetta and Rigler, 1972); suffice it to say that such a research tradition hopelessly confounds causal variables with variables related to being publicly identified or labeled as deviant.

(2) *Lack of comparison groups.* In addition to limitations of sampling methods used in research on family violence, a good number of studies of child and wife abuse fail to employ comparison groups (see, for example, Walker, 1979). Thus, investigators are unable to establish patterns of associations, as they have no group of nonabusers to which to compare their samples of victims and their families.

(3) *Lack of generalizability.* The nature of the sampling methods means that it is impossible to generalize from one sample to a larger population. Researchers and clinicians reading the results of a study conducted in a regional medical center cannot know for sure that the results of the study are generalizable to anyone other than the isolated sample chosen from that medical center. Findings and implications from such research can be applied to other patients, settings, and populations only with greatest hesitancy and caution (although this does not always happen).

(4) *Simplistic theoretical models.* The field of family violence abounds with simplistic theoretical models. In the earliest research reports the model advanced was that of psychopathology—mental illness caused child abuse. Others have advanced explanations which posit that if a person was abused as a child, he or she will become an abuser as an adult. Others propose that abuse and violence is caused by alcoholism, drugs, stress, low income, or patriarchy. While nearly each one of these factors is certainly related to child and wife abuse, the fact remains that it is extremely unlikely that family violence will be amenable to the simplistic, single variable explanations which have proliferated in the early years of research on this emotion-laden social problem.

(5) *The Woozle Effect.* The Woozle Effect has been defined and explained in an earlier paper (Gelles, 1980b). Its essential line of reasoning is that simple empirical results or statements are repeated by many authors until the statement or finding gains the status of a "law,"—without so much as a single bit of additional data being

collected. This has been quite common as researchers and clinicians struggle to find ideas and data to fill important theoretical and practical gaps in their work.

(6) *The perpetuation of myths.* In sum, the newness of both clinical and research work in the field of family violence has led to the creation and generation of myths concerning the extent, patterns, and causes of family violence. These myths have found their way into clinical practice and are frequently the only research which is noted and applied to diagnostic and therapeutic intervention in cases of family violence.

Advantages. A review of the weaknesses of current research and theory on family violence is not to say that there is not solid research which could be applied to clinical practice. Considerable research has been conducted during the decade of the 1970s. Despite sampling and measurement differences and limitations, considerable data have been gathered which agree as to certain factors which are related to abuse and violence (see Chapter 1 for a review of these). Moreover, there has been theoretical work which attempts to advance causal modeling beyond the simple, deterministic models which were popular in early writings. After just one decade of intensive research, there are abundant data which can be brought to bear in attempting to answer both research and clinical questions.

Incompatibilities Between Research and Clinical Practice

Clearly, good intentions and a sound and extensive background in the empirical data and theory on family violence do not necessarily make for a good clinician. It is not my intention to consider or discuss my own personal qualities as a clinician, my failings, or my strengths. Rather, the essential point of this work was to consider the interface, or lack of one, between research and practice. Initially, my strongest impressions concerned the constraints, barriers, and incompatibilities between the paradigm of research and the paradigm of clinical practice. There were striking incompatibilities between the worldview of a trained researcher compared to the outlook of a clinician.

IDIOGRAPHIC VERSUS NOMOTHETIC PERSPECTIVES

It is axiomatic that sound research training prepares a social scientist to use nomothetic explanations of social behavior (Babbie, 1975). The nomothetic perspective views phenomena by isolating relatively few factors associated with the phenomena in order to help explain the underlying trends and patterns associated with the phenomena. While *nomothetic* comes from the Greek word *nomo-*, which means law, the laws applied by social scientists are typically stochastic. Thus, in viewing child abuse or wife abuse, a researcher would be interested in identifying factors which are associated with abuse, and with constructing models to identify a number of variables which explain a certain percentage of the variance in the dependent variable (child or wife abuse, family violence).

The world of clinical practice is much more an idiographic world. An idiographic approach leads one to analyze the many special circumstances that differentiate a particular event from other similar ones. The result is individualized explanations of single cases. Idiographic approaches are the central outlook of clinicians who need to explain why a particular person is emotionally disturbed, suicidal, or violent.

Researchers trained in the nomothetic paradigm come to realize the shortcomings of their perspective when asked to apply their relatively few variables to single clinical cases. When conducting a diagnostic assessment it is often little help to know that families with similar composition, stress, or socioeconomic status are more likely to engage in certain phenomena than other families. My research background did little to prepare me for the massive amount of data and number of variables one could obtain in a single 50-minute diagnostic session. My clinical supervisors were most unimpressed with my early tendency to summarize my diagnostic sessions by trying to pigeonhole my patient according to previous research. Such pigeonholing, they said, ignored, diminished, and overlooked many other factors which might be critical to understanding the situation of the particular family. The nomothetic perspective often constrained and constricted my clinical attempts to explain what was happening in one particular family. Knowing how little of the variance in family violence we were actually explaining in our research, it did not take me long to see the shortcomings of applying stochastic, nomothetic paradigms to my clinical work. But, in gradually giving up the nomothetic perspective and adopting the idiographic approach, I realized that I was leaving behind most of what I thought I had to offer—extensive empirical knowledge of what researchers had found to be related (statistically) to family violence. While the lawyers and professionals who abused their children could safely be overlooked by the researcher as deviant cases, when they presented in the emergency room or clinic with injured children they could no longer be safely categorized as exceptions to the rule.

TIME

A second important difference between research and clinical practice is the time element. Researchers who concentrate on family studies (and most other specializations in social science) typically use survey research methods to gather their data (Nye and Bayer, 1963; Phillips, 1971). Since the vast majority of social surveys are cross-sectional, and since most interviews or questionnaires are designed to take about 1 hour to 90 minutes to complete, researchers' time with their subjects is rather fleeting. Even the rare in-depth interview rarely lasts longer than four hours, and the rarer longitudinal study typically involves 1-to-2 hour interviews three to four times per year. Thus, researchers are trained to make the most of their rather limited temporal contact with research subjects. Little time can be wasted with small talk or useless questions. In fact, many interviewers develop techniques which allow them to "go for the jugular" in the course of an interview (LaRossa et al., 1981). "Going for the jugular" means that when an opening occurs for asking a question which is crucial for the research, the researcher, pressed by time, must take immediate advantage of such an opportunity.

I found that my experience in both qualitative and quantitative interviewing prepared me well for the intense and emotional diagnostic and therapy sessions in which I became involved. But I also found that I was ill-prepared in terms of patience and time usage. I struggled to gather all my information in one 50-minute session. If my supervisor suggested a line of questioning, I would use it immediately in the next session. I was unprepared for the idea that a therapy patient would, and could, be seen once a week for a year or more. Somehow, even though colleagues and supervisors tried to point out the pace of therapy and diagnostic interviewing, my research training had made me doubt that time was not as scarce a resource in clinical practice as it was in research.

Thus, time has different meanings and different values to researchers and clinicians. Once again I found that a virtue of research, the ability to ask questions, seek answers, and use time wisely, was not necessarily a virtue and was possibly a roadblock to effective clinical work.

CLOSURE

The nomothetic paradigm of research, together with the time pressure of the typical social survey, combine to generate a need for closure as part of the research process. The goal of sound research is, as always, to explain, predict, and understand social behavior. Toward that end researchers are constantly sifting, arranging, and analyzing data in search of social patterns. Those who use the logical, deductive approach state hypotheses, gather data, test hypotheses, and build theory. Analytic induction calls for constant testing of the data against the emerging pattern and explanation. In either case the researcher is concerned with and moves toward closure (identification of a social pattern) as the product of research.

Such a pressure for closure is desired in diagnostic clinical work but tends not to be the goal of therapy. My general impression of clinical work, both diagnostic and therapeutic, was that clinicians attempt to remain receptive to all kinds of data and information, at the expense of closure. Again, the idiographic model does not have as a goal or desired end product the fitting of a case into a general pattern. Since each case is different, the clinician must constantly be available to receive information, clues, and data. I found that while my teammates in both diagnostic work and therapy were searching for new and different information, I was already fitting our patient into a broader social pattern. I could quickly sum up our sessions and draw tentative conclusions after even a 50-minute session—but often I could not adequately or accurately describe what the patient looked like, dressed like, or report on various pieces of information which had been presented in the course of our session. My partners could remember a wealth of information, but struggled, even after two sessions, to bring the information together into a coherent picture of what was going on in the patients' families.

LISTENING SKILLS

If there was one aspect of my training which I was sure would be transferrable to clinical work, it was my experience in conducting unstructured, in-depth intrerviews. I felt that this experience had trained me well as a listener and question asker. I found, however, that it is one thing to ask questions, it is quite another to listen to answers.

By dint of my nomothetic, time-pressured-search-for-closure training, I tended to listen to my patients and search for meanings in their statements as a way of establishing a social pattern. For instance, a family had presented with a young son who was acting out at school and at home. Both parents were concerned about his aggressive tendencies and were at their wits' ends to explain why he was doing so poorly at school. They noted that his sisters had done much better. I asked how many sisters he had and what their ages were, and found that the son was the first male child born after six girls. Immediately, I remembered Morris Rosenberg's study of adolescence and self-image, and his notion of the "young minority boy"—the male child with two or more older siblings who were girls (Rosenberg, 1965). These boys tended to be described as "underachievers" but also had very good self-concepts. As it turned out, the young minority boy aspect of the case was only marginally useful in forming our diagnostic opinion; but it does illustrate my tendency, as someone with a research background, to listen for the meaning of statements in terms of how they fit a social pattern.

Clinicians, on the other hand, have different listening skills and interpretive frameworks. After a number of weeks of clinical work, it began to dawn on me that my supervisors expected me to listen to statements made by individuals and families and search for their interpretations of the statements. Had I been a better symbolic interactionist, I might have applied this framework to my listening. But my research training and my own recent survey research experiences had taught me, to a certain extent, that what a statement means to a person, what it indicates about his or her needs and motivations, is often irrelevant. As an example, my 65-year-old woman patient, near the end of the year, began to balk at coming in for her therapy sessions. One week she would say she forgot, another week it was transportation problems, a third week she was sick. My supervisor asked me why I thought the woman was not coming in. I in turn noted that she was sick, without a car, or had a memory lapse. I was told that I was taking my subject too literally and that, in fact, the woman was expressing her need to avoid terminating our relationship. Of course, my supervisor knew this mostly as a consequence of the social pattern she had seen in her years of clinical work; but the point is that researchers, especially those whose specialty is large-scale surveys with closed-ended items, tend not to look for or care to be bothered with listening to statements in terms of what meaning the statements hold for the individuals.

SUMMARY

Without question, many, if not most, of what I saw as incompatibilities between a sound research paradigm and the skills needed for good clinical practice were the results of my own inexperience and naiveté. Indeed, many of the difficulties were cleared up as my clinical work expanded and I gained more experience. But the central point is that these incompatibilities were there and could only be overcome with increased clinical experience. Without clinical experience the researcher will tend to view the nonclosure-sensitive clinician as a "sloppy thinker." Unless one has actually tried to see the differences between families which have similar social characteristics, it is easy to note that clinicians and their idiographic approach "cannot see the forest for the trees." Of course, to the clinicians, they can neither see nor even be bothered by the forest: they have a job to do for the tree!

Applicability of Research
to Clinical Practice

Perhaps the biggest surprise and disappointment of my clinical experience was how little of the actual research and theory on family violence I actually drew up in diagnostic work and therapy. Sometimes I would apply the results of our discriminant function analysis of the factors related to child and wife abuse (Straus et al., 1980: 201-220). However, as time went on I realized that the number of variables we had analyzed in the national survey was minute in comparison to the data I had access to through hospital records, diagnostic interviews, and other information provided to me.

I found that I did have an opportunity to apply my familiarity with the knowledge base in situations when other clinicians were applying inaccurate assumptions to their diagnostic work. For instance, at one case conference, there was considerable discussion over whether a child who had been admitted with a fractured skull had been injured by her parents. A social worker noted that when she visited the family's home, she found it dirty and disorganized; and that indicated that the family was abuse-prone. I noted that this assumption that cleanliness of the home was associated with abuse was not supported by research. Moreover, if such an association was actually found in research reports, it was probably a consequence of clinicians selectively labeling injured children "abused" if they lived in dirty and disorganized homes. I would react similarly to circumstances in which clinicians would apply deterministic statements about the causes of child abuse (e.g., the parent was abused as a child, therefore, he or she must have abused his or her child; or poverty is related to child abuse, and this family is poor, so the injury must have been caused by the parents).

However, with the exception of such applications of actual research findings and theory to clinical practice, I did not tap my knowledge of the field of family violence on a continuing and regular basis.

CONCEPTUAL FRAMEWORKS

If the specific research and theory on family violence was not as helpful as I had anticipated, what was? I found that after 11 months of clinical practice, the most useful aspect of my research training and experience was the variety of conceptual frameworks which I could apply to trying to understand and assist my patients.

Others have addressed the utility of various conceptual frameworks from family studies and sociology which are applicable to clinical work. Hurvitz (1979) has discussed the applicability of a symbolic inter-actionist framework to marital and family therapy. Kargman (1957) applies social systems theory to marital counseling.

Having previously reviewed 17 theories of family violence (Gelles and Straus, 1979), I had a wealth of conceptual frameworks which I could apply to clinical work. As the year progressed, I found that I was continually applying propositions and ideas from exchange theory.

Applying exchange theory to clinical issues in the treatment of family violence results in the proposition that if people abuse family members because they can (e.g., costs are low), then a central goal of treatment is to make it so they cannot (raise the costs or lower the rewards).

Obviously, increasing the costs of family violence is not as easy as it would seem. A consistent finding in child abuse and family violence research is that perpetrators of domestic violence typically have poor self-concepts. Thus, if a clinician tries to raise the costs of family violence by directing the offender to accept the pejorative label "abuser," one of the unanticipated consequences of this approach would be to undermine further the patient's self-concept and further exacerbate the factors which may have caused the abuse.

Nevertheless, in applying exchange theory to clinical practice, I felt that it was important to try to "cancel the hitting license" and move the patient to accept the responsibility for his or her violent and abusive behavior. This meant that I would not accept accounts of rational-izations which attributed the violent behavior to drugs, alcohol, or a loss of control. An example of how a clinician can "cancel the hitting license" by rejecting such accounts is the case of a husband who hit his wife on several occasions:

> Each time he felt he was wrong. He apologized—very genuinely. But still, he did it again. The husband explained that he and his wife got so worked up in their arguments that he "lost control." In his mind, it was almost involuntary, and certainly not something he did according to a rule or

norm which gives one the right to hit his wife. But the marriage counselor in the case brought out the rules which permitted him to hit his wife. He asked the husband why, if he had "lost control" he didn't stab his wife! (Straus et al., 1980).

The norms which accept certain levels of permissible family violence are so pervasive that a clinician must be aware not to accept them him or herself in the course of therapy.

A variety of innovative treatment approaches to family violence, including EMERGE, the first men's counseling service for domestic violence, now advocate the "canceling of the hitting license" and the acceptance of responsibility for violence as a necessary part of treatment.

A second clinical application of exchange theory is for the clinician to try to reduce the social isolation experienced by violent families. Research tends to find that child abusers, wife abusers, and their families are more socially isolated than nonviolent families (Straus et al., 1980). Not only does isolation deprive families of social, psychological, and economic resources in times of stress, but it greatly reduces the possibility of external social control over family relations. Families with considerable stress and conflict could be well served by having community linkages on which they could draw for help or assistance in meeting stress and reducing conflict.

SHARPENING THE DIAGNOSTIC PROCESS

Latent culture is difficult to escape, and I was not totally able to disassociate myself from the social scientist's bias for the nomothetic approach to human behavior.

Even while becoming comfortable with the idiographic nature of diagnostic work, I was drawn to identify social patterns. I soon found that diagnostic assessments drew primarily on three types of data— medical, psychological, and social. The sources of these data could be primary—physical examinations for medical data, psychological testing for psychological data, or social histories for social data. Data could also come from secondary sources—previous medical information reported in the medical record, psychological reports written by other clinicians, or information on social factors reported by clinicians who had interviewed the family or made a home visit. Finally, data could come from tertiary sources—a social worker who reports on a medical examination or a school counselor's assessment of a child.

DIAGNOSTIC ASSESSMENT MODEL

		Type of Data		
		Medical	Psychological	Social
Source of Data	Primary			
	Secondary			
	Tertiary			

Types of data and sources can be arranged in the nearly indispensable tool of the social scientist—a three-by-three table (see example above).

Having created the table, I could then check and see which cells I had filled in and which data and from which source I was leaning on in drawing my conclusions. I applied the same model to case conferences which were periodically held to assess the progress of a clinical case in therapy or in the Family Development Clinic. The three-by-three model allowed me to chart the direction of the conference and to point out that on some occasions conclusions were being based primarily on tertiary or secondary sources. This frequently led to the suggestion that the clinic or the therapy team could seek primary data to test their assumptions and conclusions.

INTERVIEWING FAMILIES

I was heartened that my experience in conducting unstructured and structured interviews as part of my research on family violence was of some help in clinical work (in spite of the previously mentioned drawbacks of skills used to develop one's research interviewing ability). By the time I arrived at Children's Hospital, I had gotten over most of my anxieties about asking people to discuss private, intimate, and taboo aspects of their marriages. I had most recently used the Conflict Tactics Scales which had been developed by Straus and Steinmetz, and which were used in our national survey of domestic violence (Straus et al., 1980).[5] Since I was familiar with the scales, I began to use them as part of my diagnostic interviewing. At first my coworkers were astonished that I would ask questions such as, "How often did your husband use a gun or knife against you or the children?" Their astonishment grew when the patients began to discuss various violent episodes, including the use of guns and knives. By the end of the year, the Conflict Tactics Scales had become a routine part of the diagnostic interview in the Family Development Clinic, and the Scales are still used by the clinic staff in their work.

INTERRELATEDNESS OF TYPES OF FAMILY VIOLENCE

The administration of the Conflict Tactics Scales in the Family Development Clinic opened another avenue where research could be applied to clinical practice. The administration of the scales and the responses soon revealed to the clinical staff that if there is violence in one family relationship (e.g., parent to child), there is a significant chance that other relationships will also be violent (e.g., spousal violence). Soon the clinic found that it was not only identifying and treating abused children, but battered wives, battered husbands, battered siblings, and occasional battered parents. Because the clinic was housed in a Children's Hospital, there had been a tendency to look only for and find cases of child abuse. But the use of the Conflict Tactics Scales, coupled with the presence of a researcher who held the theory that types of family violence are interrelated, led to the broadening of the clinic's focus and mandate.

Whereas previously the finding that an injury had been inflicted by a sibling caused the clinical staff to breathe a sigh of relief and drop plans of filing a child abuse report, now such a finding is considered cause for concern and further diagnostic probing (albeit with the understanding that such relationships are probabilistic, not predictive).

Conclusions

My one-year sabbatical from research and the role of researcher and my tentative entry into clinical practice were both sobering and exhilarating. It was sobering to find that after only a few months of clinical work I would find myself forgetting or ignoring the results of my research as I struggled with the emotions, complexities, and responsibilities of conducting clinical diagnoses and doing therapy. On more than one occasion I found myself publicly stating that I thought alleged abusers of a child were crazy. Once, when reminded that I had earlier written a paper which tried to discredit the psychopathological perspective (Gelles, 1973), I replied, "I don't care what I wrote—these people are nuts!"

On the other hand, there were gratifying instances when I could directly apply a fact, theory, idea, or suggestion to a case and find that my coworkers would accept and be grateful for these insights. During the year following my experience at Children's Hospital, the Family Development Clinic has institutionalized the use of the Conflict Tactics Scales as an interviewing instrument. The clinic staff have broadened their perspectives and now see family violence, rather than just child abuse, as their clinical mandate. Fathers, typically the "missing persons" of social histories conducted in the clinic and in the Department of Psychiatry, are now matters of concern as a result of my suggestion that fathers, fathers' employment, and fathers' family roles are important in understanding family violence.

It was also no small relief that the section of this chapter on incompatibilities between research and clinical practice is about as long as is the section on applying research to clinical practice.

My experience and this chapter do lend support to the assumption that research can inform clinical practice, especially in terms of the value of researchers' conceptual frameworks to clinical work.

Notes

1. The assumed applicability of research and theory to clinical practice can also be seen in the renewed interest which is being paid to "clinical sociology." For a definition and discussion of clinical sociology, see Glassner and Freedman, 1979; the March/April, 1979 issue of *American Behavioral Scientist* devoted to clinical sociology; and Franklin, 1979.

2. Of course, the research was not free from the bias caused by selective reporting by the subjects of the interviews.

3. I was paired with other "interns" for both diagnostic work and therapy. Two of my partners were social work students, while a third was enrolled in a psychiatric nursing program.

4. The decision of the mother to move out of state and take her child and herself out of therapy after two visits did little to help my fragile clinical self-concept.

5. The Conflict Tactics Scales consist of 19 questions designed to measure intrafamily conflict in the sense of the means used to resolve conflicts of interest. Three different sets of questions measure three different tactics: (1) reasoning: the use of rational discussion and

argument (e.g., how often did you get information to back up your side of things); (2) verbal aggression: the use of verbal and symbolic means of hurting (e.g., how often did you insult or swear at your partner); and (3) violence: the actual use of physical force (e.g., how often did you beat up your partner/child). One of the advantages of the Conflict Tactics Scales as a research tool and diagnostic interviewing technique, is that the order in which the questions are asked increases the likelihood of the interviewer establishing rapport with the subject/patient. The scales begin with questions such as, How often did you discuss the issue calmly? The rational discussion questions are followed by the verbal aggression items, with the force and violence questions coming at the end. For a complete discussion of the items, scale, and a sample Scale, see Straus, 1979b, or Straus et al., 1980: 253-266.

REFERENCES

ADELSON, L. (1972) "The battering child." Journal of the American Medical Association 222 (October): 159-161.

ALEXANDER, T. (1952) "The adult-child interaction test: a projective test for use in research." Monographs in Social Research and Child Development 17, 2: Serial 55.

ALFARO, J. (1977) "Report on the relationship between child abuse and neglect and later socially deviant behavior." Presented at Exploring the Relationship Between Child Abuse and Delinquency Symposium, University of Washington, Seattle.

ALLEN, C. and M. STRAUS (1980) "Resources, power, and husband-wife violence," pp. 188-208 in M. Straus and G. Hotaling (eds.) The Social Causes of Husband-Wife Violence. Minneapolis: University of Minnesota Press.

American Association for Protecting Children (1985) Highlights of Official Child Neglect and Abuse Reporting, 1983. Denver: American Humane Association.

American Humane Association (1982) National Analysis of Official Child Neglect and Abuse Reporting, 1980. Denver: Author.

American Humane Association (1983) Highlights of Official Child Neglect and Abuse Reporting, 1981. Denver: Author.

AMIR, M. (1971) Patterns of Forcible Rape. Urbana, IL: University of Chicago Press.

ARIES, P. (1962) Centuries of Childhood. New York: Knopf.

BABBIE, E. R. (1975) The Practice of Social Research. Belmont, CA: Wadsworth.

BAKAN, D. (1971) Slaughter of the Innocents: A Study of the Battered Child Phenomenon. Boston: Beacon.

BALDWIN, J. and J. OLIVER (1975) "Epidemiology and family characteristics of severely abused children." British Journal of Preventive Social Medicine 29: 202-221.

BANDURA, A. (1973) Aggression: A Social Learning Analysis. Englewood Cliffs, NJ: Prentice-Hall.

BANDURA, A., D. ROSS, and S. ROSS (1961) "Transmission of aggression through imitation of aggressive models." Journal of Abnormal Sociology and Psychology 63: 575-582.

BANE, M. J. (1976) Here to Stay: American Families in the Twentieth Century. New York: Basic Books.

BARD, M. (1969) "Family intervention police teams as a community mental health resource." Journal of Criminal Law, Criminology, and Police Science 60, 2: 247-250.

BARD, M. and B. BERKOWITZ (1969) "Family disturbance as a police function," in S. Cohen (ed.) Law Enforcement Science and Technology II. Chicago: I.I.T. Research Institute.

BARD, M. and J. ZACKER (1971) "The prevention of family violence: Dilemmas of community intervention." Journal of Marriage and the Family 33 (November): 677-682.

BART, P. (1975) "Rape doesn't end with a kiss." Viva 39-42: 100-102.

BECKER, H. (1963) Outsiders: Studies in the Sociology of Deviance. New York: Free Press.

BENDER, L. (1959) "Children and adolescents who have killed." American Journal of Psychiatry 116 (December): 510-513.

BENNIE, E. and A. SCLARE (1969) "The battered child syndrome." American Journal of Psychiatry 125, 7: 975-979.

BERARDO, F. (1976) "Beyond the college student: an editorial comment." Journal of Marriage and the Family 38 (May): 211.

BERGER, P. and H. KELLNER (1964) "Marriage and construction of reality." Diogenes 46: 1-25.

Berkeley Planning Associates (1978) Executive Summary: Evaluation of the Joint OCD/SRS National Demonstration Program in Child Abuse and Neglect. (mimeo)

BERKOWITZ, L. (1962) Aggression: A Social Psychological Analysis. New York: McGraw-Hill.

BILLINGSLEY, A. and J. GIOVANNONI (1972) Children of the Storm. New York: Harcourt.

BLOCK, M. and J. SINNOTT [eds.] (1979) "The battered elder syndrome: an exploratory study." University of Maryland. (unpublished)

BLOOD, R. O. and D. W. WOLFE (1960) Husbands and Wives. New York: Free Press.

BLUM, F. (1970) "Getting individuals to give information to the outsider," pp. 83-90 in W. Filstead [ed.] Qualitative Methodology: Firsthand Involvement with the Social World. Chicago: Markham.

BLUM, G. (1949) "A study of the psychoanalytic theory of psychosexual development." Genetic Psychology Monographs 39: 3-99.

BLUMBERG, M. (1964) "When parents hit out." Twentieth Century 173 (Winter): 39-44.

BOHANNAN, P. (1960) African Homicide and Suicide. New York: Athenium.

BOLTON, F. C., Jr., R. H. LANER, D. S. GAI, and S. P. KANE (1981) "The 'study' of child maltreatment: When is research . . . research?" Journal of Family Issues 2 (December): 531-539.

BOSSARD, J. and E. BOLL (1966) The Sociology of Child Development. New York: Harper & Row.

BOUDOURIS, J. (1971) "Homicide and the family." Journal of Marriage and the Family 33 (November): 667-676.

BOWKER, L. H. (1983) Beating Wife-Beating. Lexington, MA: D. C. Heath.

BRILEY, M. (1979) "Battered parents." Dynamic Years 14, 2: 24-27.

BROWNMILLER, S. (1975) Against Our Will: Men, Women and Rape. New York: Simon & Shuster.

BULCROFT, R. and M. A. STRAUS (1980) "Validity of husband, wife, and child reports of intrafamily violence." (mimeo)

BURGDORF, K. (1980) Recognition and Reporting of Child Maltreatment. Rockville, MD: Westat.

BURGESS, R. L. (1979) "Family violence: some implications from evolutionary biology." Presented at the annual meeting of the American Society of Criminology, Philadelphia.

BURGESS, R. L. and J. GARBARINO (1983) "Doing what comes naturally? An evolutionary perspective on child abuse," pp. 88-101 in D. Finkelhor et al. (eds.) The Dark Side of Families. Current Family Violence Research. Newbury Park, CA: Sage.

BURSTON, G. R. (1975) "Granny-battering." British Medical Journal, 3, 5983: 592.

BYRD, D. E. (1979) "Intersexual assault: a review of empirical findings." Presented at the annual meeting of the Eastern Sociological Society, New York.

CAFFEY, J. (1946) "Multiple fractures in the long bones of infants suffering from chronic subdural hematoma." American Journal of Roentgenology, Radium Therapy, and Nuclear Medicine 56: 163-173.

CAFFEY, J. (1957) "Some traumatic lesions in growing bones other than fractures and dislocations." British Journal of Radiology 23: 225-238.

CALVERT, R. (1974) "Criminal and civil liability in husband-wife assaults," pp. 88-90 in S. Steinmetz and M. Straus (eds.) Violence in the Family. New York: Harper & Row.

CAMPBELL, D. and C. STANLEY (1963) Experimental and Quasi-Experimental Designs for Research. Chicago: Rand McNally.

CAPLOW, T. (1964) Sociology of Work. New York: McGraw-Hill.

CARR, A. (1977) Some Preliminary Findings on the Association Between Child Maltreatment and Juvenile Misconduct in Eight New York Counties. Report to the Administration for Children, Youth, and Families. National Center of Child Abuse and Neglect, Kingston, RI.

CATE, R. M., J. M. HENTON, F. S. CHRISTOPHER, and S. LLOYD (1982) "Premarital abuse: a social psychological perspective." Journal of Family Issues 3 (March): 79-90.

CENTERS, R. (1949) "Marital selection and occupational strata." American Journal of Sociology 54 (May): 530-535.

CHAPA, D., P. SMITH, F. RINDON, R. VALDEZ, M. YOST, and T. CRIPPS (1978) "The relationship between child abuse and neglect and substance abuse in a predominantly Mexican-American population," pp. 116-125 in M. Lauderdale et al. (eds.) Child Abuse and Neglect: Issues on Innovation and Implementation, Vol. 1: Proceedings of the Second Annual Conference on Child Abuse and Neglect, 1977. Washington, DC: Department of Health, Education and Welfare.

COLEMAN, D. H. and M. A. STRAUS (1986) "Marital power, conflict, and violence." Violence and Victims 1, 1: 139-153.

COLES, R. (1964) "Terror-struck children." New Republic 150 (May 30): 11-13.

COLMAN, A. and L. COLMAN (1973) Pregnancy: The Psychological Experience. New York: Seabury Press.

CONGDON, T. (1970) "What goes on in his head when you're pregnant? Glamour (December): 102ff.

CONGER, R. D. (1978) "Family change and child abuse," pp. 74-79 in M. Lauderdale et al. (eds.) Child Abuse and Neglect: Issues on Innovation and Implementation, Vol. 1: Proceedings of the Second Annual Conference on Child Abuse and Neglect, 1977. Washington, DC: Department of Health, Education and Welfare.

CORNELL, C. P., and R. J. GELLES (1982a) "Adolescent to parent violence." Urban and Social Change Review 15 (Winter): 8-14.

CORNELL, C. P., and R. J. GELLES (1982b) "Elder abuse: the status of current knowledge." Family Relations 31 (July): 457-465.

COSER, L. A. (1967) Continuities in the Study of Social Conflict. New York: Free Press.

CRONAN, S. (1969) Marriage. New York: Feminist Press.

CUMMINGS, J. (1952) "Family pictures: a projective test for children." British Journal of Psychology 43: 53-60.

CURTIS, L. (1974) Criminal Violence: National Patterns and Behavior. Lexington, MA: D. C. Heath.

DAVIS, A. (1970) "Sexual assaults in the Philadelphia prison system," pp. 107-124 in J. Gagnon and W. Simon (eds.) The Sexual Scene. Chicago: Aldine.

DELLI QUADRI, T. C. (1978) "Changing family roles and structures: impact on child abuse and neglect," pp. 70-73 in M. Lauderdale et al. (eds.) Child Abuse and Neglect: Issues on Innovation and Implementation, Vol. 1: Proceedings of the Second Annual Conference on Child Abuse and Neglect, 1977. Washington, DC: Department of Health, Education and Welfare.

De MAUSE, L. [ed.] (1974) The History of Childhood. New York: Psychohistory Press.

De MAUSE, L. (1975) "Our forebears made childhood a nightmare." Psychology Today 8 (April): 85-87.

DEXTER, L. (1958) "A note on selective inattention in social science." Social Problems 6 (Fall): 176-182.

DOBASH, R. E. and R. DOBASH (1979) Violence Against Wives. New York: Free Press.

DOLLARD, J. C., L. DOOB, N. MILLER, O. MOWRER and R. SEARS (1939) Frustration and Aggression. New Haven, CT: Yale University Press.

DOUGLASS, R., T. HICKEY, and C. NOEL (1980) "A study of maltreatment of the elderly and other vulnerable adults." University of Michigan. (unpublished)

DRAPKIN, I. and E. VIANO [eds.] (1974) Victomology. Lexington, MA: D. C. Heath.

DUNHAM, H. (1964) "Anomie and mental disorder," pp. 128-157 in M. Clinard (ed.) Anomie and Deviant Behavior. New York: Free Press.

DYER, E. (1963) "Parenthood as crisis: a re-study." Marriage and Family Living 25 (May): 196-201.

ECKLUND, B. (1968) "Theories of mate selection." Eugenics Quarterly 15 (June): 71-84.

EGELAND, B. and L. JACOBVITZ (1984) "Intergenerational continuity of parental abuse: cause and consequence." Presented at the Social Science Research Council Conference on Biosocial Perspectives on Child Abuse and Neglect, York, ME.

ELMER, E. (1967) Children in Jeopardy: A Study of Abused Minors and Their Families. Pittsburgh: University of Pittsburgh Press.

ERICKSON, K. (1966) Wayward Puritans. New York: John Wiley.

ERLANGER, H. (1974) "Social class and corporal punishment in childrearing: a reassessment." American Sociological Review 39 (February): 68-85.

FARBEROW, N. [ed.] (1966) Taboo Topics. New York: Atherton.

FAULK, M. (1977) "Sexual factors in marital violence." Medical Aspects of Human Sexuality 11 (October): 30-38.

Federal Contracts Opportunities (1980) "Aging committees consider programs to curb growing problems of elder abuse." Volume 5: 1.

FIDLER, D. and R. KLEINKNECHT (1977) "Randomized response versus direct questioning: two data-collection methods for sensitive information." Psychological Bulletin 84, 5: 1045-1049.

FIELD, M. and H. FIELD (1973) "Marital violence and the criminal process: neither justice nor peace." Social Service Review 47, 2: 221-240.

FINKELHOR, D. and G. HOTALING (1984) "Sexual abuse in the national incidence study of child abuse and neglect: an appraisal." Child Abuse Neglect: The International Journal 8: 23-33.

FINKELHOR, D. and K. YLLO (1985) License to Rape: Sexual Abuse of Wives. New York: Holt Rinehart, & Winston.

FONTANA, V. (1971) The Maltreated Child: The Maltreatment Syndrome in Children. Springfield, IL: Charles C Thomas.

FONTANA, V. (1973) Somewhere a Child is Crying: Maltreatment—Causes and Prevention. New York: Macmillan.

FRAMO, J. L. [ed.] (1972) Family Interaction: A Dialogue Between Family Researchers and Family Therapists. New York: Springer.

FRANKLIN, B. J. (1979) "Clinical sociology: the sociologist as practitioner." Psychology: A Quarterly Journal of Human Behavior 16 (Fall): 51-56.

FREIDSON, E. (1960) "Client control and medical practice." American Journal of Sociology 65 (January): 374-382.

FRENCH, J., W. RODGERS, and S. COBB (1974) "Adjustment as person-environment fit," pp. 316-333 in G. Coelho et al. (eds.) Coping and Adaption. New York: Basic Books.

FRIEDRICH, W. and J. BORISKIN (1976) "The role of the child in abuse: a review of literature." American Journal of Orthopsychiatry 46, 4: 580-590.

GALDSTON, R. (1965) "Observations on children who have been physically abused and their parents." American Journal of Psychiatry 122, 4: 440-443.

GALDSTON, R. (1975) "Preventing abuse of little children: the parent's center project for the study and prevention of child abuse." American Journal of Orthopsychiatry 45 (April): 372-381.

GALLEN, R. (1967) Wives' Legal Rights. New York: Dell.

GARBARINO, J. (1976) "A preliminary study of some ecological correlates of child abuse: the impact of socioeconomic stress on mothers." Child Development 47: 178-185.

GARBARINO, J. (1977) "The human ecology of child maltreatment." Journal of Marriage and the Family 39 (November): 721-735.

GARBARINO, J. and M. C. PLANTZ (1984) "An ecological perspective on the outcomes of child maltreatment: what difference will the differences make?" Presented at the Social Science Research Council Conference on Biosocial Perspectives on Child Abuse and Neglect, York, ME.

GELLES, R. (1973) "Child abuse as psychopathology: A sociological critique and reformulation." American Journal of Orthopsychiatry 43 (July): 611-621.

GELLES, R. (1974) The Violent Home: A Study of Physical Aggression Between Husbands and Wives. Newbury Park, CA: Sage.

GELLES, R. (1975a) "On the association of sex and violence in the fantasy production of college students." Suicide 5 (Summer): 78-85.

GELLES, R. (1975b) "The social construction of child abuse." American Journal of Orthopsychiatry 45 (April): 363-371.

GELLES, R. (1975c) "Violence and pregnancy: a note on the extent of the problem and needed services." Family Coordinator 24 (January): 81-86.

GELLES, R. (1976) "Abused wives: why do they stay?" Journal of Marriage and the Family 38 (November): 659-668.

GELLES, R. (1977) "Power, sex, and violence: the case of marital rape." Family Coordinator 26 (October): 339-347.

GELLES, R. (1978) "Violence towards children in the United States." American Journal of Orthopsychiatry 48 (October): 580-592.

GELLES, R. (1980a) "A profile of violence towards children in the United States," pp. 82-105 in G. Gerbner et al. (eds) Child Abuse: An Agenda For Action. New York: Oxford University Press.

GELLES, R. (1980b) "Violence in the family: a review of research in the seventies." Journal of Marriage and the Family 42 (November): 873-885.

GELLES, R. (1982) "Applying research on family violence to clinical practice." Journal of Marriage and the Family 44 (February): 9-20.

GELLES, R. (1983) "An exchange/social control theory," pp. 151-165 in D. Finkelhor et al. (eds.) The Dark Side of Families: Current Family Violence Research. Newbury Park, CA: Sage.

GELLES, R. and C. CORNELL [eds.] (1983) International Perspectives on Family Violence. Lexington, MA: D. C. Heath.

GELLES, R. and M. STRAUS (1979) "Determinants of violence in the family: toward a theoretical integration," pp. 549-581 in W. Burr et al. (eds.) Contemporary Theories About the Family, Vol. 1. New York: Free Press.

GIL, D. (1970) Violence Against Children: Physical Child Abuse in the United States. Cambridge, MA: Harvard University Press.

GIL, D. (1971) "Violence against children." Journal of Marriage and the Family 33 (November): 637-648.

GIL, D. (1975) "Unraveling child abuse." American Journal of Orthopsychiatry 45 (April): 364-358.

GILES-SIMS, J. (1983) Wife-Beating: A Systems Theory Approach. New York: Guilford.

GILLEN, J. (1946) The Wisconsin Prisoner: Studies in Crimogenesis. Madison: University of Wisconsin Press.

GILLESPIE, D. (1971) "Who has the power? The marital struggle." Journal of Marriage and the Family 33 (August): 445-458.

GIOVANNONI, J. and R. BECERRA (1979) Defining Child Abuse. New York: Free Press.

GLASSNER, B. and J. FREEDMAN (1979) Clinical Sociology. New York: Longman.

GOFFMAN, E. (1961) Asylums. New York: Anchor Books.

GOODE, E. (1969) "Multiple drug use among marijuana smokers." Social Problems 17 (Summer): 48-64.

GOODE, W. (1971) "Force and violence in the family." Journal of Marriage and the Family 33 (November): 624-636.

GRIFFEN, S. (1971) "Rape: the all-American crime." Ramparts (September): 26-35.

GROVES, R. and R. KAHN (1979) Surveys By Telephone: A National Comparison With Personal Interviews. New York: Academic Press.

GUTTMACHER, M. (1960) The Mind of the Murderer. New York: Farrar, Straus, & Cudahy.

HAKEEM, M. (1957) "A critique of the psychiatric approach to the prevention of juvenile delinquency." Social Problems 5 (Fall): 194-206.

HAMPTON, R. and E. NEWBERGER (1984) "Child abuse incidence and reporting by hospitals: significance of severity, class and race." Presented at the Second National Conference for Family Violence Researchers, Durham, NH:

HARBIN, H. and D. MADDEN (1979) "Battered parents: a new syndrome." American Journal of Psychiatry 136 (October): 1288-1291.

HARRIS, C. (1975) Fact Book on Aging: A Profile of America's Older Population. Washington, DC: National Council on the Aging.

HARRIS, L. and Associates (1979) A Survey of Spousal Abuse Against Women in Kentucky. New York: Author.

HAWORTH, M. (1966) The CAT: Facts and Fantasy. New York: Grune & Stratton.

HELFER, R. and C. KEMPE [eds.] (1968) The Battered Child. Chicago: University of Chicago Press.

HELFER, R. and C. KEMPE (1972) Helping the Battered Child and His Family. Philadelphia: Lippincott.

HENRY, J. (1971) Pathways to Madness. New York: Vintage.

HENTON, J. M., R. CATE, J. KOVAL, S. LLOYD, and S. CHRISTOPHER (1983) "Romance and violence in dating relationships." Journal of Family Issues 4 (September): 467-482.

HINTON, C. and J. STERLING (1975) "Volunteers serve as an adjunct to treatment for child-abusing families." Hospital and Community Psychiatry 26 (March): 136-137.

HOBBS, D. (1965) "Parenthood as crisis: a third study." Journal of Marriage and the Family 27 (August): 367-372.

HOFFMAN, L. W. (1961) "Effects of maternal employment on the child." Child Development 32: 187-197.

HOFFMAN, L. W. (1974) "Effects of maternal employment on the child—a review of the research." Developmental Psychology 10: 204-228.

HOLLINGSHEAD, A. (1950) "Cultural factors in the selection of mates." American Sociological Review 15 (October): 619-627.

HOLMS, T. H. and R. H. RAHE (1967) "The social readjustment rating scale." Journal of Psychosomatic Research 11: 213-218.

HOOKER, E. (1966) "Male homosexuality," pp. 44-55 in N. Farberow (ed.) Taboo Topics. New York: Atherton Press.

HORNUNG, C., B. McCULLOUGH, and T. SUGIMOTO (1981) "Status relationships in marriage: risk factors in spouse abuse." Journal of Marriage and the Family 43 (August): 675-692.

HOROWITZ, A. (1978) "Families who care: a study of natural support systems of the elderly." (unpublished)

HOROWITZ, I. and M. LIEBOWITZ (1967) "Social deviance and political marginality: toward a redefinition of the relation between sociology and politics." Social Problems 15: 280-296.

HORVITZ, D., B. GREENBERG, and J. ABERNATHY (1975) "Recent developments in randomized response designs," pp. 271-285 in J. Strivastava (ed.) A Survey of Statistical Design and Linear Models. New York: American Elsevier.

HOUGHTON, B. (1979) "Review of research on women abuse." Presented at Annual Meeting of the American Society of Criminology, Philadelphia.

HRDY, S. B. (1979) "Infanticide among animals: a review classification, and examination of the implications for reproductive strategies of females." Ethological Sociobiology 1: 13-40.

HUERTA, F. (1976) "Incest: the neglected form of child abuse." Presented to the Western Social Science Association, Phoenix, AZ.

HUGGINS, M. and M. STRAUS (1980) "Violence and the social structure as reflected in children's books from 1850-1970," in M. Straus and G. Hotaling (eds.) The Social Causes of Husband-Wife Violence. Minneapolis: University of Minnesota Press.

HUMPHREYS, L. (1970) Tearoom Trade: Impersonal Sex in Public Places. Chicago: Aldine.

HUNT, M. (1973) "Sexual behavior in the 1970's—Part II: premarital sex." Playboy (November): 74-75.

HURT, M. (1975) Child Abuse and Neglect: A Report on the Status of the Research. U.S. Department of Health, Education, and Welfare, Office of Human Development/Office of Child Development.

HURVITZ, N. (1979) "The sociologist as a marital and family therapist." American Behavioral Scientist 23 (March/April): 557-576.

JAMES, H. (1975) The Little Victims: How America Treats Its Children. New York: David McKay.

JAMESON, P. A. and C. J. SCHELLENBACH (1977) "Sociological and psychological factors in the background of male and female perpetrators of child abuse." Child Abuse and Neglect: The International Journal 1, 1: 77-83.

JOHNSON, B. and H. MORSE (1968) "Injured children and their parents." Children 15: 147-152.

JONES, A. (1980) Women Who Kill. New York: Holt, Rinehart, & Winston.

JORGENSEN, S. R. (1977) "Social class heterogamy, status striving, and perception of marital conflict: a partial replication and revision of Perlin's contingency hypothesis." Journal of Marriage and the Family 39 (November): 653-661.

JUSTICE, B. and D. F. DUNCAN (1975) "Child abuse as a work-related problem." Presented at Child Abuse Session, A.P.H.A., Mental Health Section.

JUSTICE, B. and D. F. DUNCAN (1976) "Life crisis as a precursor to child abuse." Public Health Reports 91, 2: 110-115.

JUSTICE B. and R. JUSTICE (1976) The Abusing Family. New York: Human Sciences Press.

KAGAN, J. (1958) "Socialization of aggression and the perception of parents in fantasy." Child Development 29: 311-320.

KAGAN, J., B. HOSKEN, and S. WATSON (1961) "Child's symbolic conceptualization of parents." Child Development 32 (March-December): 625-636.

KAPLAN, H. (1972) "Toward a general theory of psychosocial deviance: the case of aggressive behavior." Social Sciences and Medicine 6, 5: 593-617.

KARGMAN, M. W. (1957) "The clinical use of social system theory in marriage counseling." Marriage and Family Living 19 (August): 263-269.

KEMPE, C. et al. (1962) "The battered-child syndrome." Journal of the American Medical Association 181 (July 7): 17-24.

KEMPE, C. (1971) "Pediatric implications of the battered baby syndrome." Archives of Disease in Children 46: 28-37.

KERLINGER, F. (1973) Foundations of Behavioral Research. New York: Holt, Rinehart, & Winston.

KINSEY, A., B. WARDELL, and C. MARTIN (1948) Sexual Behavior in the Human Male. Philadelphia: W. B. Saunders.

KITSUSE, J. (1964) "Societal reaction to deviant behavior: problems of theory and method," pp. 87-102 in H. Becker (ed.) Perspectives on Deviance—The Other Side. New York: Free Press.

KOCH, L. and J. KOCH (1980) "Parent abuse—a new plague." Washington Post (January 27): 14-15.

KORBIN, J. (1978) "Changing family roles and structures: impact on child abuse and neglect? A cross cultural perspective," pp. 98-107 in M. Lauderdale et al. (eds.) Child Abuse and Neglect: Issues on Innovation and Implementation, Vol. 1: Proceedings of the Second Annual Conference on Child Abuse and Neglect, 1977. Washington, DC: Department of Health, Education and Welfare.

KORBIN, J. (1981) Child Abuse and Neglect: Cross-Cultural Perspectives. Berkeley: University of California Press.

KORBIN, J. (1984) "Child maltreatment and the cultural context: current knowledge and future directions." Presented to Social Science Research Council Conference on Biosocial Perspectives on Child Abuse and Neglect, York, ME.

LAING, R. (1971) The Politics of the Family. New York: Vintage.

LAKIN, M. (1957) "Assessment of significant role attitudes in primiparous mothers by means of a modification of the TAT." Psychosomatic Medicine 19: 50-60.

LANDIS, J. (1957) "Values and limitations of family research using student subjects." Marriage and Family Living 19 (February): 100-105.

LaROSSA, R. (1976) "Couples expecting their first child: use of in-depth interviews." Presented to the Population Association of America, Montreal.

LaROSSA, R. (1977) Conflict and Power in Marriage: Expecting the First Child. Newbury Park, CA: Sage.

LaROSSA, R., L. A. BENNETT, and R. J. GELLES (1981) "Ethical dilemmas in qualitative family research." Journal of Marriage and the Family 43 (May): 303-313.

LASLETT, B. (1973) "The family as a public and private institution: a historical perspective." Journal of Marriage and the Family 35 (August): 480-492.

LASLETT, B. and R. RAPOPORT (1975) "Collaborative interviewing and interactive research." Journal of Marriage and the Family 37 (November): 968-977.

LAU, E. and J. KOSBERG (1979) "Abuse of the elderly by informal care providers." Aging 299: 10-15.

Legal Research and Services for the Elderly (1979) "Elderly abuse in Massachusetts: a survey of professionals and paraprofessionals." Boston: (mimeo)

LeMASTERS, E. (1957) "Parenthood as crisis." Marriage and Family Living 19 (November): 352-355.

LENA, H. and S. WARKOV (1974) "Occupational perceptions of child abuse: common and divergent conceptions of a social problem." Presented at the Forty-Fourth Annual Meeting of the Eastern Sociological Society, Philadelphia.

LEON, C. (1969) "Unusual patterns of crime during 'la Violencia' in Columbia." American Journal of Psychiatry 125, 11: 1564-1575.

LEVINE, R. (1959) "Gussi sex offenses: a study in social control." American Anthropologist 61: 965-990.

LEVINGER, G. (1966) "Sources of marital dissatisfaction among applicants for divorce." American Journal of Orthopsychiatry 26 (October): 803-897. (reprinted in P. Glasser and L. Glasser [eds.] Families in Crisis. New York: Harper & Row.

LIGHT, R. (1974) "Abused and neglected children in America: a study of alternative policies." Harvard Educational Review 43 (November): 556-598.

LITMAN, T. (1971) "Health care and the family: a three generational analysis." Medical Care 9, 1: 67-81.

LONDON, J. (1978) "Images of violence against women." Victimology 2: 510-524.

LOVENS, H. and J. RAKO (1975) "A community approach to the prevention of child abuse." Child Welfare 54 (February): 83-87.

LYMAN, S. and M. SCOTT (1970) A Sociology of the Absurd. New York: Appleton-Century-Crofts.

McCARTHY, M. (1963) The Group. New York: Harcourt Brace Jovanovich.

MADDOX, G. L. (1975) "The patient and his family," in S. Sherwood (ed.) The Hidden Patient: Knowledge and Action in Long Term Care. New York: Spectrum.

MADEN, M. F. and D. F. WRENCH (1977) "Significant findings in child abuse research." Victimology 2: 196-224.

MAGNUSON, E. (1983) "Child abuse: the ultimate betrayal." Time 122 (September 5): 20-22.

MAHMOOD, T. (1978) "Child abuse in Arabia, India and the West—comparative legal aspects," pp. 281-289 in J. Eekelaar and S. Katz (eds.) Family Violence: An International and Interdisciplinary Study. Toronto: Butterworth.

MAKEPEACE, J. M. (1981) "Courtship violence among college students." Family Relations 30 (January): 97-102.

MAKEPEACE, J. M. (1983) "Life events stress and courtship violence." Family Relations 32 (January): 101-109.

MARTIN, D. (1976) Battered Wives. San Francisco, Glide.

MARTIN, H. L. (1970) "Antecedents of burns and scalds in children." British Journal of Medical Psychology 43: 39-47.

MARTIN, H. P. (1972) "The child and his development," pp. 93-114 in C. H. Kempe and R. E. Helfer (eds.) Helping the Battered Child and His Family. Philadelphia: Lippincott.

MEDIA, A. and K. THOMPSON (1974) Against Rape. New York: Farrar, Straus, & Giroux.

Medical News (1980) "The elderly: newest victims of familial abuse." Volume 243: 1221-1225.

MERTON, R. (1938) "Social structure and anomie." American Sociological Review 3 (October): 672-682.

MERTON, R. and R. NISBET (1976) Contemporary Social Problems. New York: Harcourt Brace Jovanovich.

MEYER, M. and R. TOLMAN (1955) "Correspondence between attitudes and images of parent figures in TAT stories and therapeutic interviews." Journal of Consulting Psychology 19: 79-82.

MILLER, N. (1941) "The frustration-aggression hypothesis." Psychological Review 48, 4: 337-342.

MILLS, C. W. (1940) "Situated actions and vocabularies of motive." American Sociological Review 5 (October): 904-913.

MILNE, A. A. (1926) Winnie-the-Pooh. New York: Dell.

Mindout (1974) What About Battered Wives? London: MIND National Association for Mental Health.

MITCHELL, M. (1936) Gone with the Wind. New York: Macmillan.

MORGAN, P. and E. GAIER (1956) "The direction of aggression in the mother-child situation." Child Development 27: 447-457.

NELSON, B. J. (1984) Making an Issue of Child Abuse: Political Agenda Setting for Social Problems. Chicago: University of Chicago Press.

New York Radical Feminists (1974) Rape: The First Sourcebook for Women. New York: New American Library.

NEWBERGER, E. et al. (1977) "Pediatric social illness: toward an etiologic classification." Pediatrics 60 (August): 178-185.

NEWBERGER, E., G. HAAS, and R. MULFORD (1973) "Child abuse in Massachusetts: incidence, current mechanism for intervention and recommendations for effective control." Massachusetts Physician 32 (January): 31-38.

NEWBERGER, E., J. J. HAGENBUCH, N. B. EBELING, E. P. COLLIGAN, J. S. SHEEHAN, and S. H. McVEIGH (1973) "Reducing the literal and human cost of child abuse: impact of a new hospital management system." Pediatrics 51 (May): 840-848.

NEWBERGER, E. and J. HYDE (1975) "Child abuse: principles and implications of current pediatric practice." Pediatric Clinics of North America 22 (August): 695-715.

NEWBERGER, E. and E. H. McANULTY (1976) "Family intervention and the pediatric clinic: a necessary approach to the vulnerable child." Clinical Pediatrics 15 (December): 1155-1161.

NEWBERGER, E., R. REED, J. DANIEL, J. HYDE, and M. KOTELCHUCK (1975) "Toward an etiologic classification of pediatric social illness: a descriptive epidemiology of child abuse and neglect, failure to thrive accidents, and poisonings in children under four years of age. Presented at the biennial meetings of the Society for Research on Child Development, Denver.

Newsweek, (1973) "Britain: battered wives." (July 9): 39.

NYE, F. and A. BAYER (1963) "Some recent trends in family research." Social Forces 41 (March): 290-301.

OAKLAND, L. and R. L. KANE (1973) "The working mother and child neglect on the Navajo reservation." Pediatrics 51: 849-853.

O'BRIEN, J. (1971) "Violence in divorce prone families." Journal of Marriage and the Family 33 (November): 692-698.

ORNE, M. (1962) "On the social psychology of the psychological experiment: with particular reference to demand characteristics and their importance." American Psychologist 17: 776-783.

OWENS, D. and M. STRAUS (1975) "Childhood violence and adult approval of violence." Aggressive Behavior 1, 2: 193-211.

PAGELOW, M. (1979) "Research on woman battering," pp. 334-349 in J. B. Fleming (ed.) Stopping Wife Abuse. New York: Anchor.

PAGELOW, M. (1981) Women-Battering: Victims and Their Experiences. Newbury Park, CA: Sage.

PALMER, S. (1962) The Psychology of Murder. New York: Thomas Y. Crowell.

PARKE, R. D. and C. W. COLLMER (1975) "Child abuse: an interdisciplinary analysis," pp. 1-102 in M. Hetherington (ed.) Review of Child Development Research, Vol. 5. Chicago: University of Chicago Press.

PARNAS, R. (1967) "The police response to domestic disturbance." Wisconsin Law Review 914 (Fall): 914-960.

PAULSON, M. and P. BLAKE (1969) "The physically abused child: a focus on prevention." Child Welfare 48 (February): 86-95.

Pediatric News (1975) "One child dies daily from abuse: parent probably was abuser." Volume 9 (April): 3.

PELTON, L. (1978) "Child abuse and neglect: the myth of classlessness." American Journal of Orthopsychiatry 48 (October): 608-617.

PELTON, L. G. (1979) "Interpreting family violence data." American Journal of Orthopsychiatry 49 (April): 194.

PETERS, J. (1975) "The Philadelphia rape victim study," pp. 181-199 in I. Drapkin and E. Viano (eds.) Victimology: A New Focus, Vol. 3. Lexington, MA: D. C. Heath.

PHILLIPS, D. (1971) Knowledge From What? Theories and Methods in Social Research. Chicago: Rand McNally.

PITTMAN, D. and W. HANDY (1964) "Patterns in criminal aggravated assault." Journal of Criminal Law, Criminology, and Police Science 55, 4: 462-470.

PLECK, E., J. PLECK, M. GROSSMAN, and P. BART (1977-78) "The battered data syndrome: a comment on Steinmetz's article." Victimology 2(3/4): 680-683.

POKORNY, A. D. (1965) "Human violence: a comparison of homicide, aggravated assault, suicide, and attempted suicide." Journal of Criminal Law, Criminology, and Police Science 56 (December): 488-497

POLAKOW, R. and D. PEABODY (1975) "Behavioral treatment of child abuse." International Journal of Offender Therapy and Comparative Criminology 19: 100ff.

POLSKY, N. (1969) Hustlers, Beats and Others. Garden City, NY: Anchor.

POMEROY, W. (1966) "Human sexual behavior," pp. 22-32 in N. Farberow (ed.) Taboo Topics. New York: Atherton.

PRESCOTT, J. and C. McKAY (1973) "Child abuse and child care: some cross cultural and anthropological perspectives." Presented at the National Conference on Child Abuse in Washington, D.C., June.

PRESCOTT, S. and C. LETKO (1977) "Battered women: a social psychological perspective," pp. 72-96 in M. Roy (ed.) Battered Women: A Psychosociological Study of Domestic Violence. New York: Van Nostrand Reinhold.

PUZO, M. (1969) The Godfather. New York: Putnam.

RADBILL, S. (1974) "A history of child abuse and infanticide," pp. 3-21 in R. Helfer and C. Kempe (eds.) The Battered Child. Chicago: University of Chicago Press.

RADKE, M. (1946) "The relation of parental authority to children's behavior and attitudes." University of Minnesota Child Welfare Monographs, 22.

RATHBONE-McCUAN, E. (1980) "Elderly victims of family violence and neglect." Social Casework 61, 4: 296-304.

REINER, B. and I. KAUFMAN (1959) Character Disorders in Parents of Delinquents. New York: Family Service Association of America.

REISS. I. (1960) Premarital Sexual Standards in America. New York: Free Press.

RESNICK, P. (1969) "Child murder by parents: a psychiatric review of filicide." American Journal of Psychiatry 126, 3: 325-334.

RIEKEN, H. et al. (1954) "Narrowing the gap between field studies and laboratory experiment in social psychology: A statement of the summer seminar." Social Science Research Council Items 8 (December): 37-42.

ROBINSON, J., R. ATHANASIOU, and K. HEAD (1969) Measures of Occupational Attitudes and Occupational Characteristics. Ann Arbor, MI: Survey Research Center.

ROHNER, R. P. (1975) They Love Me, They Love Me Not. A Worldwide Study of the Effects of Parental Acceptance and Rejection. New Haven, CT: HRAF Press.

ROSENBERG, M. (1965) Society and Adolescent Self Image. Princeton, NJ: Princeton University Press.

ROSENBERG, M. L., R. J. GELLES, P. C. HOLINGER, E. STARK, M. A. ZAHN, J. M. CONN, N. N. FAJMAN, and T. A. KARLSON (1984) Violence. Homicide, Assault, and Suicide. (mimeo)

ROSSI, A. (1968) "Transition to parenthood." Journal of Marriage and the Family 30 (February): 26-39.

ROTH, J. (1966) "Hired hand research." American Sociologist 1 (August): 190-196.

ROUSE, L. (1984) "Conflict tactics used by men in marital disputes." Presented at Second National Conference for Family Violence Researchers, Durham, NH.

RUSSELL, D. (1975) The Politics of Rape: The Victim's Perspective. New York: Stein and Day.

RUSSELL, D. (1982) Rape in Marriage. New York: Macmillan.
SANDERS, R. (1972) "Resistance to dealing with parents of battered children." Pediatrics 50 (December): 853-857.
SARGENT, D. (1962) "Children who kill—a family conspiracy." Social Work 7 (January): 35-42.
SCANZONI, J. (1972) Sexual Bargaining. Englewood Cliffs, NJ: Prentice-Hall.
SCHAFER, S. (1968) The Victim and His Criminal: A Study in Functional Responsibility. New York: Random House.
SCHULTZ, D. (1969) Coming Up Black: Patterns of Ghetto Socialization. Englewood Cliffs, NJ: Prentice-Hall.
SCHULTZ, L. G. (1960) "The wife assaulter." Journal of Social Therapy 6, 2: 103-112.
SCHUMAN, W. (1981) "The violent American way of life," pp. 101-103 in Celeste Borg (ed.) Social Problems 81/82. Guilford: Dushkin.
SEITES, J. (1975) "Marital rape: dispelling the myth." (unpublished)
SELLTIZ, C. et al. (1959) Research Methods in Social Relations. New York: Holt, Rinehart & Winston.
SHAH, S. (1970a) "Recent developments in human genetics and their implication for problems of social deviance." Presented at the American Association for the Advancement of Science, Chicago.
SHAH, S. (1970b) Report on the XYY Chromosomal Abnormality. National Institutes of Mental Health Conference Report. Washington, DC: Government Printing Office.
SHERMAN, L. W. and R. A. BERK (1984) "Deterrent effects of arrest for domestic violence." American Sociological Review 49 (April): 261-272.
SHIELDS, N. M. and C. R. HANNEKE (1983) "Battered wive's reactions to marital rape," pp. 132-150 in D. Finkelhor et al. (eds.) The Dark Side of Families: Current Family Violence Research. Newbury Park, CA: Sage.
SIMMEL, G. (1950) The Sociology of Georg Simmel (K. Wolf, ed.). Glencoe, IL: Free Press.
SHNEIDMAN, E. (1966) "Suicide," pp. 33-43 in N. Farberow (ed.) Taboo Topics. New York: Atherton Press.
SHORTER, E. (1975) The Making of the Modern Family. New York: Basic Books.
SILVER, L., C. DUBLIN, and R. LOURIE (1971) "Agency action and interaction in cases of child abuse." Casework 52, 3: 164-171.
SILVERMAN, F. (1953) "The roentgen manifestations of unrecognized skeletal trauma in infants." American Journal of Roentgenology, Radium Therapy, and Nuclear Medicine 69 (March): 413-427.
SILVERMAN, S. (1976) "Rape in marriage: is it legal?" Do It Now (June): 10.
SIMONS, B., E. DOWNS, M. HURSTER, and M. ARCHER (1969) "Child abuse: epidemiologic study of medically reported cases." New York State Journal of Medicine 66: 2738-2788.
SINGER, J. [ed.] (1971) The Control of Aggression and Violence. New York: Academic Press.
SKOLNICK, A. and J. SKOLNICK [eds.] (1977) The Family in Transition. Boston: Little, Brown.
SMITH, S. (1965) "The adolescent murder." Archives of General Psychiatry 13 (October): 310-319.
SMITH, S., R. HANSON, and S. NOBLE (1973) "Parents of battered babies: a controlled study." British Medical Journal 4 (November): 388-391.

SNELL, J., R. ROSENWALD, and A. ROBEY (1964) "The wifebeater's wife: a study of family interaction." Archives of General Psychiatry 11 (August): 107-112.
SOKOL, R. (1976) "Some factors associated with child abuse potential." Presented at the annual meetings of the American Sociological Association, New York.
SPINETTA, J. and D. RIGLER (1972) "The child abusing parent: a psychological review." Psychological Bulletin 77 (April): 296-304.
SPRENKLE, D. H. (1976) "In my opinion: the need for integration among theory, research, and practice in the family field." Family Coordinator 25 (July): 261-263.
SROLE, L., T. LANGNER, S. MICHAEL, M. OPLER, and T. RENNIE (1962) Mental Health in the Metropolis. New York: McGraw-Hill.
STAR, B. (1980) "Patterns of family violence." Social Casework 61 (June): 339-346.
STARK, R. and J. McEVOY (1970) "Middle class violence." Psychology Today 4 (November): 52-54; 110-112.
STARR, R. H., S. J. CERESNIE, and R. STEINLAUF (1978) "Social and psychological characteristics of abusive mothers." Presented at the meeting of the Eastern Psychological Association, Washington, DC.
STEELE, B. and C. POLLOCK (1968) "A psychiatric study of parents who abuse infants and small children," pp. 103-147 in R. Helfer and C. Kempe (eds.) The Battered Child. Chicago: University of Chicago Press.
STEELE, B. and C. POLLOCK (1974) "A psychiatric study of parents who abuse infants and small children," pp. 89-134 in R. Helfer and C. Kempe (eds.) The Battered Child. Chicago: University of Chicago Press.
STEINMETZ, S. (1971) "Occupation and physical punishment: a response to Straus." Journal of Marriage and the Family 33 (November): 664-666.
STEINMETZ, S. (1974a) "The sexual context of social research." American Sociologist 9, 3: 111-116.
STEINMETZ, S. (1974b) "Occupational environment in relation to physical punishment and dogmatism," pp. 166-172 in S. Steinmetz and M. Straus (eds.) Violence in the Family. New York: Harper & Row.
STEINMETZ, S. (1975) "Intra-familial patterns of conflict resolution: husband/wife; parent/child; sibling/sibling." Ph.D. dissertation, Case Western Reserve University.
STEINMETZ, S. (1977a) "The battered husband syndrome." Victimology 2 (3/4): 499-509.
STEINMETZ, S. (1977b) The Cycle of Violence: Assertive, Aggressive, and Abusive Family Interaction. New York: Praeger.
STEINMETZ, S. (1978a) "Violence between family members." Marriage and Family Review 1, 3: 1-16.
STEINMETZ, S. (1978b) "Battered parents." Society 15, 5: 54-55.
STEINMETZ, S. (1984) "Family violence towards elders," pp. 137-163 in S. Saunders et al. (eds.) Violent Individuals and Families: A Handbook for Practitioners. Springfield, IL: Charles C Thomas.
STEINMETZ, S. and M. STRAUS (1971) "Some myths about violence in the family." Presented at the meetings of the American Sociological Association.
STEINMETZ, S. and M. STRAUS (1973) "The family as a cradle of violence." Society 10, 6: 50-56.
STEINMETZ, S. and M. STRAUS (1974) Violence in the Family. New York: Harper & Row.

STRAUS, M. (1969) "Phenomenal identity and conceptual equivalence of measurement in cross-national research." Journal of Marriage and the Family 31 (May): 233-239.

STRAUS, M. (1971) "Some social antecedents of physical punishment: a linkage theory interpretation." Journal of Marriage and the Family 33 (November): 658-663.

STRAUS, M. (1973) "A general systems theory approach to a theory of violence between family members." Social Science Information 12 (June): 105-125.

STRAUS, M. (1974a) "Forward," pp. 13-17 in R. J. Gelles (ed.) The Violent Home: A Study of Physical Aggression Between Husbands and Wives. Newbury Park, CA: Sage.

STRAUS, M. (1974b) "Cultural and social organizational influences on violence between family members," pp. 53-69 in R. Prince and D. Barrier (eds.) Configurations: Biological and Cultural Factors in Sexuality and Family Life. Lexington, MA: D. C. Heath.

STRAUS, M. (1974c) "Leveling, civility, and violence in the family." Journal of Marriage and the Family 36 (February): 13-29.

STRAUS, M. (1975) "Cultural approval and structural necessity of intrafamily assaults in sexist societies." Presented at the International Institute of Victimology, Bellagio, Italy, July.

STRAUS, M. (1976) "Sexual inequality, cultural norms, and wife beating." Victimology 1 (Spring): 54-76.

STRAUS, M. (1977) "Societal morphogenesis and intrafamily violence in cross-cultural perspective." Annals of the New York Academy of Science 285: 717-730.

STRAUS, M. (1978) "Wife beating: how common and why?" Victimology 2 (3/4): 443-458.

STRAUS, M. (1979a) "Family patterns and child abuse in a nationally representative American sample." Child Abuse and Neglect: The International Journal 3, 1: 213-225.

STRAUS, M. (1979b) "Measuring intrafamily conflict and violence: the conflict tactics (CT) scales." Journal of Marriage and the Family 41 (February): 75-88.

STRAUS, M. (1981) "Societal change and change in family violence." Presented at the National Conference for Family Violence Researchers, University of New Hampshire, July.

STRAUS, M. and S. CYTRYNBAUM (1961) A Scoring Manual for Intrafamilial Power and Affective Support. Minneapolis: Minnesota Family Study Center.

STRAUS, M. and R. GELLES (1986) "Societal change and family violence from 1975 to 1985 as revealed by two national surveys." Journal of Marriage and the Family 48 (August): 465-479.

STRAUS, M., R. GELLES, and S. STEINMETZ (1973) "Theories methods, and controversies in the study of violence between family members." Presented at the meetings of the American Sociological Association, New York.

STRAUS, M., R. GELLES, and S. STEINMETZ (1980) Behind Closed Doors: Violence in the American Family. New York: Doubleday/Anchor.

STRAUS, M. and G. HOTALING (1980) The Social Causes of Husband-Wife Violence. Minneapolis, MN: University of Minnesota Press.

STRAUS, M. and I. TALLMAN (1971) "SIMFAM: a technique for observational measurement and experimental study of families," pp. 378-438 in J. Aldous et al. (eds.) Family Problem Solving. Hinsdale, IL: Dryden.

STRUBE, M. J. and L. S. BARBOUR (1983) "The decision to leave an abusive relationship: economic dependence and psychological commitment." Journal of Marriage and the Family 45 (November): 785-793.

STURGESS, T. and K. HEAL (1967) Non-Accidental Injury to Children under the Age of 17 (Res 663/2/25): A Study to Assess Current Probation Service Involvement With Cases of Non-Accidental Injury. London: Home Office Research Unit, House of Commons Select Committee on Violence in the Family, Session 350.

SUDNOW, D. (1964) "Normal crimes: sociological features of the penal code in a public defender office." Social Problems 12, 3: 255-276.

SZASZ, T. (1960) "The myth of mental illness." American Psychologist 15 (February): 113-118.

SZASZ, T. (1961) The Myth of Mental Illness: Foundations of a Theory of Personal Conduct. New York: Delta.

SZASZ, T. (1970) The Manufacture of Madness. New York: Harper & Row.

TANAY, E. (1969) "Psychiatric study of homicide." American Journal of Psychiatry 125(a): 1252-1258.

TAYLOR, L. and E. H. NEWBERGER (1979) "Child abuse in the International Year of the Child." New England Journal of Medicine 301: 1205-1212.

TEN BROECK, E. (1974) "The extended family center: 'a home away from home' for abused children and their parents." Children Today 3 (April): 2-6.

THORNTON, A., D. F. ALWIN, AND D. CAMBURN (1983) "Causes and consequences of sex-role attitudes and attitude change." American Sociological Review 48 (April): 211-227.

TREAS, J. (1977) "Family support systems for the aged." Gerontologist 17, 6: 486-491.

TRUNINGER, E. (1971) "Marital violence: the legal solutions." Hastings Law Review 23 (November): 259-276.

TURBETT, J. P. and R. O'TOOLE (1980) "Physician's recognition of child abuse." Presented at the Annual Meeting of the American Sociological Association, New York.

U.S. Bureau of the Census (1978) Statistical Abstracts of the United States, 1978. Washington, DC: Government Printing Office.

U.S. Department of Commerce, Bureau of the Census (1977) Current Population Reports: 1977, Series P-20, Population Characteristics, No. 306.

U.S. Department of Commerce, Bureau of the Census (1978) Current Population Reports: 1976-1978, Series P-25, Population Estimates and Projections, No. 800.

U.S. Congress, Select Committee On Aging, Subcommittee on Human Services (1980) Domestic Violence Against the Elderly. Washington, DC: Government Printing Office.

U.S. Department of Health, Education and Welfare (1969, July) Bibliography on the Battered Child. Social and Rehabilitation Service.

U.S. Department of Justice (1980) Intimate Victims: A Study of Violence Among Friends and Relatives. Washington, DC: Government Printing Office.

U.S. Department of Justice (1984) Family Violence. Washington, DC: Bureau of Justice Statistics.

United States Senate (1973) Hearing Before the Subcommittee on Children and Youth of the Committee on Labor and Public Welfare. United States Senate, 93rd Congress, First Session on S.1191 Child Abuse Prevention Act. Washington, DC: Government Printing Office.

VIANO, E. (1974) "Attitudes toward child abuse among American professionals." Presented at the First Meetings of the International Society for Research on Aggression, Toronto, Canada.

VON HENTIG, H. (1948) The Criminal and His Victim: Studies in the Sociology of Crime. New Haven, CT: Yale University Press.

WALKER, L. (1979) The Battered Woman. New York: Harper & Row.

WARDELL, L., D. L. GILLESPIE, and A. LEFFLER (1983) "Science and violence against wives," pp. 69-84 in D. Finkelhor et al. (eds.) The Dark Side of Families: Current Family Violence Research. Newbury Park, CA: Sage.

WARNER, S. (1965) "Randomized response: a survey technique for eliminating evasive answer bias." American Statistical Association 60: 63-69.

WARREN, C. (1978) "Parent batterers: adolescent violence and the family." Presented at the annual meetings of the Pacific Sociological Association, Anaheim, CA, April.

WASSERMAN, S. (1967) "The abused parent of the abused child." Children 14 (September-October): 175-179.

WEBB, E. et al. (1966) Unobtrusive Measures. Chicago: Rand McNally.

Webster's New Collegiate Dictionary (1975) Springfield, MA: Merriam.

WHITING, B. (1972) Work and the Family: Cross-Cultural Perspectives. Proceedings of the Conference on Women: Resource for a Changing World, Cambridge, England.

WHYTE, W. (1955) Street Corner Society. Chicago: University of Chicago Press.

WOLFGANG, M. (1957) "Victim-precipitated criminal homicide." Journal of Criminal Law, Criminology and Police Science 48 (June): 1-11.

WOLFGANG, M. (1958) Patterns in Criminal Homicide. Philadelphia: University of Pennsylvania Press.

WOLFGANG, M. and F. FERRACUTI (1967) The Subculture of Violence. London: Tavistock Publications.

WOLKENSTEIN, A. (1975) "Hospital acts on child abuse." Journal of the American Hospital Association 49 (March): 103-106.

WOOLLEY, P. and W. EVANS (1955) "Significance of skeletal lesions resembling those of traumatic origin." Journal of the American Medical Association 158: 539-543.

YARROW, M., P. SCOTT, L. DeLEEUW, and C. HEINIG (1962) "Child-rearing in families of working and non-working mothers." Sociometry 25, 2: 122-140.

YOUNG, L. (1964) Wednesday's Child: A Study of Child Neglect and Abuse. New York: McGraw-Hill.

ZALBA, S. (1971) "Battered children." Transaction 8 (July-August): 58-61.

ZIGLER, E. (1976) "Controlling child abuse in America: an effort doomed to failure." Presented at the First National Conference on Child Abuse and Neglect, Atlanta, January.

ABOUT THE AUTHOR

Richard J. Gelles is Dean of the College of Arts and Sciences, Professor of Sociology and Anthropology at the University of Rhode Island, and Lecturer on Pediatrics at the Harvard Medical School. He directs the Family Violence Research Program at the University of Rhode Island and has published extensively on the topics of child abuse, wife abuse, and family violence. He is the author of *The Violent Home* (1974) and *Family Violence* (1979), coauthor of *Behind Closed Doors: Violence in the American Family* (1980), *Intimate Violence in Families* (1985), and coeditor of *The Dark Side of Families: Current Family Violence Research* (1983) and *International Perspectives on Family Violence* (1983).

NOTES

NOTES

NOTES

NOTES

NOTES